New Jersey
State Road Atlas

Table of Contents

New Jersey Cities

MILEAGE CHART	Atlantic City	Camden	Cape May	Jersey City	Long Branch	Morristown	Newark	New Brunswick	New Hanover	Paterson	Phillipsburg	Princeton	Rutherford	Somerville	Toms River	Trenton	Union	Vineland	Wildwood
Atlantic City		60	48	94	80	120	104	88	64	118	136	81	114	100	52	68	114	30	46
Camden	60		80	80	68	69	78	55	34	92	56	45	88	51	52	32	56	36	78
Cape May	48	80		144	108	172	150	140	100	164	160	125	154	150	85	112	136	48	2
Jersey City	94	80	144		44	20	2	22	62	16	58	37	10	52	64	50	47	116	142
Long Branch	80	68	108	44		52	40	36	47	54	84	40	50	48	32	44	72	88	106
Morristown	120	39	172	20	52		18	32	67	22	46	34	26	18	76	47	30	115	170
Newark	104	78	150	2	40	18		20	60	14	60	35	10	24	56	48	45	114	148
New Brunswick	88	55	140	22	36	32	20		44	34	48	16	30	12	44	28	36	91	138
New Hanover	64	34	100	62	47	67	60	44		74	60	33	70	49	32	20	48	62	98
Paterson	118	92	164	16	54	22	14	34	74		65	49	4	38	70	62	16	128	162
Phillipsburg	136	56	160	58	84	46	60	48	60	65		40	75	26	83	40	12	92	158
Princeton	81	45	125	37	40	34	35	16	33	49	40		45	16	43	13	28	81	123
Rutherford	114	88	154	10	50	26	10	30	70	4	75	45		34	66	58	55	127	152
Somerville	100	51	150	52	48	18	24	12	49	38	26	16	34		56	29	14	87	148
Toms River	52	52	85	64	32	76	56	44	32	70	83	43	66	56		43	80	68	83
Trenton	68	32	112	50	44	47	48	28	20	62	40	13	58	29	43		36	68	110
Union	114	56	136	47	72	30	45	36	48	16	12	28	55	14	80	36		92	134
Vineland	30	36	48	116	88	115	114	91	62	128	92	81	127	87	68	68	92		46
Wildwood	46	78	2	142	106	170	148	138	98	162	158	123	152	148	83	110	134	46	

Interstate Highways

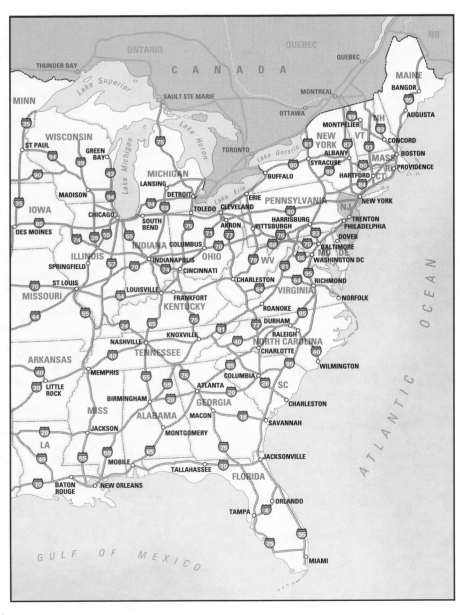

Eastern US Cities

MILEAGE CHART	Atlanta, GA	Baltimore, MD	Boston, MA	Charlotte, NC	Chicago, Il	Dallas, TX	Detroit, MI	New York, NY	Philadelphia, PA	Pittsburgh, PA	Raleigh, NC	St. Louis, MO	Washington, DC
Annapolis, MD	663	26	435	367	730	1339	539	232	123	271	252	828	33
Atlantic City, NJ	832	160	387	536	777	1487	625	145	60	360	460	997	202
Baltimore, MD	669		409	372	697	1347	511	201	97	245	324	833	41
New Brunswick, NJ	813	161	257	585	772	1475	620	42	60	345	472	899	210
Cambridge, MD	718	79	490	422	785	1394	594	287	129	326	307	883	88
Camden, DE	779	111	281	483	808	1455	622	82	80	351	435	938	145
Camden, NJ	763	94	330	519	760	1424	588	95	3	295	409	971	136
Cape May, NJ	866	130	427	622	857	1527	695	159	97	392	512	878	195
Dagsboro, DE	807	105	429	511	816	1425	625	192	126	337	338	914	119
Dover, DE	759	91	381	463	788	1435	602	163	77	289	415	918	100
Elkton, MD	719	51	341	423	748	1395	562	163	49	249	325	878	89
Frankford, DE	761	93	383	409	772	1381	581	274	116	313	294	870	115
Hagerstown, MD	701	73	482	405	678	1377	435	274	196	148	354	866	71
Harrington, DE	774	78	396	478	803	1450	617	178	92	304	430	933	92
Jersey City, NJ	845	181	213	615	784	1515	610	10	83	391	620	931	231
Long Branch, NJ	801	172	378	597	791	1492	605	50	70	267	487	1033	228
Middletown, DE	734	68	356	438	763	1410	577	141	57	264	390	893	103
Newark, DE	722	56	338	426	251	1398	565	132	45	252	378	811	94
Newark, NJ	843	189	213	617	782	1515	608	12	78	369	518	929	226
New Castle, DE	773	66	349	437	762	1469	376	121	40	263	389	892	104
Oakland, MD	825	197	606	529	64	1501	476	398	320	94	478	742	195
Paterson, NJ	858	204	200	632	770	1530	593	23	93	384	533	944	239
Princeton, NJ	793	144	350	569	780	1464	610	46	42	239	459	915	181
Rockville, MD	646	34	443	350	611	1322	430	235	131	276	299	811	16
Rutherford, NJ	850	198	208	640	778	1538	601	20	86	392	526	937	234
Seaford, DE	796	86	48	500	825	1472	639	201	115	379	452	955	100
Smyrna, DE	749	80	370	452	777	1424	591	110	65	278	404	907	118
Trenton, NJ	781	132	362	557	792	1452	622	58	29	227	447	903	170
Washington, DC	630	41	430	334	151	1306	506	230	133	219	283	795	
Wilmington, DE	794	72	320	444	769	1416	583	121	28	312	396	899	110
Wildwood, NJ	884	188	425	620	855	1125	693	157	95	389	510	876	193

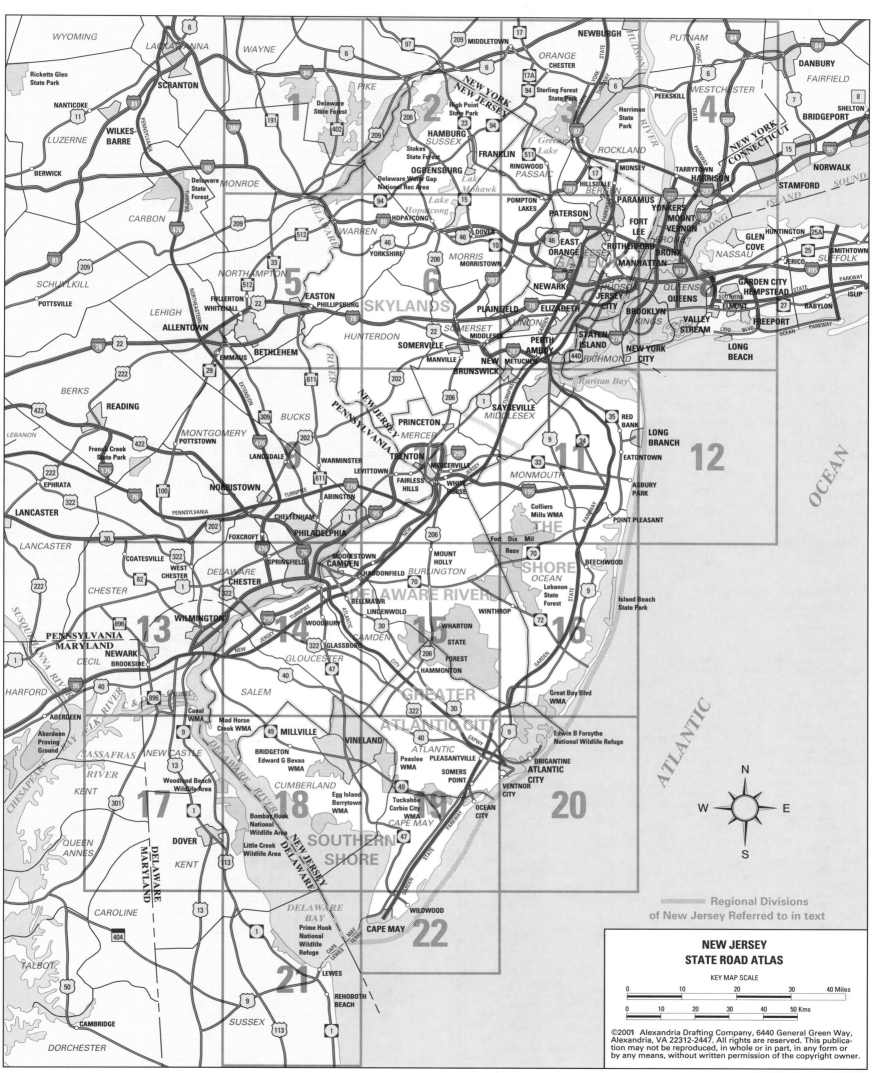

Regional Divisions
of New Jersey Referred to in text

**NEW JERSEY
STATE ROAD ATLAS**

KEY MAP SCALE

0   10   20   30   40 Miles

0   10   20   30   40   50 Kms

A Step-By-Step Guide To Using Your State Road Atlas

Thank you for buying our New Jersey State Road Atlas

We've included these directions just in case you need help getting used to your new atlas. After using it once or twice, you won't need any help at all.

1. It all starts with the Index to Map Features.

The Index to Map Features includes place names, parks and recreation areas, colleges and universities, lakes and streams, points of interest, and more. If you know only the name of a feature, these index listings will help you find the location.

Let's say you want to visit Lebanon State Forest, which is located in Burlington and Ocean Counties, New Jersey, but don't know the location of the Forest. First, you turn to the Forest and Wildlife Areas section on pages 53 of the index and find Lebanon State Forest. Note the letters and numbers listed after the name.

Section from index page 53

2. Finding your map and using the grid coordinates.

As you can see, there are three entries for Lebanon State Forest. Each entry is followed by a set of letters and numbers. The first letters in each set are the territory codes that tell you in which county (and State) the Forest is located (see explanation of codes on index page 47). The following numbers identify the map pages on which Lebanon State Forest can be found (you will find these numbers at the upper corners of the maps). The letter/number combinations that follow the map pages are the grid coordinates (these letters and numbers are shown in blue in the margins of the maps).

First, look up the symbol for forests in the legend on page 5. Then, following the example above, find Lebanon State Forest on Map 15, in grid square F2. If you read the notation in the margin — "Joins Map 16" — you will also know that Lebanon State Forest continues on the next map page.

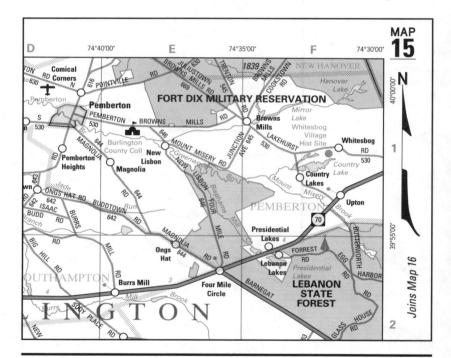

3. Now you've got two choices.

If you wish, you can just turn to Map 16 and, taking a visual cue from Map 15, find Lebanon State Forest. Or you can go back to the index where you'll see again, that Lebanon State Forest is also in grid square A1 on Map 16. But how do you get to that area form where you are now?

4. The big picture.

Use the Key Map on page 3 to get a general overview of your route to Lebanon State Forest, and which maps to use.

You know that you're headed for the part of Lebanon State Forest, which is on Map 15. Assuming you're in Sayreville, you will see that your current location is in square 11 (square numbers correspond to map numbers) and your destination is in square 15.

Section from key map on page 3

5. ■ There is more

You'll find that the front pages of this atlas contain visitors information on state regions, points of interest, parks, golf courses, wineries, mileage charts, and general information for the driver. Browse these pages and you'll see that this is the only book you need to travel New Jersey.

You'll find it particularly useful if you study the map legend below. Familiarity with the various symbols will permit you to more quickly find any information on the maps.

Finally, let us hear from you. We appreciate getting ideas and information from our atlas users. This helps us to improve the product's usefulness and value.

Write to: Hagstrom Map Company, 46-35 54th Road, Maspeth, NY 11378. Your suggestions are always welcome.

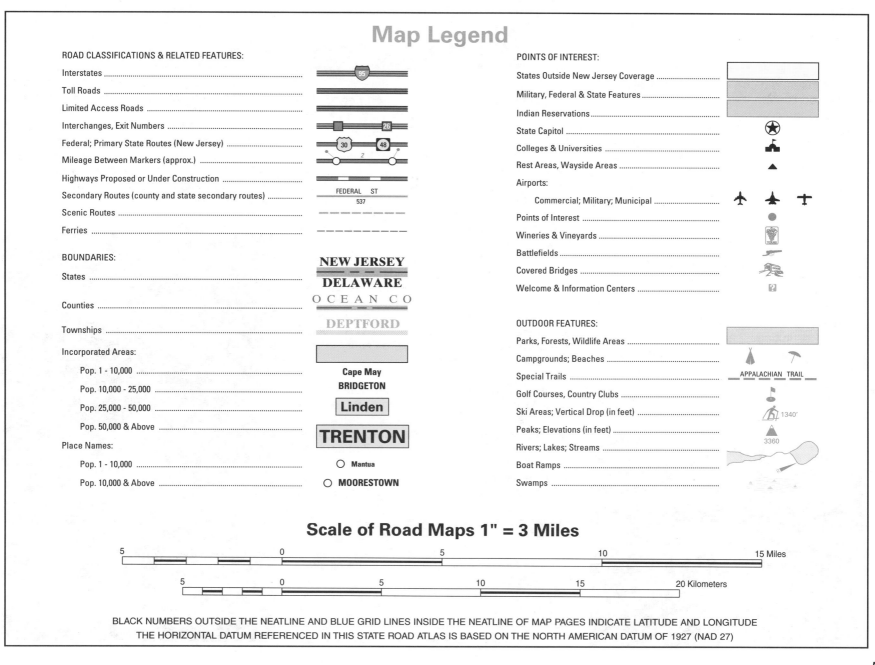

Map Legend

ROAD CLASSIFICATIONS & RELATED FEATURES:

Interstates
Toll Roads
Limited Access Roads
Interchanges, Exit Numbers
Federal; Primary State Routes (New Jersey)
Mileage Between Markers (approx.)
Highways Proposed or Under Construction
Secondary Routes (county and state secondary routes)
Scenic Routes
Ferries

BOUNDARIES:

States
Counties
Townships
Incorporated Areas:
  Pop. 1 - 10,000
  Pop. 10,000 - 25,000
  Pop. 25,000 - 50,000
  Pop. 50,000 & Above
Place Names:
  Pop. 1 - 10,000
  Pop. 10,000 & Above

POINTS OF INTEREST:

States Outside New Jersey Coverage
Military, Federal & State Features
Indian Reservations
State Capitol
Colleges & Universities
Rest Areas, Wayside Areas
Airports:
  Commercial; Military; Municipal
Points of Interest
Wineries & Vineyards
Battlefields
Covered Bridges
Welcome & Information Centers

OUTDOOR FEATURES:

Parks, Forests, Wildlife Areas
Campgrounds; Beaches
Special Trails
Golf Courses, Country Clubs
Ski Areas; Vertical Drop (in feet)
Peaks; Elevations (in feet)
Rivers; Lakes; Streams
Boat Ramps
Swamps

Scale of Road Maps 1" = 3 Miles

BLACK NUMBERS OUTSIDE THE NEATLINE AND BLUE GRID LINES INSIDE THE NEATLINE OF MAP PAGES INDICATE LATITUDE AND LONGITUDE
THE HORIZONTAL DATUM REFERENCED IN THIS STATE ROAD ATLAS IS BASED ON THE NORTH AMERICAN DATUM OF 1927 (NAD 27)

Salute to New Jersey

State Building, Trenton

When you look at all that New Jersey has to offer, you suddenly understand the state's tourism slogan "What a Difference a State Makes."

New Jersey's attractions run the gamut from the cultural sophistication and excitement of Atlantic City, to the stillness and solitude of the sprawling Pine Barrens, to the sunny beaches and busy amusements of the Jersey Shore, to the austere black basalt cliffs of the Palisades that tower over the Hudson River.

Although New Jersey covers a mere 7,500 square miles, ranking only 46th in size among the United States, its park system is the third largest in the country. Indeed, forests blanket fully 40 percent of the state. Some 20 percent of New Jersey is devoted to farmland — hence its nickname "Garden State." In addition, New Jersey counts 1,400 miles of trout-filled waters among its 100 rivers and streams, 800 navigable lakes and ponds, 90 preserved nature areas, national and state parks and forests, and nearly 130 miles of protected beaches.

New Jersey is also an important commercial center. Aside from many plants, factories, and other industrial works located here, it has become the home of corporate headquarters for many of the nation's leading publishers, banking institutions, chemical and pharmaceutical corporations, insurance companies, and other businesses.

No matter which of its six recreational regions you visit, you'll find that New Jersey is

Lady Liberty at New Jersey Gateway

synonymous with diversity. Each offers its own blend of family-style attractions, historic sites, sports and outdoor activities, cultural events, and even winery tours and wine tastings. As you discover each of these six regions, you'll see why one of the country's smallest states now ranks fifth in tourist popularity.

Gateway

Situated in the northeastern corner of New Jersey, Gateway encompasses Bergen, Essex, Union, Hudson, Passaic, and Middlesex counties. The region is a gateway to the entire northeastern megalopolis, being linked to New York by spectacular bridges and tunnels, as well as ferry boats. Newark International Airport (one of the country's largest and fastest growing), excellent highways, and an extensive mass transit network make the Gateway region New Jersey's transportation hub.

Liberty State Park covers over 2 miles of waterfront in Jersey City and celebrates the immigrant experience in America each year, during the fall, with a popular ethnic festival. The Gateway region itself has been a melting pot for newcomers settling in the U.S., where you'll find the country's ethnic diversity reflected in the neighborhoods.

Gateway is also New Jersey's center for culture and history. Dramatic and musical productions are staged at Millburn's Paper Mill Playhouse. You can view contemporary art at the Newark Museum, or more traditional masterpieces at the Jane Voorhees Zimmerli Art Museum at renowned Rutgers University in New Brunswick.

The past is recalled throughout the Gateway region. West Orange contains Thomas Edison's laboratory, while a recreation of the world's first movie studio can be toured at the inventor's home. Paterson was the birthplace of both the Colt revolver and the submarine. The city was both a leading silk-producing center and the principal builder of locomotives—industries that can be traced at the Paterson Museum and in the city's historic district.

Natural beauty is another unmistakable fea-

ture of Gateway. Visit the New Jersey Botanical Gardens in Ringwood State Park or enjoy one of the breathtaking overlooks at the Stone Mountain Reservation in West Orange. "Great Falls," the second largest waterfall east of the Mississippi, crashes down right in the middle of downtown Paterson. The cherry blossoms that bloom in Newark's Branch Brook Park are said to surpass their more famous rivals in the nation's capital.

The Meadowlands Sports Complex, a marvel of modern engineering, is home to football's Giants and Jets, hockey's Devils, and basketball's Nets. Meadowlands Race Track offers annual harness and thoroughbred racing. Its Hambeltonian event is the most prestigious in harness racing. Continental Airlines Arena sponsors family fare, amateur track and wrestling events, concerts, and more.

Skylands

The Skylands region, located in the northwest corner of the state and including the counties of Sussex, Warren, Hunterdon, Somerset and Morris is known for its physical beauty and challenging recreational activities. With natural attractions such as Great Gorge and the Delaware Water Gap, there's no end to the opportunities to enjoy your favorite seasonal sports. Lake Hopatcong, New Jersey's largest lake, is also embraced by the Skylands region, as is the 8,000-acre Great Swamp National Wildlife Refuge, a wetlands haven for migratory birds, with miles of hiking trails. In addition, there are opportunities for ballooning and the downhill ski resorts of Hidden Valley and Mountain Creek.

High Point State Park offers 14,000 acres of spectacular scenery in the Kittatinny Mountains. From its obelisk-topped overlook, the highest point in the state, you'll receive a panoramic view of the mountains and river valley that fan out around you.

Balloon Fest at Readington

Stretching for 37 miles along the Delaware River, Delaware Water Gap National Recreation Area is a favorite for tubing, rafting, canoeing, and swimming. If you prefer a more sedentary visit, it's also an idyllic spot to stroll, picnic, or simply contemplate nature's beauty.

The Skylands region is also Revolutionary War territory. Visit the Ford Mansion in Morristown National Historic Park—George Washington's headquarters during the winter of 1778—or his 1779 headquarters at the Wallace house in Somerville; or Rockingham, in Rocky Hill, where he wrote his farewell address to the Continental army.

The Waterloo Village recalls its heritage as an 18th-century iron town and a 19th-century canal town. Industrial history and ingenuity are remembered at such places as Bell Laboratories, an enormous complex near Morristown with technological displays and exhibits, and the Thomas Edison National Historic Site, which allows visitors to see the great inventor's laboratory and library, as well as a museum filled with his inventions.

Morris County, known as "corporate county" because of all the corporate headquarters located there, also offers many of the region's historical and cultural attractions. Morristown was a base for Washington's troops during the winter of 1779-1780. The National Park here features restorations of log huts the troops built to keep warm. Morristown also features a 19th-century working farm and Historic Speedwell, where the telegraph was developed.

Delaware River

Princeton University

History and outdoor majesty accent the Delaware River region, which encompasses Mercer, Burlington, Gloucester, Camden, and Salem counties. Most of the Pine Barrens, the largest U.S. wilderness area east of the Mississippi, lies within the region's perimeters. In addition, it was in this area that George Washington crossed the Delaware River on December 25, 1776 to stage a surprise attack on soldiers stationed in Trenton. One of the world's most venerable institutions, Princeton University, also lies within the Delaware River region.

The 18th-century town of Princeton is steeped in history. You can visit historic houses such as Bainbridge House, Thomas Clarke House, and Morven; marvel at the mansions on State Street, or see the stately Greek Revival governor's residence, Drumthwacket. Needless to say, the most visited site in town is Princeton University, revered internationally for its excellence in education and research. Among the on-campus highlights are the Gothic Chapel, the University Art Museum, McCarter Theatre, and the Center for the Performing Arts.

Not far from Princeton lie the forests, cranberry bogs, and farmlands of the Pine Barrens. Beribboned by sand roads flanked by pine, oak, and ash trees, this remote area is home mostly to birds; however, fine camping, fishing, hiking, swimming, and canoeing attract many visitors.

Reminders of events and characters that shaped this state can be found just about everywhere. Salem, with its 500-year-old oak tree, has some 60 buildings along Market Street that date from the 18th century. In Burlington, visit the houses of James Fenimore Cooper and Captain James Laurence. Bordentown boasts Clara Barton's school as well as Thomas Paine's home. The oldest schoolhouse in New Jersey, the Historic Prison Museum, and the Smithville Mansion can all be found near Mount Holly. The woodwork in Hancock House, at Hancock's Bridge, still bears bayonet scars made by British soldiers when they massacred a group of Quakers for selling beef to Washington's army. The oldest log cabin in America stands in Gibbstown. Presidential First Lady Dolly Madison spent the night at a tavern in Haddonfield. Point Breeze Mansion, in Bordentown, was the home of Napoleon's older brother, who had escape tunnels incorporated into the design. The region's industrial heritage can be traced at the restored Batsto Village near Hammonton. New Jersey's state capital, Trenton, was briefly the capital of the United States in 1794. Among its historic

Cranberry Bogs, Burlington

sites is the Eagle Tavern, the state's oldest watering hole.

Other regional highlights include the Cowtown Rodeo in Sharptown, the oldest on the East Coast, and Camden, the town where Walt Whitman lived. Camden's attractions include Walt Whitman's House, with his original manuscripts and library, and the Walt Whitman Center for the Arts and Humanities.

The Shore

The Shore region refers to New Jersey's northeastern coastal area and the counties of Monmouth and Ocean. It's known for its lively amusement centers, pristine natural areas and sparkling beaches along the ocean. Hundreds of privately owned—and four state-owned marinas dot the shore.

Gateway National Recreation Area at Sandy Hook, the northernmost point of the state's Atlantic coast, forms a barrier peninsula. In addition to undeveloped shoreline, you'll find historic Fort Hancock, nature trails, and Sandy Hook Light, the oldest operating lighthouse in the country.

Island Beach State Park is another shore preserve, where 10 miles of unspoiled beaches stretch between Seaside Park and Barnegat Inlet.

In addition to the preserved coastal areas, there are the resorts such as Point Pleasant, with its arcades and amusement rides; Seaside Heights, with its lively boardwalk; and the family communities along Long Beach Island.

Monmouth Battlefield State Park, just west of Freehold, commemorates the June 1778 his-

Jersey Shore

Atlantic City

toric event when the Continental army, led by George Washington, engaged the British army in the largest and longest sustained battle of the American Revolution.

Jackson Township boasts the largest family entertainment complex in the northeast at Six Flags Great Adventure Theme Park & Wild Safari. Thrill to hundreds of rides and attractions, as well as live entertainment and an enormous drive-through safari park.

Greater Atlantic City

The Greater Atlantic City region combines everything New Jersey has to offer. Here you'll find the excitement of fast-paced Atlantic City, thrilling thoroughbred racing, beach resort communities, watersports, and a 22,000-acre wildlife refuge.

The "Queen of Resorts," Atlantic City shines year round with its luxurious casinos, glamorous nightlife, and special events. Top-name entertainers perform regularly in this world-class resort town. Its famed 6-mile boardwalk, built in 1881, is the oldest and largest in the world. The annual Miss America Pageant is one of its most famous events.

In contrast to the glittery resort city, the region also contains some of the finest parklands in the state. The Estell Manor County Park offers fishing, playing fields, and hiking trails spread over 1,672 acres, and hosts the annual Pinelands Festival. A haven for migrating

shore birds, the Absecon Wildlife Management Area has a number of hiking trails cutting through its 3,500 acres. The spectacular 22,000-acre Brigantine division of the Edwin B. Forsythe National Wildlife Refuge offers sanctuary to shore birds and is a satisfying destination for birdwatchers.

Local history can be seen in any number of the communities in the Greater Atlantic City region. The real estate developer responsible for creating Atlantic City, Dr. Jonathan Pitney, lived in an early 19th-century home in Absecon. "Lucy the Elephant" is a national landmark in Margate City. Built in 1881, the 3-story-high, 90-ton "elephant" was once used as a hotel. "Lucy" was originally built as a publicity stunt to bring people to the area.

One of the region's more unusual sites is the Marine Mammal Stranding Center in Brigantine. Here, injured whales, dolphins, turtles, and other aquatic creatures are rescued, rehabilitated, and returned to the sea.

Southern Shore

The Southern Shore region mixes some of New Jersey's most crowded, fun-filled family resorts with its most dignified and serene shore communities. Here you can jet ski in the ocean, meander through wildlife preserves, or cruise across the Delaware Bay.

The Southern Shore lies below the northern latitude of the Mason-Dixon Line. Southern Shore hospitality is not just a phrase, it's a way of life. The region blends history with recreation and offers creature comforts in an unspoiled, natural environment. This is why the Southern Shore is known as a vacation paradise.

The region has many extremely popular family resorts. Ocean City, founded in 1879, spans 8 miles of beach. Its 3-mile-long boardwalk features a Music Pier with year round events and the Discovery Shell Museum. The Wildwoods include the overlapping resort communities of North Wildwood, Wildwood Crest, and Wildwood.

East Point Lighthouse, Heislerville

Cape May is considered to be the Grand Dame of the Southern Shore. The nation's first planned seaside resort, it retains its lovely gas-lit streets, gingerbread and wedding-cake-style cottages, and wide verandas, encompassed by a genteel Victorian atmosphere.

Avalon and Stone Harbor lie at almost opposite ends of a 7-mile barrier island. Both communities cherish their solitude and protected high dunes.

Many historic areas and wildlife refuges lie inland. Bridgeton is a living museum with over 2,000 registered historic Colonial and Victorian structures. It also features the 1,000-acre Cohanzick Zoo. Millville's Wheaton Village offers glassmaking demonstrations in a 19th-century glass factory. The 11,000-acre Belleplain State Forest in Woodbine is great for camping, fishing, swimming and hiking.

"Lucy the Elephant", Margate

Mainstay Inn, Cape May

Points of Interest

Skylands

Black River and Western Railroad 908-782-9600
Antique steam and diesel trains travel from Flemington to Ringoes and Lambertville. (Ringoes) 10 B1

Miniature Kingdom 908-698-6866
Exact replicas of European castles and cathedrals in miniature. (Washington) 6 A3

Peters Valley Craft Center 973-948-5200
Local craftsmen sell their handmade wares. (Peters Valley) 2 B4

Rockingham Historic Site 609-921-8835
Washington's farewell address to his army was written here. (Rocky Hill) 10 E2

Space Farms Zoo & Museum 973-875-5800
Zoo and museum complex containing 500 animals within their 100 acres. (Beemerville) 2 D4

USGA National Headquarters Golf House Museum & Library 908-234-2300
A fascinating collection of golf memorabilia & artifacts. (Far Hills) 6 E5

Gateway

East Jersey Olde Towne 732-463-9077
Colonial village reconstructed from 20 houses found throughout central New Jersey. (Piscataway) 7 A6

Edison National Historic Site 732-736-0550
Edison's invention laboratory & home have been turned into museums. (West Orange) 7 D3

Ellis Island National Monument 212-269-5755
Self-guided tours of the Ellis Island immigration Museum. For ferry information call 212-269-5755. (New York Harbor) Map 26

Great Falls National Landmark District 973-279-9587
First Planned industrial city in America. Most known for submarines, locomotives and silk. (Paterson) Map 30

Grover Cleveland Birthplace 973-226-1810
Birthplace of the only US president elected to two non-consecutive terms of office. (Caldwell) 7 C2

Jane Voorhees Zimmerli Art Museum 732-932-7237
19th Century French and American; Contemporary Art. (New Brunswick) Map 28

Liberty Science Center 201-200-1000
Four floors of exhibits. Laser light show, living salt marsh, science theater, touch tunnel, and nation's largest IMAX Theater. (Jersey City) Map 26

Liberty State Park/Statue of Liberty 201-915-3400
International symbol of America's freedom. (Jersey City) 7 F4

New Jersey Meadowlands Sports Complex 201-935-8500
Major site for sports and concerts. (East Rutherford) Map 31

Paper Mill Playhouse 973-376-4343
The State Theater of New Jersey. (Millburn) 7 C4

Statue of Liberty 212-363-3200
This 152-foot copper statue was presented to the U.S. by France in 1886. Its 150-foot-high island pedestal houses a museum devoted to the immigrant experience and the history of "Lady Liberty." For ferry information call 212-809-0808. (New York Harbor) 7 F4

Thomas A. Edison Memorial Tower and Museum 732-549-3299
Shows where the lightbulb was invented. (Menlo Park) 7 B6

Delaware River

Clara Barton School 609-298-1740
Located within Bordentown historic district. (Bordentown) 10 C5

Historic Burlington County Prison Museum 609-265-5958
Built in 1810, designed by Robert Mills to be maintenance-free, fireproof, heated and ventilated. (Mount Holly) 10 C6

James Fenimore Cooper House 609-386-1012
Adjoining this is Captain James Lawrence's house. (Burlington) 10 B6

New Jersey State Aquarium 856-365-3300
Features a large open ocean tank, seal pool, auditorium, and the new Ocean Base Atlantic interactive adventure. Accessible by car or ferry. (Camden) Map 25

New Jersey State Police Museum & Learning Center 609-882-2000 Ext. 2556
Contains the Lindbergh Kidnapping Archives and evidence. (Ewing) 10 B3

Old Barracks Museum 609-396-1776
A national landmark, the Revolution barracks where Hessians were surprised by Washington's troops Christmas 1776. (Trenton) Map 32

Smithville Mansion 609-256-5068
1840 Greek Revival Museum. (Eastampton) 15 D1

Thomas Paine's Home 609-298-1740
Located within Bordentown historic district. (Bordentown) 10 C5

Walt Whitman House 856-298-5383
Extensive collection of manuscripts, photos and memorabilia in the only home of one of America's finest poets. (Camden) Map 25

Wharton State Forest- Batsto Historic Village (within the Pine Barrens) 609-561-0024
Over one million acres of wilderness land make up the Pine Barrens. (Hammonton) 15 C4

The Shore

Barnegat Lighthouse 609-494-2016
Nicknamed "Old Barny" the lighthouse stands 172 feet, marking the entrance to Barnegat Inlet. (Barnegat Light) 16 E3

Fantasy Island Amusement Park 609-492-4000
Adult casino arcade, adult and children's amusement rides and spectacular miniature golf course. (Beach Haven) 16 D6

Fort Hancock/Sandy Hook Lighthouse 732-872-0115
Oldest operating lighthouse in the U.S. stands over historic Fort Hancock. (Sandy Hook Island) 11 F1

PNC Bank Arts Center 732-442-9200
Outdoor amphitheater hosts ethnic festivals, dance, opera, classical and popular music fests. (Holmdel) 11 D2

Navesink Light Station at Twin Lights State Historic Site 732-872-1814
Two-beacon lighthouse marks the western entrance into New York harbor. (Highlands) 12 A2

Greater Atlantic City

Atlantic City Boardwalk 609-348-7100
Built in 1881, the World's first boardwalk has hotels, casinos, and amusements. Map 24

Atlantic City Convention Hall 609-348-7100
Built in 1928, this recently restored meeting hall contains the world's largest pipe organ. Map 24

Lucy The Elephant 609-823-6473
Historic landmark overlooking the ocean. This 3-story, 90-ton elephant was once used as a hotel. Restored and tours given. (Margate) 19 F3

Towne of Historic Smithville 609-652-7777
Twelve miles from Atlantic City, where tourists will find cobblestone paths and craft shops. (Smithville) 20 A1

Southern Shore

Cape May Lighthouse 609-884-8656
Scenic view from Watch Room Gallery of this restored 1859 structure. (Cape May Point State Park) 22 A1

Discovery Sea Shell Museum 609-398-2316
Spectacular collection of seashells. (Ocean City) 19 E3

Leaming's Run Gardens & Colonial Farm 609-465-5871
One of the most beautiful gardens on the East Coast. (Swainton) 19 C5

Mid-Atlantic Center for the Arts 609-884-5404
Year-round tours of Victorian Cape May. (Cape May) 22 A1

Vineyards & Wineries

NEW JERSEY WINE LINE 800-524-0043

SKYLANDS:

Alba Vineyard 908-995-7800
(Milford) 5 D5

Amwell Valley Vineyard 908-788-5852
(Ringoes) 10 C1

Four Sisters Winery 908-475-3671
(Belvidere) 5 F2

Kings Road Vineyard 908-479-6611
(Asbury) 5 F5

La Follette Vineyard & Winery 908-359-5018
(Bell Mead) 10 E1

Poor Richards Winery 908-996-6480
(Frenchtown) 5 F6

Tamuzza Vineyards 908-459-5878
(Hope) 5 F2

Unionville Vineyards 908-788-0400
(Ringoes) 10 C1

DELAWARE RIVER:

Amalthea Cellars 856-768-8585
(Atco) 15 B4

Valenzano Winery 609-268-6731
(Shamong) 15 D3

THE SHORE:

Cream Ridge Vineyards & Champagne Cellars 609-259-9797
(Cream Ridge) 10 E5

GREATER ATLANTIC CITY:

Balic Winery 609-625-2166
(Mays Landing) 19 C1

Renault Winery 609-965-2111
(Egg Harbor City) 15 E6

Sylvin Farms Winery 609-965-1548
(Germania) 15 F6

Tomasello Winery 609-561-0567
(Hammonton) 15 C4

SOUTHERN SHORE:

Cape May Winery & Vineyard 609-884-1169
(Cape May) 22 A1

Marimac Vineyards 856-459-1111
(Bridgeton) 18 C2

Recreation

Downhill Ski Areas

Belle Mountain Ski Area   609-397-0043
190' vertical drop (Lambertville) 10 A2

Campgaw Mountain Ski Center   201-327-7800
270' vertical drop (Mahwah) 3 D6

Hidden Valley   201-764-6161
620' vertical drop (Vernon) 3 A4

Mountain Creek   973-827-2000
1033' vertical drop (Vernon) 2 F4

Racing Tracks

Atco Raceway   856-768-2167
Funnycars, dragsters, prostocks (Atco) 15 B3

Atlantic City Race Course   609-641-2190
Thoroughbred racing and fine dining (McKee City) 19 D1

Bridgeport Speedway   856-467-4407
Stock car racing (Bridgeport) 14 B3

East Windsor Speedway   609-448-8510
Stock car racing (Hightstown) 10 F3

Flemington Speedway   908-782-2413
Stock car racing (Flemington) 6 B6

Freehold Raceway   732-462-3800
Historic Park with harness racing, trotters and pacers (Freehold) 11 C3

Garden State Park Race Track   856-488-8400
Harness and thoroughbred racing (Cherry Hill) 14 C3

Island Dragway   908-637-6060
NHRA Drag Racing (Great Meadows) 6 A2

Meadowlands Race Track   201-460-4043
Harness and thoroughbred racing (East Rutherford) Map 31

Monmouth Park Racetrack   732-222-5100
Thoroughbred racing and dining (Oceanport) 11 F3

New Egypt Speedway   732-370-5968
Stock Car Racing (New Egypt) 11 A6

Old Bridge Township Raceway Park   732-446-7800
Drag racing, motocross, jet-ski racing (Englishtown) 11 B3

Wall Stadium   732-681-6400
Stock Car Racing (Belmar) 11 E4

Public Golf Courses

Apple Mountain GC   908-453-3023
18 holes (Belvidere) 5 F3

Ashbrook GC   908-756-0414
18 holes (Scotch Plains Twp) 7 B5

Avalon GC   609-465-4653
18 holes (Swainton) 19 C5

BL England GC   609-390-0472
9 holes (Beesley's Point) 19 E3

Ballyowen GC   973-293-8899
18 holes (Hamburg) 2 E5

Beaver Brook CC   908-735-4022
18 holes (Clinton) 6 B5

Beckett CC   856-467-4700
27 holes (Swedesboro) 14 C4

Bel-Aire GC   732-449-6024
27 holes (Allenwood) 11 E5

Bey Lea GC   732-349-0566
18 holes (Toms River) 16 D1

Black Bear G & CC   973-209-2226
18 holes (Franklin) 2 F5

Blair Academy GC   908-362-6218
9 holes (Blairstown) 6 A1

Blue Heron Pines GC   609-965-4653
18 holes (Cologne) 19 E1

Bowling Green GC   973-697-8688
18 holes (Milton) 2 F6

Brigantine Golf Links   609-266-1388
18 holes (Brigantine) 20 B1

Buena Vista CC   609-697-3733
18 holes (Buena) 15 B6

Bunker Hill GC   908-359-6335
18 holes (Princeton) 10 F1

Cape May National GC   609-884-1563
18 holes (Cape May) 19 B6

Cedar Creek GC   732-269-4460
18 holes (Bayville) 16 D2

Centerton GC   856-358-2220
18 holes (Centerton) 14 E6

Charleston Springs GC   732-409-7227
18 holes (Millstone Township) 11 B4

Cohanzick CC   856-455-2127
18 holes (Fairton) 18 D2

Colonial Terrace GC   732-775-3636
9 holes (Wanamassa) 11 F4

Cranbury GC   609-799-0341
18 holes (Cranbury) 10 E3

Cream Ridge GC & CC   609-259-2849
18 holes (Cream Ridge) 10 F5

Cruz Farm GC   732-938-3378
18 holes (Farmingdale) 11 E4

Crystal Springs GC   973-827-1444
18 holes (Hamburg) 2 F5

Culver Lake GC   973-948-6959
9 holes (Branchville) 2 D4

Darlington GC   201-327-8770
18 holes (Mahwah) 3 D6

Deerwood CC   609-265-1800
18 holes (Westampton) 15 C1

Eagle Ridge GC   732-901-4900
18 holes (Lakewood) 11 D6

Eastlyn GC   609-691-5588
18 holes (Vineland) 19 A1

East Orange GC   973-379-6775
18 holes (Short Hills) 7 B3

Emerson GC   201-261-1100
18 holes (Emerson) 7 F1

Fairway Valley GC   908-689-1530
9 holes (Washington) 6 A3

Farmstead G & CC   973-383-1666
27 holes (Lafayette) 2 E5

Fernwood GC   973-226-9661
9 holes (Roseland) 7 C3

Flanders Valley GC   973-584-5382
18 holes (Flanders) 6 E3

Francis Byrne GC   973-736-2306
18 holes (West Orange) 7 C3

Freeway GC   856-227-1115
18 holes (Sicklerville) 14 F3

Galloping Hill GC   908-686-1556
18 holes (Union) 7 C4

Gambler Ridge GC   609-758-3588
18 holes (Cream Ridge) 10 F5

Glenwild Greens GC   973-283-0888
9 holes (Bloomingdale) 3 B6

Golden Pheasant GC   609-267-4276
18 holes (Medford) 15 C1

Great Gorge CC   973-827-5757
27 holes (McAfee) 2 F4

Great Gorge Golf Resort   973-209-2226
45 holes (Franklin) 2 E5

Greate Bay Resort GC   609-927-0066
18 holes (Somers Point) 19 E3

Green Knoll GC   908-722-1301
18 holes (Bridgewater) 6 E5

Green Pond GC   973-983-9494
9 holes (Marcella) 7 A1

Green Tree GC   609-267-8440
18 holes (Egg Harbor Twp) 19 D2

Hamilton Trails CC   609-641-6824
9 holes (Mays Landing) 19 E1

Hammonton CC   609-561-5504
18 holes (Hammonton) 15 C5

Hanover CC   609-758-8301
18 holes (Jacobstown) 10 F6

Harbor Pines CC   609-927-0006
18 holes (Egg Harbor) 19 E2

Hendricks Field GC   973-751-0178
18 holes (Belleville) 7 D3

Hidden Acres GC   973-948-9804
9 holes (Hainesville) 2 C3

High Mountain GC   201-891-4653
18 holes (Franklin Lakes) 7 D1

High Point CC   973-293-3282
18 holes (Montague) 2 C3

Hillsborough CC   908-369-3322
18 holes (Flemington) 10 C1

Holly Hills GC   856-935-2412
18 holes (Alloway) 14 C6

Hominy Hill GC   732-462-9222
18 holes (Colts Neck) 11 D3

Hyatt Hills GC   732-388-3600
9 holes (Clark) 7 C5

Howell Park GC   732-939-4771
18 holes (Farmingdale) 11 D4

Indian Spring GC   609-983-0222
18 holes (Marlton) 15 B2

Jumping Brook GC   732-922-6140
18 holes (Neptune) 11 F4

Knob Hill CC   732-446-4800
18 holes (Englishtown) 11 B3

Knoll East GC   973-263-7115
9 holes (Parsippany) 7 B2

Knoll West GC   973-263-7110
18 holes (Parsippany) 7 B2

Kresson GC   856-435-3355
18 holes (Voorhees) 15 B2

Lake Lackawanna GC   973-347-9701
9 holes (Stanhope) 6 D1

Lakewood CC   732-364-8899
18 holes (Lakewood) 11 C5

Latona G & CC *9 holes* (Buena) 15 A6	856-692-8149	**Ponderlodge GC** *18 holes* (Villas) 19 A6	609-886-8065
Maple Ridge GC *18 holes* (Sewell) 14 E3	609-468-3542	**Princeton CC** *18 holes* (Princeton) 10 E3	609-452-9382
Mattawang GC *18 holes* (Belle Mead) 10 E1	908-281-0778	**Quail Brook GC** *18 holes* (Somerset) 6 F6	732-560-9199
Mays Landing CC *18 holes* (McKee City) 19 E1	609-641-4411	**Ramblewood CC** *27 holes* (Mount Laurel) 15 A1	856-235-2119
Meadows at Middlesex GC *18 holes* (Plainsboro) 10 E3	609-799-4000	**Rancocas GC** *18 holes* (Willingboro) 10 B6	609-877-5344
Meadows GC *18 holes* (Lincoln Park) 7 C2	973-696-7212	**Raritan Landing GC** *18 holes* (Piscataway) 7 A6	732-885-9600
Mercer Oaks GC *36 holes* (West Windsor) 10 D3	609-936-9603	**Rivervale CC** *18 holes* (Rivervale) 3 F6	201-391-2300
Millburn GC *9 holes* (Short Hills) 7 B4	973-379-4156	**Rockleigh GC** *27 holes* (Rockleigh) 8 A1	201-768-6353
Mine Brook GC *18 holes* (Hackettstown) 6 C2	908-979-0366	**Rockview GC** *9 holes* (Montague) 2 D2	973-293-9891
Miry Run CC *18 holes* (Robbinsville) 10 E4	609-259-1010	**Royce Brook GC** *36 holes* (Somerville) 6 E6	888-434-3673
Mountain View GC *18 holes* (Ewing) 10 C3	609-882-4093	**Rolling Greens GC** *18 holes* (Newton) 2 D6	973-383-3082
New Jersey National GC *18 holes* (Basking Ridge) 6 E5	908-781-2575	**Rutgers GC** *18 holes* (Piscataway) 7 A6	732-445-2631
Oak Ridge GC *18 holes* (Clark) 7 B5	732-574-0139	**Sand Barrens GC** *18 holes* (Swainton) 19 C5	609-465-3555
Ocean Acres CC *18 holes* (Manahawkin) 16 C4	609-597-9393	**Scotch Hills CC** *9 holes* (Scotch Plains Twp) 7 B5	908-232-9748
Ocean City GC *12 holes* (Ocean City) 19 E3	609-399-1315	**Scotland Run GC** *18 holes* (Williamstown) 14 F4	856-863-3737
Ocean County GC at Atlantis *18 holes* (Tuckerton) 16 B6	609-296-2444	**Seaview Marriott Golf Resort** *36 holes* (Absecon) 20 A1	609-652-1800
Ocean County GC at Forge Pond *18 holes* (Brick) 11 E5	732-920-8899	**Shark River GC** *18 holes* (Neptune) 11 F4	732-922-4141
Old Orchard CC *18 holes* (Eatontown) 11 F3	732-542-7666	**Sky View G & CC** *18 holes* (Sparta) 2 E6	973-729-7313
Orchard Hills CC *9 holes* (Paramus) 7 F1	201-447-3778	**Spooky Brook GC** *18 holes* (Franklin Township) 6 F6	732-873-2242
Overpeck GC *18 holes* (Teaneck) 7 F2	201-837-3020	**Springfield Golf Center** *18 holes* (Mt. Holly) 10 C6	609-267-8440
Paramus G & CC *18 holes* (Paramus) 7 E1	201-447-6067	**Spring Meadow GC** *18 holes* (Wall Township) 11 E5	732-449-0806
Pascack Brook G & CC *18 holes* (Rivervale) 7 F1	201-664-5886	**Stonybrook GC** *18 holes* (Hopewell) 10 C2	973-466-2215
Passaic County GC *36 holes* (Wayne) 7 C2	201-881-4921	**Summit Municipal GC** *9 holes* (Summit) 7 B4	908-277-6828
Pebble Creek GC *18 holes* (Colts Neck) 11 E3	732-303-9090	**Sunset Valley GC** *18 holes* (Pompton Plains) 7 C1	973-835-1515
Pennsauken CC *18 holes* (Pennsauken) 14 F1	856-662-4961	**Tamarack GC** *36 holes* (East Brunswick) 11 A1	732-821-8881
Pinelands GC *18 holes* (Winslow Township) 15 A4	609-561-8900	**Tamcrest GC** *9 holes* (Alpine) 8 A1	201-767-4610
Pinch Brook GC *18 holes* (Florham Park) 7 B3	973-377-2039	**Tara Greens GC** *18 holes* (Somerset) 11 A1	732-247-8284
Pine Barrens GC *18 holes* (Jackson) 11 C5	877-746-3227	**The Pines at Clermont GC** *9 holes* (Clermont) 19 C4	609-624-0100
Pine Brook GC *18 holes Executive* (Englishtown) 11 B3	732-536-7272	**The Spa GC** *9 holes* (McAfee) 2 F5	973-827-3710
Pitman GC *18 holes* (Sewell) 14 E3	856-589-6688	**Town & Country Golf Links** *18 holes* (Woodstown) 14 C5	856-769-8333
Plainfield West GC *9 holes* (Edison) 7 B5	908-769-3672	**Twin Brook GC** *9 holes* (Tinton Falls) 11 E4	732-922-1600
Pomona GC *9 holes* (Pomona) 15 F6	609-965-3232	**Twin Willows GC** *9 holes* (Lincoln Park) 7 C1	973-694-9726

Valleybrook GC *18 holes* (Blackwood) 14 F3	856-227-3171
Warrenbrook GC *18 holes* (Warren) 7 A5	908-754-8402
Washington Township Municipal GC *9 holes* (Turnersville) 14 F4	856-227-1435
Wedgwood CC *18 holes* (Turnersville) 14 F3	856-227-5522
Weequahic Park GC *18 holes* (Newark) 7 D4	973-923-1838
Westwood GC *18 holes* (Woodbury) 14 D3	856-845-2000
White Oaks CC *18 holes* (Newfield) 14 F6	856-694-5585
Wild Oaks GC *27 holes* (Salem) 14 A6	856-935-0705
Willowbrook CC *18 holes* (Moorestown) 10 A6	856-461-0131
Woodlake GC & CC *18 holes* (Lakewood) 11 E5	732-370-1002

New Jersey Coastal Heritage Trail

The New Jersey Coastal Heritage Trail (NJCHT) was developed cooperatively by the National Park Service, the State of New Jersey, and many organizations working to preserve the State's natural and cultural heritage. The trail is divided into five regions linked by the common bond of life on the Jersey Shore and Raritan and Delaware Bays. Each region has its own Welcome Center where one can find literature describing the unique features and themes of each region.

The trail is designed for motorized travel, with easy access to and from New Jersey's scenic roads and byways. Along the shoreline one can relax in quaint communities, explore maritime history and amusement parks, learn about wildlife migration and discover diverse wildlife habitats. Look for the multi-colored markers along the trail. As new sites are added, NJCHT logos will identify them.

For further information contact: New Jersey Division of Travel and Tourism, CN 826, Trenton, New Jersey 08625-0826 or New Jersey Coastal Heritage Trail, National Park Service, P.O. Box 118, Mauricetown, New Jersey 08329.

Region	Park	Phone	Bicycle Trails	Boating — Launch (L), Rentals	Bridle Trails	Cabins	Camping	Concession	Cross Country Skiing	Environmental Education and Interpretation	Fishing	Handicapped Facilities	Hunting	Picnic Areas	Playgrounds	Restrooms (R), Showers (S)	Snowmobile Trails	Swimming — Beach (B), Pool (P)	Trails — Hiking (H), Nature (N)	Visitors Center	Map Number	Grid Location
SKYLANDS	Allamuchy Mountain State Park	908-852-3790	●				●		●		●	●	●		●	R			H		6	C2
	Bulls Island Recreation Area	609-397-2949		L			●				●			●	●				H,N		9	F2
	Delaware & Raritan Canal State Park	732-873-3050	●	L,R	●		●		●		●	●		●		R,S			H,N		10	E1
	Farny State Park	973-962-7031							●				●						H		3	A6
	Hacklebarney State Park	908-879-5677							●		●	●		●					H		6	C4
	High Point State Park	973-875-4800	●	L		●	●	●	●					●	●	R,S	●	B	H,N	●	2	D3
	Hopatcong State Park	973-398-7010		L				●			●			●		R,S		B			6	D1
	Jenny Jump State Forest	908-459-4366				●	●					●	●	●	●	R,S			H		6	A2
	Kittatinny Valley State Park	973-786-6445	●	L	●														H		2	D6
	Round Valley Recreation Area	908-236-6355	●	L	●		●	●			●	●	●	●		R,S		B	H,N		6	B5
	Spruce Run Recreation Area	908-638-8572		L,R			●	●			●	●	●	●	●	R,S		B			6	A5
	Stephens State Park	732-852-3790	●				●	●			●	●		●	●	R			H		6	C2
	Stokes State Forest	973-948-3820	●			●	●	●	●		●	●	●	●	●	R,S	●	B	H,N		2	C3
	Swartswood State Park	973-383-5230	●	L,R	●		●	●	●		●	●	●	●	●	R,S	●	B	H,N		2	C6
	Voorhees State Park	908-638-6969	●				●	●			●	●		●	●	R,S			H		6	B4
	Washington Rock State Park	201-915-3401												●							7	A5
	Wawayanda State Park	973-853-4462	●	L,R			●	●	●		●	●	●	●		R,S	●	B	H		3	A4
	Worthington State Forest	908-841-9575	●	L			●		●		●	●	●	●		R,S	●		H		1	F6
GATEWAY	Abram S Hewitt State Forest	973-853-4462							●				●				●		H		3	B4
	Cheesequake State Park	732-566-2161	●				●	●	●		●	●		●	●	R,S		B	H,N		11	C1
	Liberty State Park	201-915-3400		L				●	●	●	●	●		●	●			P		●	7	F4
	Long Pond Ironworks State Park	973-962-7031	●	L,R	●						●	●	●						H		3	C5
	Norvin Green State Forest	973-962-7031		L					●	●	●		●						H		3	B5
	Ramapo Mountain State Forest	973-962-7031	●		●						●		●						H		3	C6
	Ringwood State Park	973-962-7031	●	L,R				●	●		●			●	●		●	B	H,N		3	D5
DELAWARE RIVER	Bass River State Forest	609-296-1114		L,R	●	●	●	●	●	●	●	●	●	●	●	R,S		B	H,N		16	A3
	Fort Mott State Park	856-935-3218								●		●		●	●						13	F5
	Lebanon State Forest	609-726-1191	●			●	●		●	●	●	●	●	●		R,S		B	H,N		15	F2
	Parvin State Park	856-358-8616	●	L,R		●	●	●	●		●	●		●	●	R,S		B	H,N		14	E6
	Penn State Forest	609-296-1114		L	●						●		●						H		16	A3
	Princeton Battlefield State Park	609-921-0074							●			●							H,N		10	D3
	Rancocas State Park	609-726-1191								●						R			H,N	●	15	B1
	Washington Crossing State Park	609-737-0623	●		●		●			●		●		●	●	R			H,N	●	10	B3
	Wharton State Forest	609-561-3262	●	L,R	●	●	●				●	●	●	●		R,S		B	H,N		15	C4
THE SHORE	Allaire State Park	732-938-2371	●		●		●	●	●		●	●		●	●	R,S			H,N	●	11	E4
	Barnegat Lighthouse State Park	609-494-2016						●						●							16	E3
	Double Trouble State Park	732-341-6642	●	L	●						●		●	●		R			H	●	16	C2
	Island Beach State Park	732-793-0506						●		●	●	●						B	N		16	F2
	Monmouth Battlefield State Park	732-462-9616	●		●									●	●				H,N	●	11	C3
SOUTHERN SHORE	Belleplain State Forest	609-861-2404	●	L,R	●		●				●	●	●	●	●	R,S		B	H,N		19	B3
	Cape May Point State Park	609-884-2159								●	●	●							H,N	●	22	A1
	Corsons Inlet State Park	609-861-2404									●		●						H,N		19	E4

General Information

Garden State Parkway Interchanges

This schematic shows full interchanges and partial interchanges. Full interchanges have entrances and exits both south and northbound. Partial interchanges may have entrances or exits, not necessarily in both directions.

Legend:

- (F) = Full interchange
- (P) = Partial interchange

▨	YES Interchange has entrance/exit in direction indicated
☐	NO Interchange has no entrance/exit in direction indicated

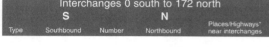

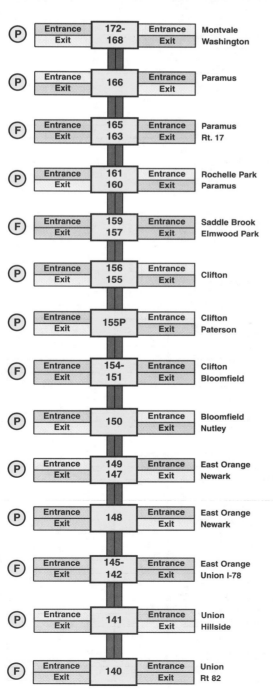

Interchanges 0 south to 172 north

Type	Southbound	Number	Northbound	Places/Highways* near interchanges
P	Entrance/Exit	172-168	Entrance/Exit	Montvale Washington
P	Entrance/Exit	166	Entrance/Exit	Paramus
F	Entrance/Exit	165-163	Entrance/Exit	Paramus Rt. 17
P	Entrance/Exit	161-160	Entrance/Exit	Rochelle Park Paramus
F	Entrance/Exit	159-157	Entrance/Exit	Saddle Brook Elmwood Park
P	Entrance/Exit	156-155	Entrance/Exit	Clifton
P	Entrance/Exit	155P	Entrance/Exit	Clifton Paterson
F	Entrance/Exit	154-151	Entrance/Exit	Clifton Bloomfield
P	Entrance/Exit	150	Entrance/Exit	Bloomfield Nutley
P	Entrance/Exit	149-147	Entrance/Exit	East Orange Newark
P	Entrance/Exit	148	Entrance/Exit	East Orange Newark
F	Entrance/Exit	145-142	Entrance/Exit	East Orange Union I-78
P	Entrance/Exit	141	Entrance/Exit	Union Hillside
F	Entrance/Exit	140	Entrance/Exit	Union Rt 82

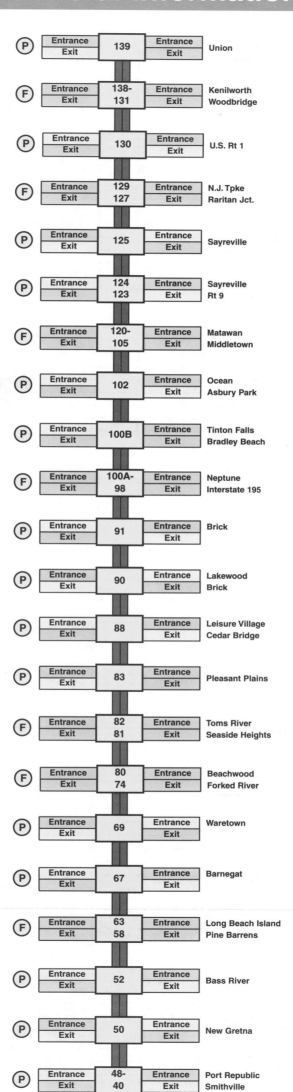

Type		Number		Places
P	Entrance/Exit	139	Entrance/Exit	Union
F	Entrance/Exit	138-131	Entrance/Exit	Kenilworth Woodbridge
P	Entrance/Exit	130	Entrance/Exit	U.S. Rt 1
F	Entrance/Exit	129-127	Entrance/Exit	N.J. Tpke Raritan Jct.
P	Entrance/Exit	125	Entrance/Exit	Sayreville
P	Entrance/Exit	124-123	Entrance/Exit	Sayreville Rt 9
F	Entrance/Exit	120-105	Entrance/Exit	Matawan Middletown
P	Entrance/Exit	102	Entrance/Exit	Ocean Asbury Park
P	Entrance/Exit	100B	Entrance/Exit	Tinton Falls Bradley Beach
F	Entrance/Exit	100A-98	Entrance/Exit	Neptune Interstate 195
P	Entrance/Exit	91	Entrance/Exit	Brick
P	Entrance/Exit	90	Entrance/Exit	Lakewood Brick
P	Entrance/Exit	88	Entrance/Exit	Leisure Village Cedar Bridge
P	Entrance/Exit	83	Entrance/Exit	Pleasant Plains
F	Entrance/Exit	82-81	Entrance/Exit	Toms River Seaside Heights
F	Entrance/Exit	80-74	Entrance/Exit	Beachwood Forked River
P	Entrance/Exit	69	Entrance/Exit	Waretown
P	Entrance/Exit	67	Entrance/Exit	Barnegat
F	Entrance/Exit	63-58	Entrance/Exit	Long Beach Island Pine Barrens
P	Entrance/Exit	52	Entrance/Exit	Bass River
P	Entrance/Exit	50	Entrance/Exit	New Gretna
P	Entrance/Exit	48-40	Entrance/Exit	Port Republic Smithville

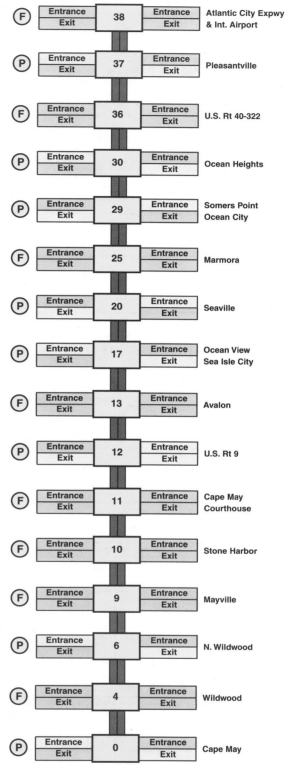

Type		Number		Places
F	Entrance/Exit	38	Entrance/Exit	Atlantic City Expwy & Int. Airport
P	Entrance/Exit	37	Entrance/Exit	Pleasantville
F	Entrance/Exit	36	Entrance/Exit	U.S. Rt 40-322
P	Entrance/Exit	30	Entrance/Exit	Ocean Heights
P	Entrance/Exit	29	Entrance/Exit	Somers Point Ocean City
F	Entrance/Exit	25	Entrance/Exit	Marmora
P	Entrance/Exit	20	Entrance/Exit	Seaville
P	Entrance/Exit	17	Entrance/Exit	Ocean View Sea Isle City
F	Entrance/Exit	13	Entrance/Exit	Avalon
P	Entrance/Exit	12	Entrance/Exit	U.S. Rt 9
F	Entrance/Exit	11	Entrance/Exit	Cape May Courthouse
F	Entrance/Exit	10	Entrance/Exit	Stone Harbor
F	Entrance/Exit	9	Entrance/Exit	Mayville
P	Entrance/Exit	6	Entrance/Exit	N. Wildwood
F	Entrance/Exit	4	Entrance/Exit	Wildwood
P	Entrance/Exit	0	Entrance/Exit	Cape May

Note: The schematic above is not drawn to scale. On the Parkway actual distances between interchanges vary. On the schematic, distances appear the same for the sake of simplification.

*Place names on the right are given for orientation and are not the actual names of the interchanges on the highway signs.

Source: Garden State Parkway Authority.

State Speed Limits
(unless otherwise posted)

Residential Highways 25mph
Primary Highways 50mph
Interstate Highways (Urban) 55mph
Interstate Highways (Rural) 65mph

Toll Information

The State of New Jersey collects tolls for its toll roads at various exits, or toll plazas, along the highways. Tolls are based on distances traveled. Toll highways include the New Jersey Turnpike (118 miles), the Garden State Parkway (173 miles), and the Atlantic City Expressway (44 miles).

E-Z Pass, a discount electronic toll collection system, is now accepted at toll plazas throughout New Jersey. Contact **E-Z Pass** at 888-288-6865 for applications and information.

ATLANTIC CITY EXPRESSWAY

Toll Plaza	Mile Post	Tolls
Pleasantville Plaza	4	$.50
Airport Ramp (Pomona)	9	.50
Mays Landing Ramp	12	.50
Egg Harbor Plaza	18	2.00
Hammonton Ramp	28	.50
Winslow Ramp	33	.50
Williamstown Ramp	38	.25
Cross Keys Ramp	41	.25

DELAWARE RIVER JOINT TOLL BRIDGE COMMISSION   215-295-5061

Milford-Montague	$.50	Both Directions	2-C3
Delaware Water Gap	1.00	Westbound Only	5-E1
Portland-Columbia	1.00	Westbound Only	5-E1
Easton-Phillipsburg	0.50	Westbound Only	5-D4
Interstate 78	0.50	Westbound Only	5-D4
New Hope - Lambertville	0.25	Both Directions	10-A2
Morrisville - Trenton	0.20	Westbound Only	10-C4

BURLINGTON COUNTY BRIDGE COMMISSION   609-829-1900

Burlington - Bristol	$2.00	Westbound Only	10-B6
Tacony - Palmyra	2.00	Westbound Only	9-F6

GARDEN STATE PARKWAY

Toll Area and Type		CAR	Car with 1-axle Trailer 2-axle, 6-Tire Camper; or 3-axle Camper	Car with 2-axle Trailer or 4-axle Camper	Car with 3 -axle Trailer	Omnibus**	HEAVY TRUCKS*** 2-axle, 4-tire Truck, 3½ tons or more	2-axle, 6-tire Truck	3-axle Truck	4-axle Truck	5-axle Truck	6-axle Truck
Hillsdale	B	.35*	.50	.70	.90	2.00						
Paramus	R	.25	.35	.50	.60	2.00						
Bergen	B	.35*	.50	.70	.90	2.00						
Saddle Brook	R	.35*	.50	.70	.90	2.00						
Clifton	R	.25	.35	.50	.60	2.00						
Passaic	R	.25	.35	.50	.60	2.00						
Watchung	R	.35*	.50	.70	.90	2.00						
Essex	B	.35*	.50	.70	.90	2.00						
Bloomfield	R	.25	.35	.50	.60	2.00						
East Orange	R	.25	.35	.50	.60	2.00						
Irvington	R	.25	.35	.50	.60	2.00						
Union	R	.35*	.50	.70	.90	2.00						
Union	R	.35*	.50	.70	.90	2.00						
Raritan North/South	B	.35	.50	.70	.90	2.00						
Matawan	R	.25	.35	.50	.60	2.00						
Keyport-Hazlet	R	.25	.35	.50	.60	2.00						
Holmdel	R	.25	.35	.50	.60	2.00						
Red Bank	R	.25	.35	.50	.60	2.00						
Eatontown	R	.35*	.50	.70	.90	2.00						
Asbury Park	B	.35*	.50	.70	.90	2.00	.70	.70	1.05	1.40	1.75	2.10
Belmar-Wall	R	.25	.35	.50	.60	2.00	.60	.50	.75	1.00	1.25	1.50
Lakewood-Brick	R	.25	.35	.50	.60	2.00	.50	.50	.75	1.00	1.25	1.50
Lakehurst	R	.25	.35	.50	.60	2.00	.50	.50	.75	1.00	1.25	1.50
Toms River	B	.35*	.50	.70	.90	2.00	.70	.70	1.05	1.40	1.75	2.10
Lacey	R	.25	.35	.50	.60	2.00	.50	.50	.75	1.00	1.25	1.50
Barnegat	B	.35*	.50	.70	.90	2.00	.70	.70	1.05	1.40	1.75	2.10
New Gretna	B	.35*	.50	.70	.90	2.00	.70	.70	1.05	1.40	1.75	2.10
Interchange 44+	R	.25	.35	.50	.60	2.00	.50	.50	.75	1.00	1.25	1.50
Atlantic City+	B	.35*	.50	.70	.90	2.00	.70	.70	1.05	1.40	1.75	2.10
Interchange 40 &/or 41+	R	.25	.35	.50	.60	2.00	.50	.50	.75	1.00	1.25	1.50
Somers Point	R	.35*	.50	.70	.90	2.00	.70	.70	1.05	1.40	1.75	2.10
Great Egg	B	.35*	.50	.70	.90	2.00	.70	.70	1.05	1.40	1.75	2.10
Cape May	B	.35*	.50	.70	.90	2.00	.70	.70	1.05	1.40	1.75	2.10
Wildwood	R	.25	.35	.50	.60	2.00	.50	.50	.75	1.00	1.25	1.50

* Car tokens available for use by cars in exact change or token only lanes.
** $.50 bus token available for regularly scheduled buses and $1.00 bus token available for all other buses for use in designated lanes.
*** Heavy trucks (3½ tons or more, 6 tires, or 3-or-more-axles) prohibited north of interchange 105 in Monmouth County.
+ To be designated   B - Barrier   R - Ramp

NEW JERSEY TURNPIKE

CLASS 1 — Passenger Cars (2 Axles)

		1 Delaware Memorial Bridge	2 US 322, Swedesboro, Chester	3 NJ 168, Woodbury, South Camden	4 NJ 73, Camden, Philadelphia	5 Burlington, Mount Holly	6 Pennsylvania Turnpike	6A Pennsylvania Turnpike, Florence	7 US 206, Bordentown, Trenton	7A I-195 Trenton, Hamilton	8 NJ 33, Hightstown, Freehold	8A Cranbury, Jamesburg	9 NJ 18, New Brunswick	10 I-287 Metuchen, Perth Amboy	11 Garden State Parkway	12 Carteret, Rahway	13 I-278, Elizabeth, Staten Island	13A Newark Airport, Elizabeth Seaport	14 Newark Airport, I-78, US 1 and 9	14A Hudson County, Ext, Bayonne	14B Jersey City, Liberty State Park	14C Holland Tunnel	15E US 1 and 9, Newark, Jersey City	15W I-280, Newark, Harrison	16E NJ 3, Lincoln Tunnel, Secaucus	16W NJ 3, Sportsplex, E. Rutherford	17 NJ 3, Lincoln Tunnel, Secaucus
1	Delaware Memorial Bridge																										
2	US 322, Swedesboro, Chester	0.55																									
3	NJ 168, Woodbury, South Camden	0.85	0.55																								
4	NJ 73, Camden, Philadelphia	1.15	0.70	0.40																							
5	Burlington, Mount Holly	1.45	1.00	0.60	0.40																						
6	Pennsylvania Turnpike	2.20	1.85	1.45	1.15	0.85																					
6A	Pennsylvania Turnpike, Florence							1.20																			
7	US 206, Bordentown, Trenton	1.75	1.20	0.85	0.60	0.40	0.70																				
7A	I-195, Trenton, Hamilton	1.85	1.45	1.00	0.70	0.55	0.85		0.40																		
8	NJ 33, Hightstown, Freehold	2.05	1.75	1.20	1.00	0.70	1.15		0.55	0.40																	
8A	Cranbury, Jamesburg	2.20	1.90	1.60	1.20	1.00	1.45		0.70	0.60	0.40																
9	NJ 18, New Brunswick	2.60	2.05	1.75	1.45	1.15	1.60		0.85	0.70	0.55	0.40															
10	I-287, Metuchen, Perth Amboy	2.65	2.20	1.85	1.60	1.20	1.75		1.00	0.85	0.60	0.55	0.40														
11	Garden State Parkway	2.90	2.45	1.90	1.75	1.45	1.85		1.15	1.00	0.70	0.60	0.40	0.40													
12	Carteret, Rahway	3.20	2.90	2.45	2.05	1.85	2.20		1.60	1.45	1.15	1.00	0.70	0.60	0.40												
13	I-278, Elizabeth, Staten Island	3.65	3.20	2.90	2.60	2.20	2.65		1.90	1.85	1.60	1.45	1.15	1.00	0.70	0.55											
13A	Newark Airport, Elizabeth Seaport	4.25	3.80	3.50	3.05	2.90	3.20		2.60	2.45	2.05	1.90	1.75	1.60	1.20	1.00	0.40										
14	Newark Airport, I-78, US 1 and 9	4.25	3.80	3.50	3.05	2.90	3.20		2.60	2.45	2.05	1.90	1.75	1.60	1.20	1.00	0.60	0.40									
14A	Hudson County, Ext, Bayonne	4.90	4.50	4.10	3.80	3.60	3.90		3.20	3.05	2.90	2.65	2.45	2.20	1.90	1.75	1.20	1.20	0.70								
14B	Jersey City, Liberty State Park	5.00	4.70	4.25	3.90	3.65	4.10		3.50	3.20	2.95	2.90	2.60	2.45	1.85	1.45	1.45	0.85	0.40								
14C	Holland Tunnel	5.30	4.80	4.40	4.10	3.80	4.25		3.60	3.50	2.95	2.65	2.60	2.20	1.90	1.60	1.60	1.00	0.55	0.40							
15E	US 1 and 9, Newark, Jersey City	4.50	4.10	3.65	3.50	3.05	3.60		2.90	2.65	2.45	2.20	1.90	1.85	1.60	1.20	0.85	0.85	0.40	1.00	1.15	1.20					
15W	I-280, Newark, Harrison	4.70	4.25	3.80	3.60	3.20	3.65		2.95	2.90	2.60	2.45	2.05	1.90	1.75	1.45	1.00	1.00	0.55	1.15	1.20	1.45	0.40				
16E	NJ 3, Lincoln Tunnel, Secaucus	5.00	4.70	4.25	3.90	3.65	4.10		3.50	3.20	2.95	2.90	2.60	2.45	2.05	1.85	1.45	1.45	0.85	1.60	1.75	1.85	0.60	0.55			
16W	NJ 3, Sportsplex, E. Rutherford	5.00	4.70	4.25	3.90	3.65	4.10		3.50	3.20	2.95	2.90	2.60	2.45	2.05	1.85	1.45	1.45	0.85	1.60	1.75	1.85	0.60	0.55			
17	NJ 3, Lincoln Tunnel, Secaucus																										0.55
18E	GWB, US 46, I-80, Ridgefield Park	5.50	5.30	4.80	4.50	4.25	4.70		3.90	3.80	3.60	3.50	3.05	2.95	2.65	2.45	1.90	1.90	1.45	2.05	2.20	2.45	1.15	1.00			
18W	GWB, US 46, I-80, Ridgefield Park	5.50	5.30	4.80	4.50	4.25	4.70		3.90	3.80	3.50	3.05			2.65	2.45	1.90	1.90	1.45	2.05	2.20	2.45	1.15	1.00		0.60	

Toll Information, Cont.

DELAWARE RIVER PORT AUTHORITY   856-968-2000

Betsy Ross	$3.00	Westbound Only	14-F1
Benjamin Franklin	3.00	Westbound Only	14-E1
Walt Whitman	3.00	Westbound Only	14-E2
Commodore John Barry	3.00	Westbound Only	14-B2

Highway Information

New Jersey Turnpike	732-247-0900
Garden State Parkway	908-442-8600
Atlantic City Expressway	609-965-6060
New Jersey Dept. of Transportation	609-530-2000

State Police

Division of State Police   609-882-2000
P.O. Box 7068
West Trenton, NJ 08628-0068

Ferry Information

RATES: CAPE MAY, NJ TO LEWES, DE

Vehicle and Driver	One Way Peak
• Passenger Car, Station Wagon, Van, Pick-up, Panel, Self-contained Camper (2 axles and 4 tires, with overall length no greater than 20 feet)	$ 20.00
• Motorbike or motorcycle	15.00
• Bicycle—ridden or hand carried	15.00

Vehicle Passengers	
Under 6 yrs of age	2.00
6 yrs of age & older	6.50
Bus Passengers	6.00

Foot Passengers	
Under 6 yrs of age	2.00
6 yrs of age & older	6.50

For Reservations	800-643-3779
For Schedule Times	800-717-7245

County Seats

County	County Seat	Map	Grid
Atlantic	Mays Landing	19	D1
Bergen	Hackensack	7	F2
Burlington	Mount Holly	15	C1
Camden	Camden	14	E1
Cape May	Cape May Courthouse	19	B5
Cumberland	Bridgeton	18	D1
Essex	Newark	7	D4
Gloucester	Woodbury	14	D2
Hudson	Jersey City	7	E4
Hunterdon	Flemington	6	B6
Mercer	Trenton	10	C4
Middlesex	New Brunswick	11	A1
Monmouth	Freehold	11	C3

County	County Seat	Map	Grid
Morris	Morristown	7	A3
Ocean	South Toms River	16	D1
Passaic	Paterson	7	D1
Salem	Salem	14	A6
Somerset	Somerville	6	E6
Sussex	Newton	2	D6
Union	Elizabeth	7	D5
Warren	Belvidere	5	E2

State Facts

State Name:	State of New Jersey
Statehood:	Admitted to the Union: December 18, 1787
Nickname:	Garden State
State Capital:	Trenton (1790)
State Motto:	"Liberty and Prosperity"
State Flower:	Common Meadow Violet
State Bird:	Eastern Goldfinch
State Tree:	Red Oak
State Insect:	Honeybee
State Animal:	Horse
State Fish:	Brook Trout
Population:	7,730,188 (1990 Census)
Land Area:	7,418.84 Sq. Mi.

State Trivia

Highest population density in the US: 1,042 persons per square mile.

Highest percent urban population in the US with nearly 90% of the people living in an urban area.

Home to the headquarters of the Boy Scouts of America.

Densest system of highways and railroads in the US.

Commonly known as "the diner capital of the world".

Home of Thomas Edison and his inventions: incandescent light bulb, phonograph, and motion picture projector.

First Drive-In Movie Theatre was opened in Camden.

New Jersey is home to the Statue of Liberty and Ellis Island.

First submarine ride —Passaic River, Paterson.

Largest chemical producing state in the nation.

Home to the Miss America pageant held in Atlantic City, which has the longest boardwalk in the world.

Known for its production of eggplant, cranberries, blueberries and tomatoes.

First organized game of baseball was played in Hoboken.

Rutgers College (now Rutgers University) played Princeton in the first intercollegiate football game.

Famous Natives & Residents

Bud Abbott & Lou Costello, Comedians
Edwin Aldrin, Astronaut
Count Basie, Big Band Leader
Jon Bon Jovi, Musician
Aaron Burr, Statesman
James Fenimore Cooper, Novelist
Allen Ginsberg, Poet
William Frederick Halsey, Jr., Admiral
Ernie Kovacs, Comedian
Jerry Lewis, Comedian
Norman Mailer, Novelist
Richard Nixon, US President
Dorothy Parker, Author
Paul Robeson, Vocalist and Activist
Ruth St. Denis, Choreographer
Antonin Scalia, Supreme Court Justice
H. Norman Schwarzkopf, General
Frank Sinatra, Vocalist and Movie Star
Bruce Springsteen, Musician
Sarah Vaughan, Vocalist
William Carlos Williams, Physician and Poet

Visitors Information

NJ Division of Travel & Tourism   609-777-0885
20 West State Street
PO Box 820
Trenton, NJ 08625
   Out Of State   800-847-4865

NJ Division of Fish, Game & Wildlife   609-292-2965
501 East State Street
PO Box 400
Trenton, NJ 08625

NJ Division of Parks & Forestry   609-843-6420
501 East State Street
PO Box 404
Trenton, NJ 08625

NJ DOT Motor Vehicles Services   609-292-6500
225 East State Street
PO Box 160
Trenton, NJ 08625

NJ Historic Trust   609-984-0473
506 East State Street
PO Box 457
Trenton, NJ 08625

NJ Campground Owners Association   609-465-8444
29 Cooks Beach Road
Cape May Court House, NJ 08210

Federal Information Center   800-688-9889

Bed & Breakfast Innkeepers Association of NJ   732-449-3535
PO Box 108
Spring Lake, NJ 07762

Regional Information

Skylands Regional Tourism Council   800-4-SKYLANDS
c/o Skylands Visitor Magazine
PO Box 329
Columbia, NJ 07832

Gateway Regional Tourism Council   201-641-7632
PO Box 602
Little Ferry, NJ 07643

Delaware River Regional Tourism Council   856-365-3300, ext. 230
Director of Marketing
c/o New Jersey State Aquarium
One Riverside Drive
Camden, NJ 08103

Shore Regional Tourism Council   732-544-9300, ext. 708
700 Hope Road
Tinton Falls, NJ 07724

Greater Atlantic City Regional Tourism Council   609-652-7777
Towne of Historic Smithville
One North New York Road
Smithville, NJ 08201

Southern Shore Regional Tourism Council   609-399-2629
c/o Ocean City Chamber of Commerce
PO Box 157
Ocean City, NJ 08226

NEW JERSEY TURNPIKE-INTERSTATES 95 & 495

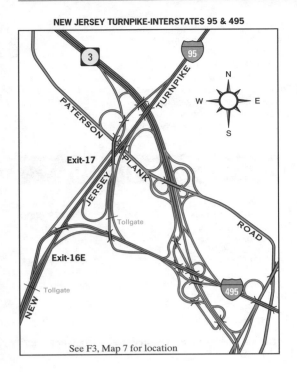

See F3, Map 7 for location

NEW JERSEY TURNPIKE-INTERSTATES 78 & 95

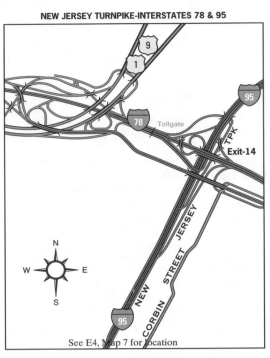

See E4, Map 7 for location

NEW JERSEY TURNPIKE-INTERSTATES 95 & 287

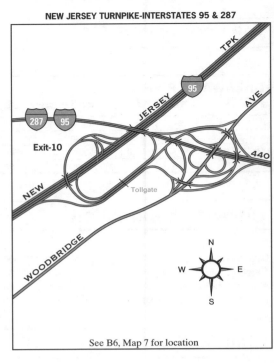

See B6, Map 7 for location

GARDEN STATE PARKWAY-INTERSTATE 80

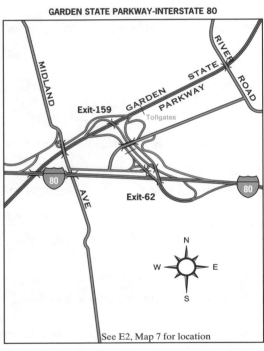

See E2, Map 7 for location

GARDEN STATE PARKWAY-ROUTES 46 & 20

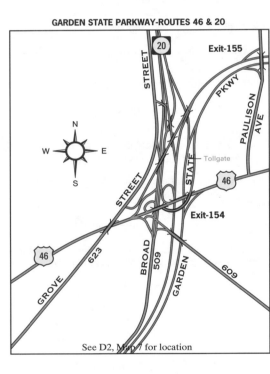

See D2, Map 7 for location

GARDEN STATE PARKWAY-ROUTE 3

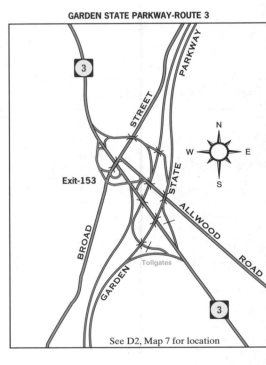

See D2, Map 7 for location

GARDEN STATE PARKWAY-INTERSTATE 78

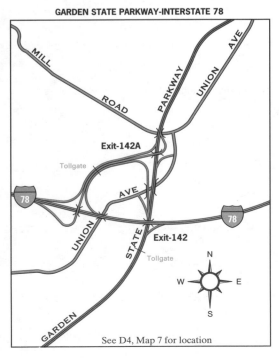

See D4, Map 7 for location

GARDEN STATE PARKWAY-ROUTE 22

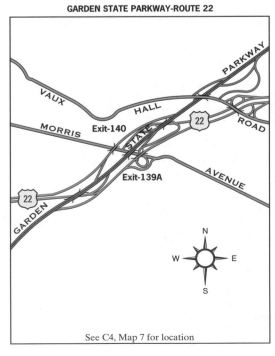

See C4, Map 7 for location

GARDEN STATE PARKWAY-ROUTES 9 & 440

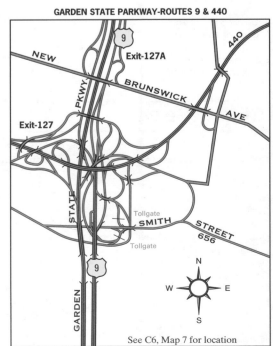

See C6, Map 7 for location

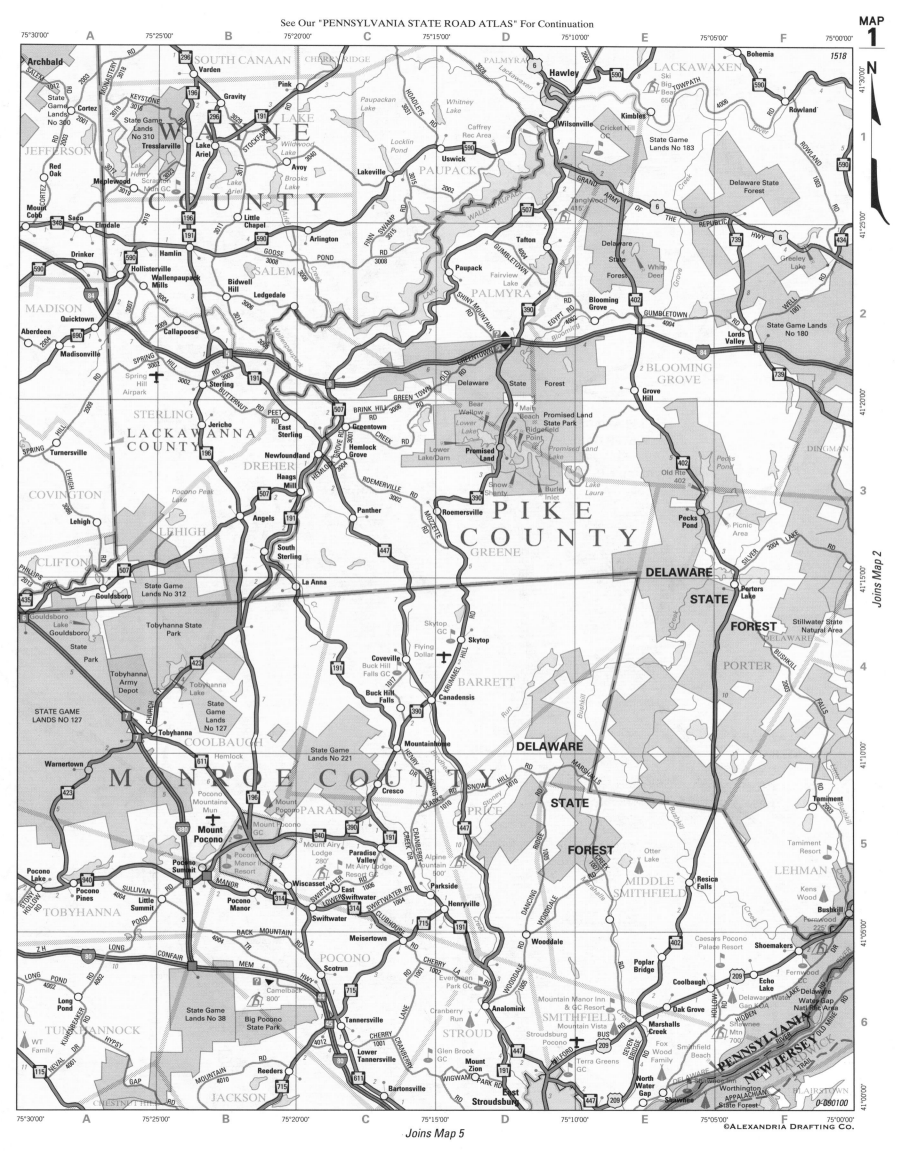

MAP
2
N

See Our "NEW YORK STATE ROAD ATLAS" For Continuation

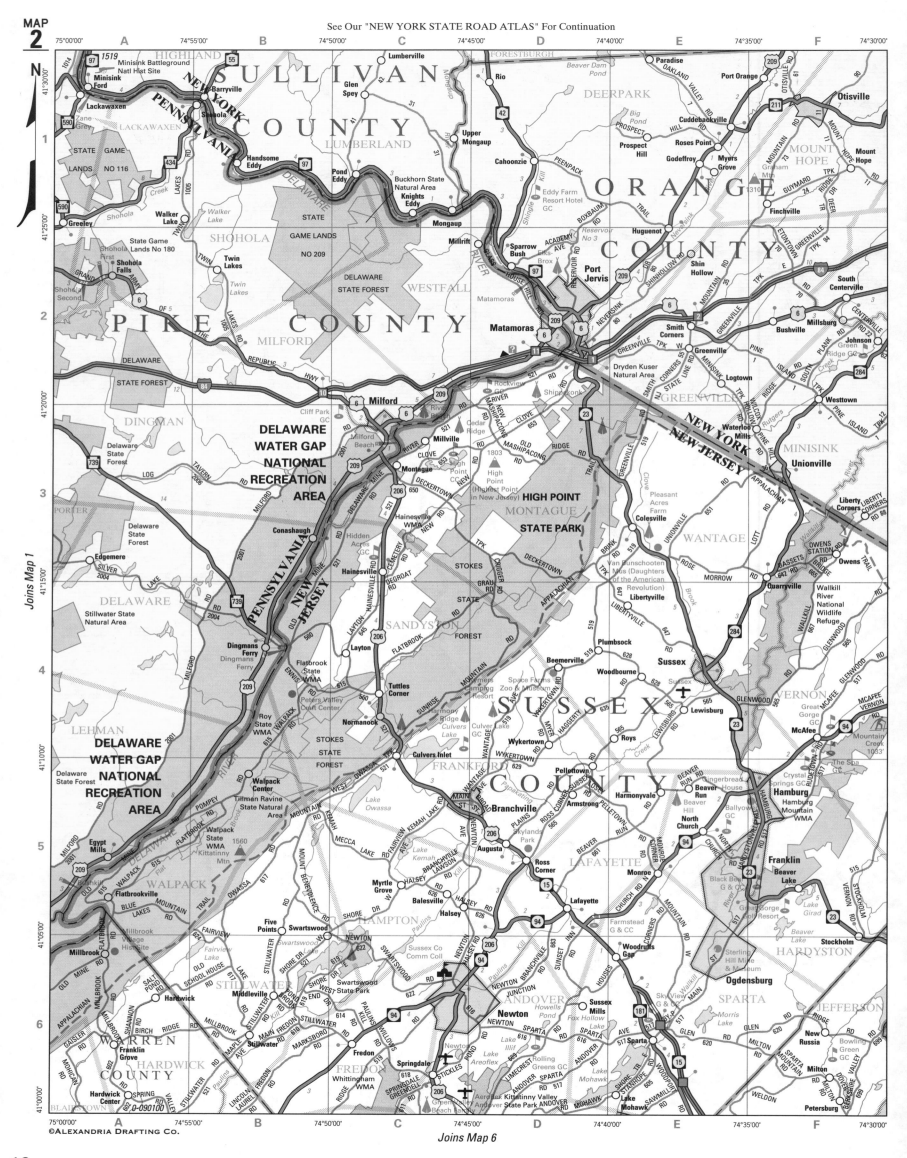

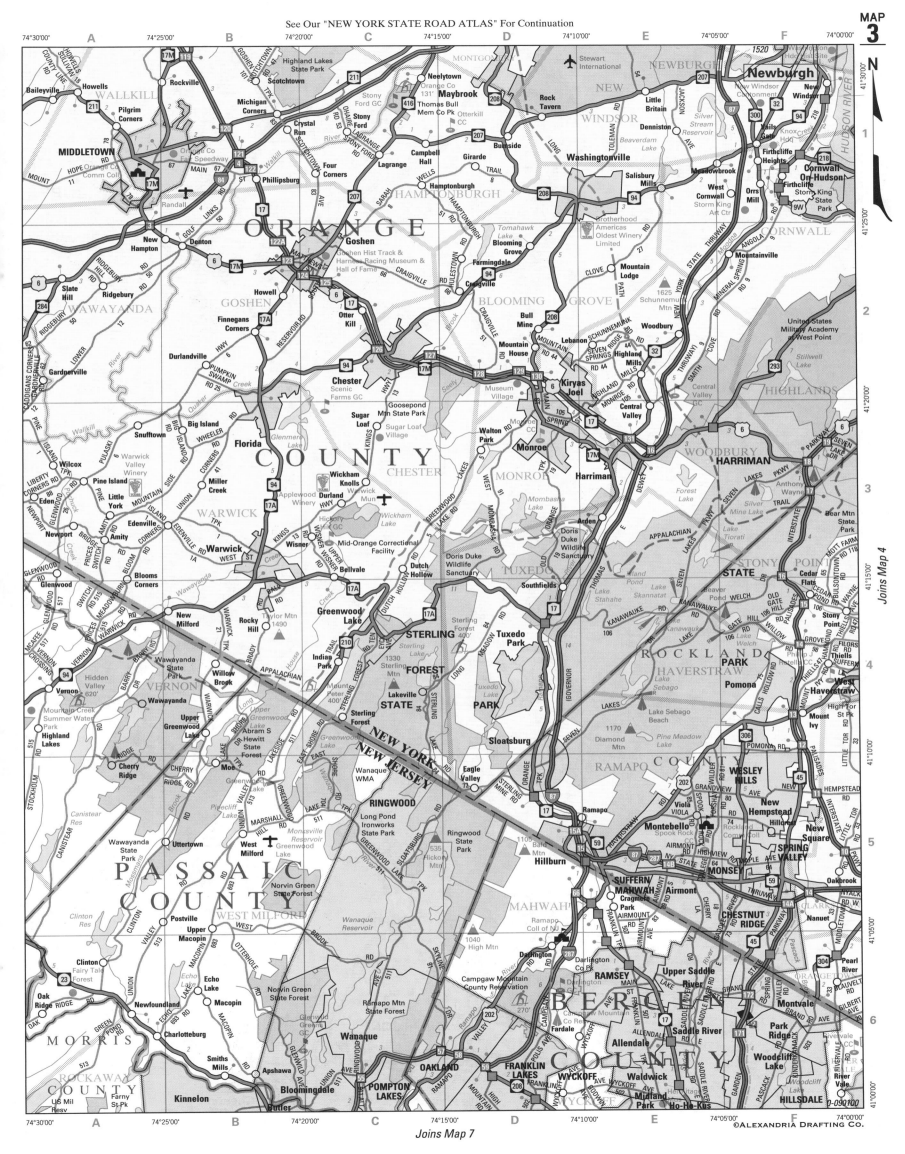

MAP
4
N

See Our "NEW YORK STATE ROAD ATLAS" For Continuation

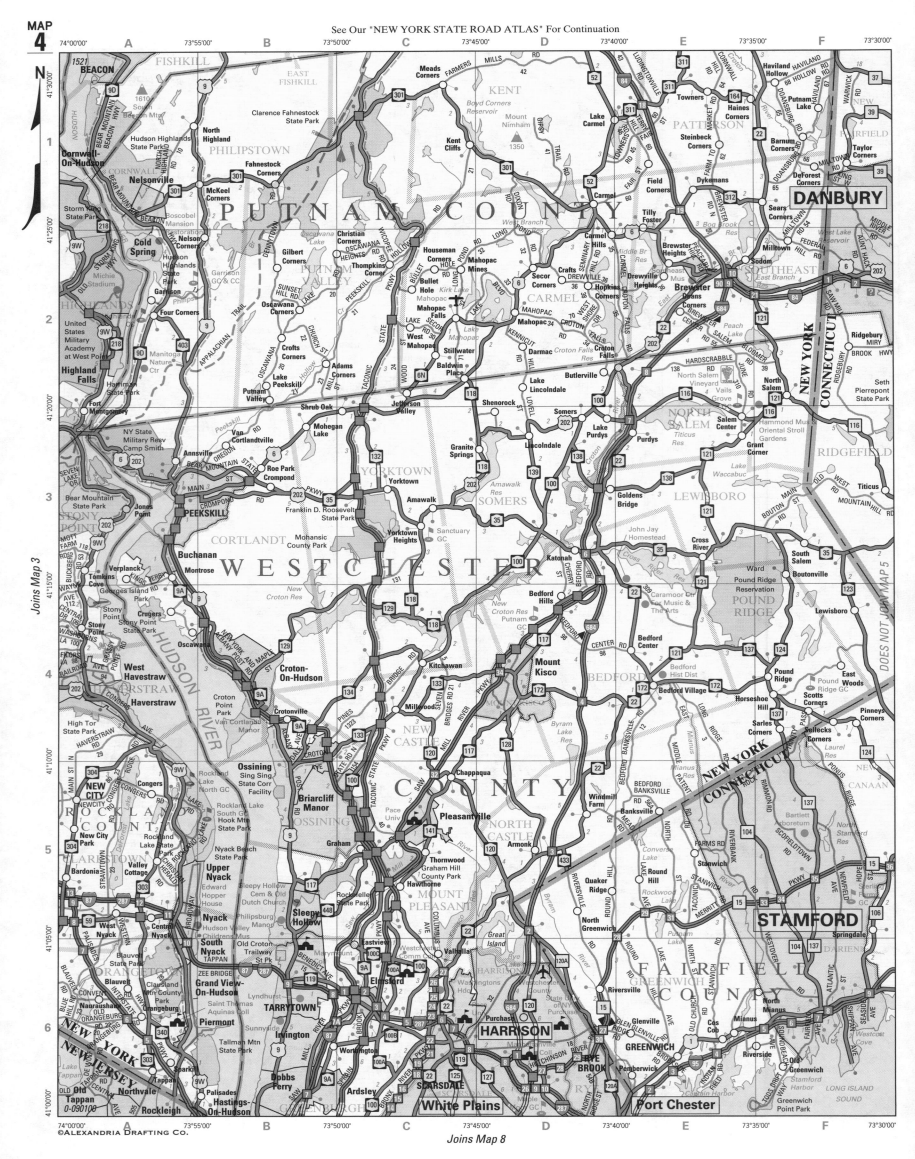

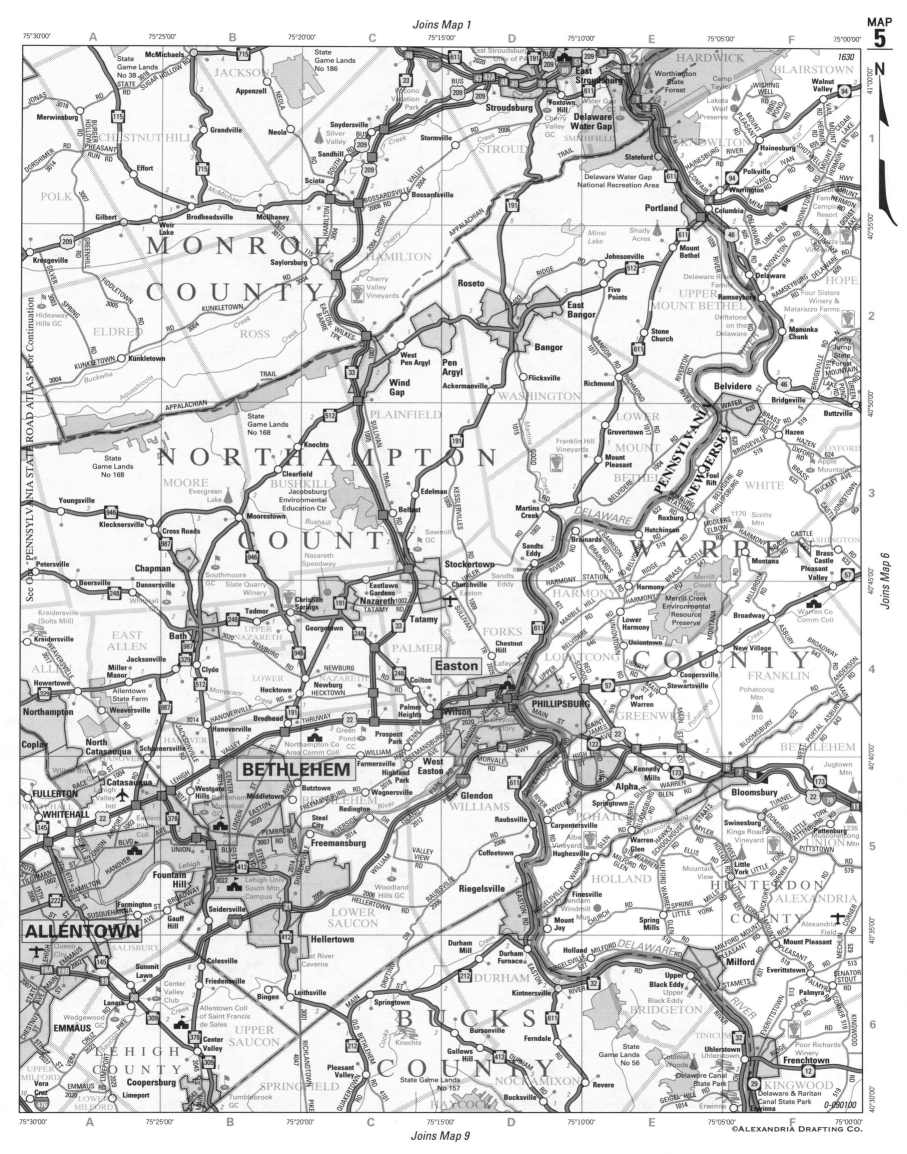

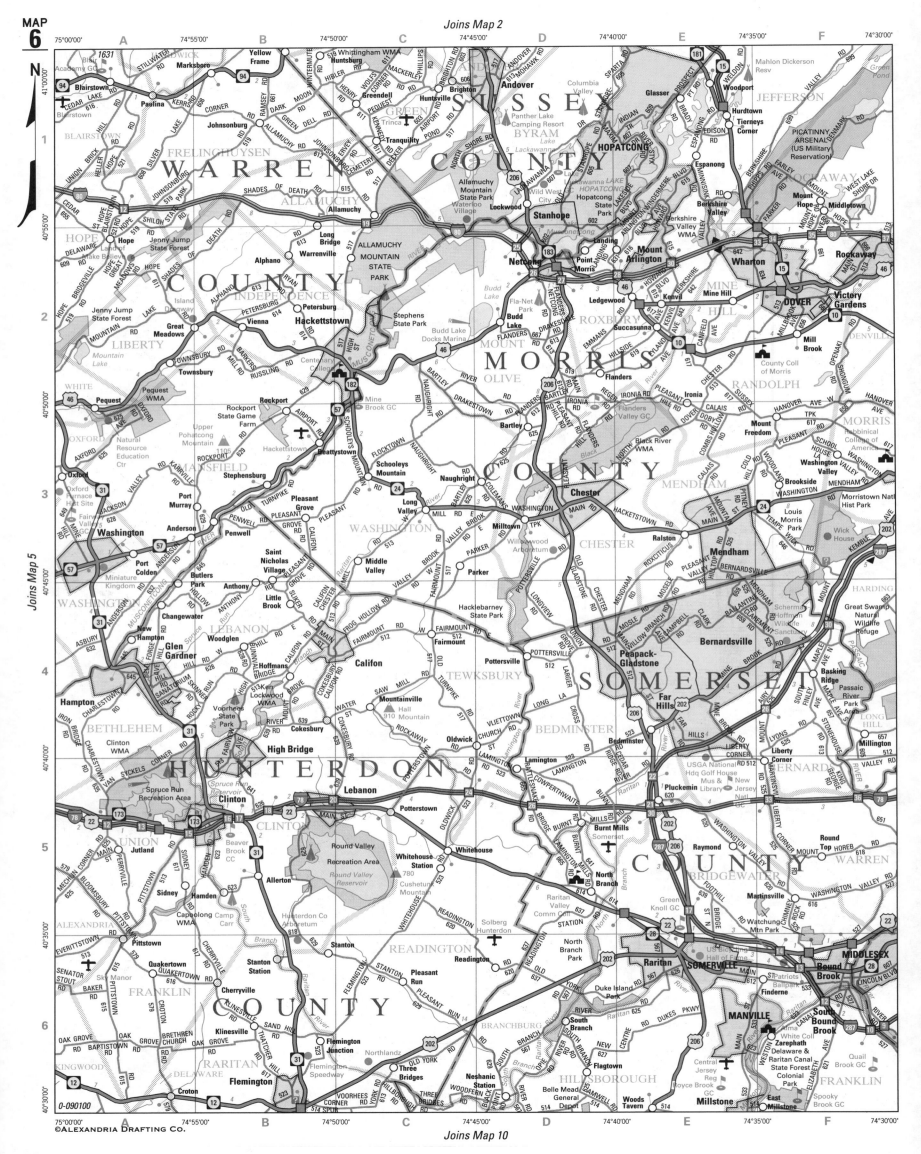

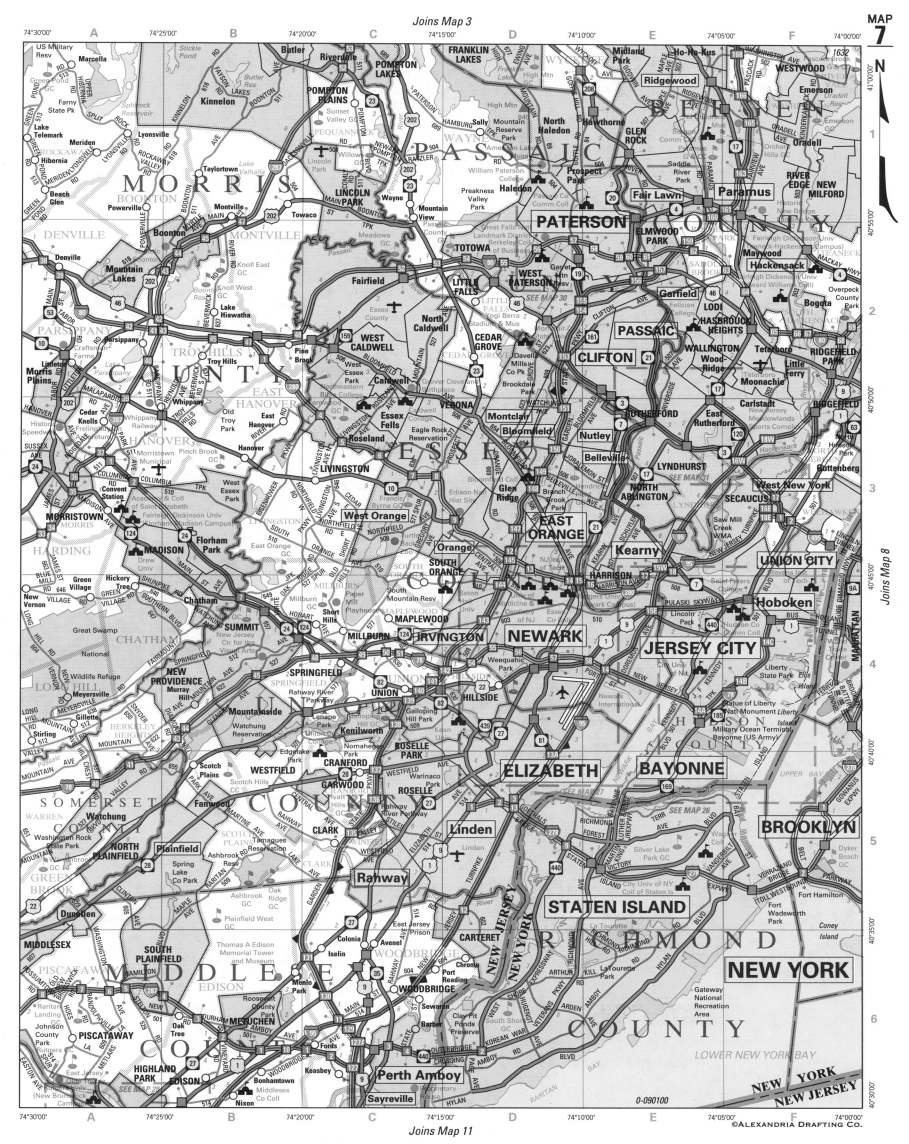

Joins Map 8

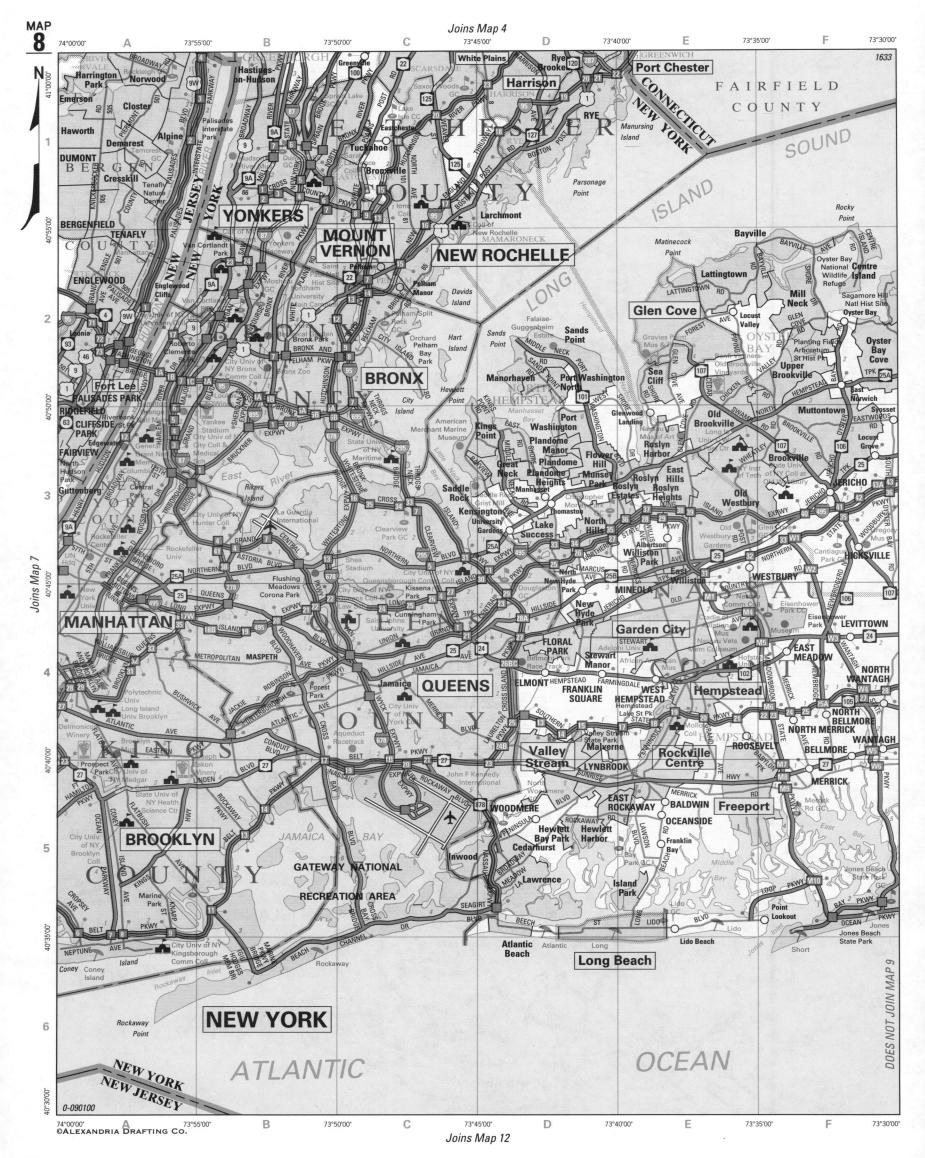

MAP
8
N
Joins Map 4
1633

©Alexandria Drafting Co.

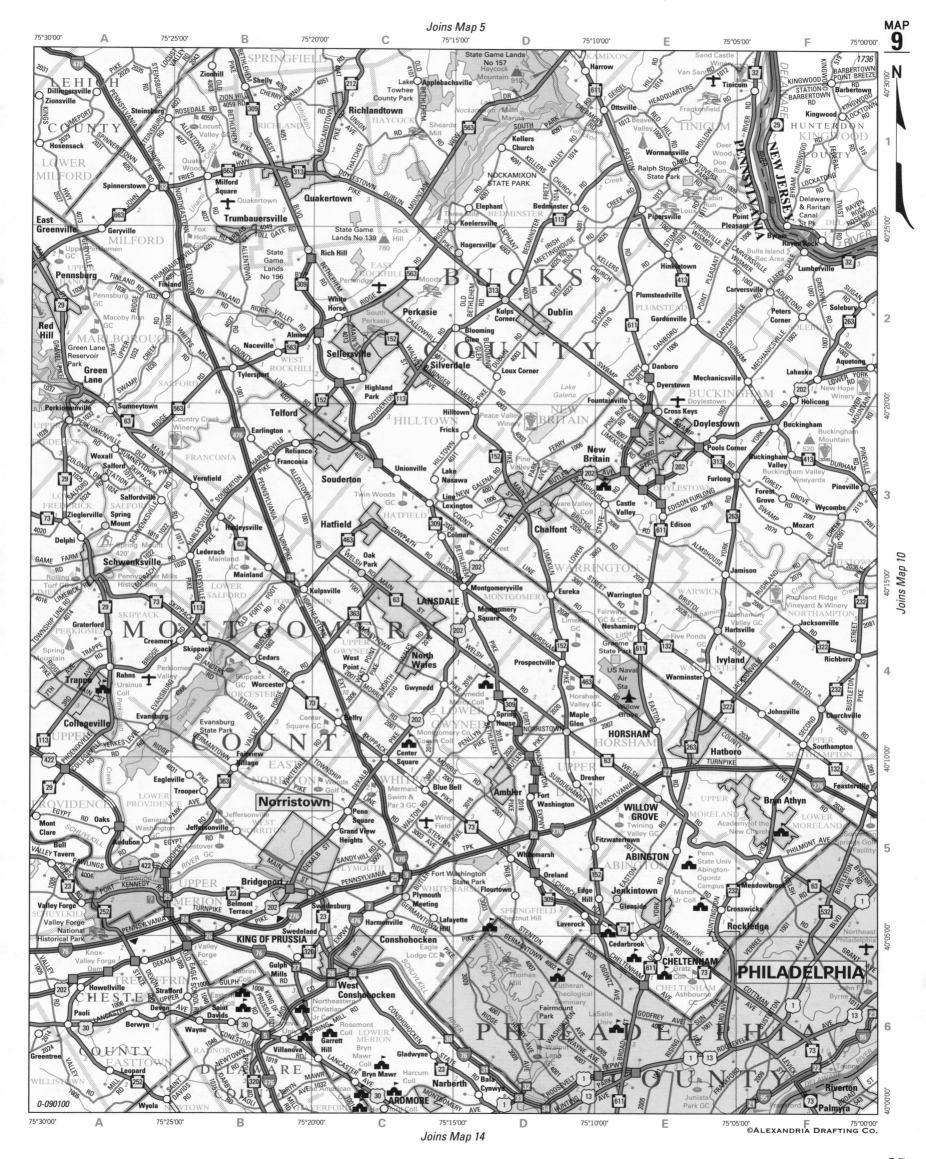

MAP
10
N
Joins Map 6

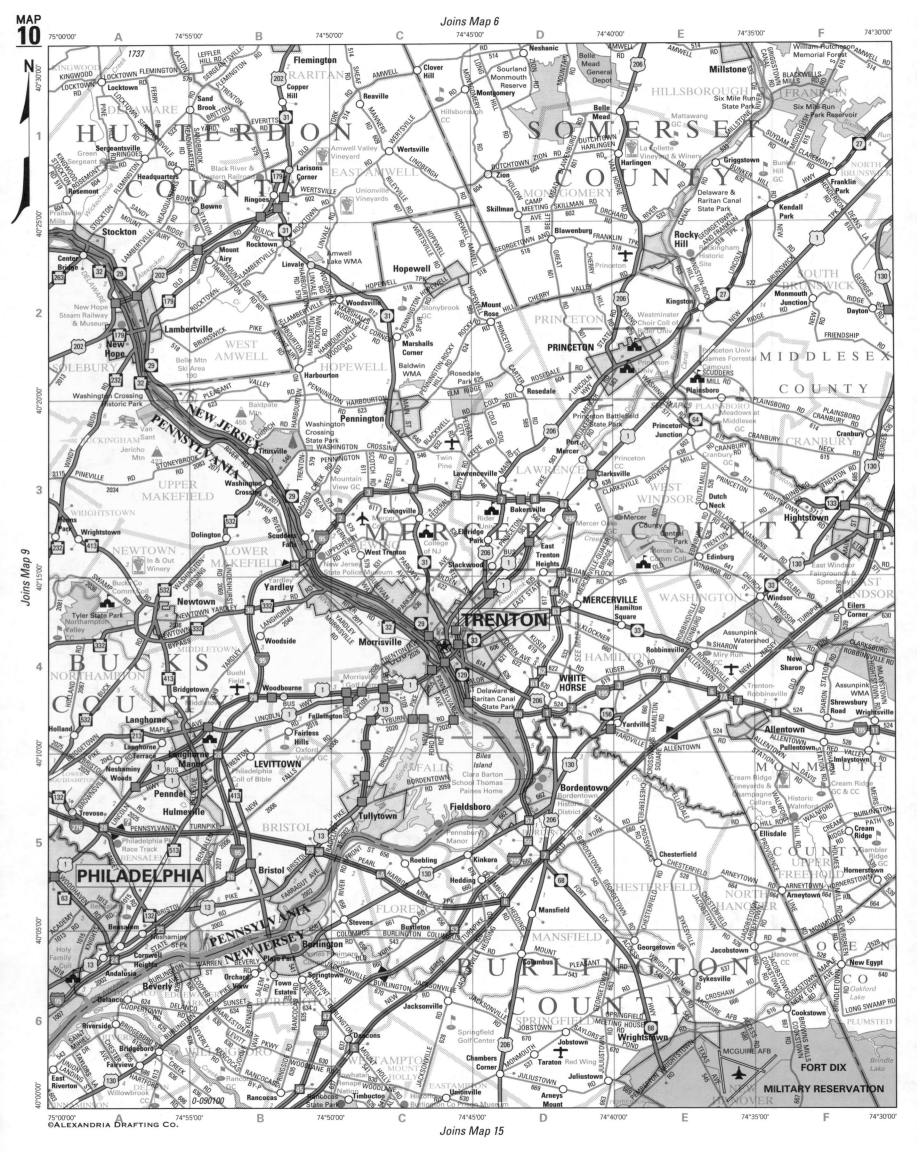

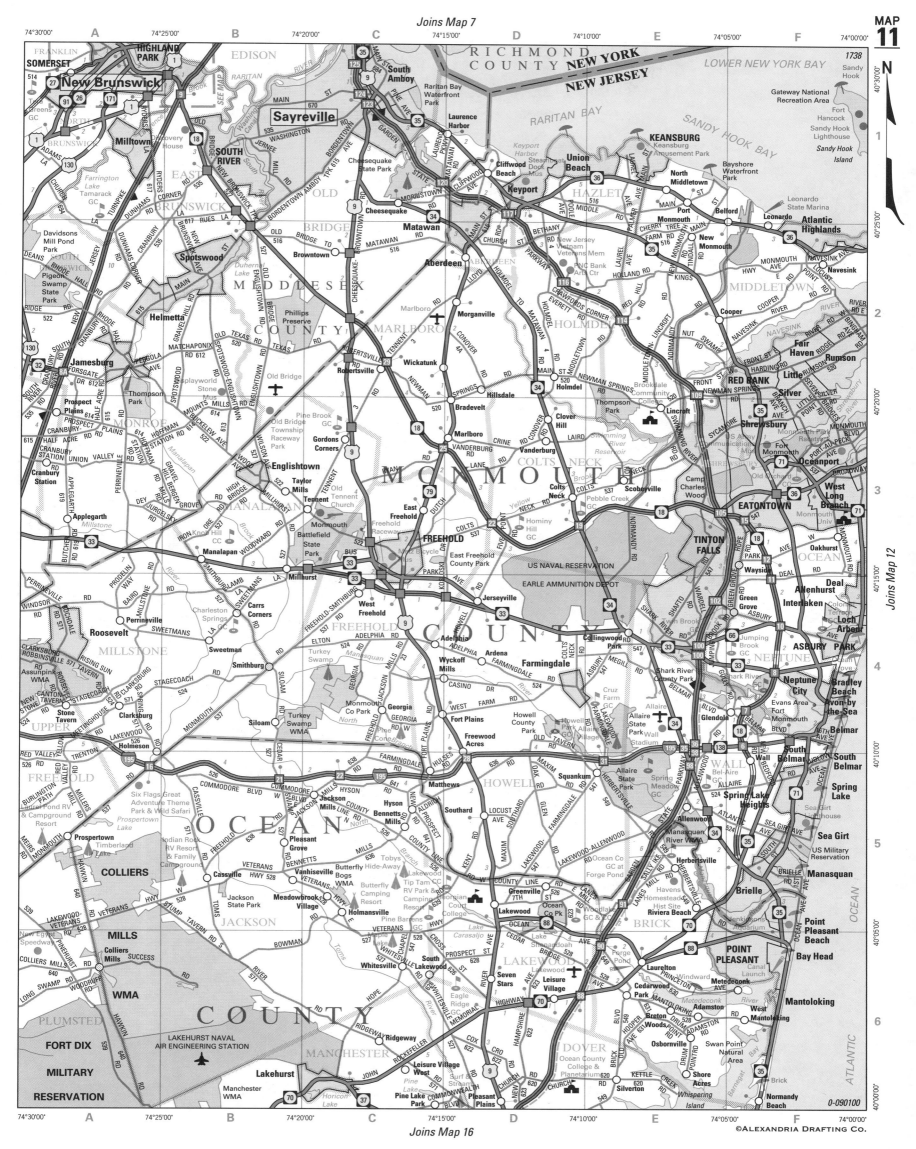

MAP
11
1738

©Alexandria Drafting Co.

Joins Map 12

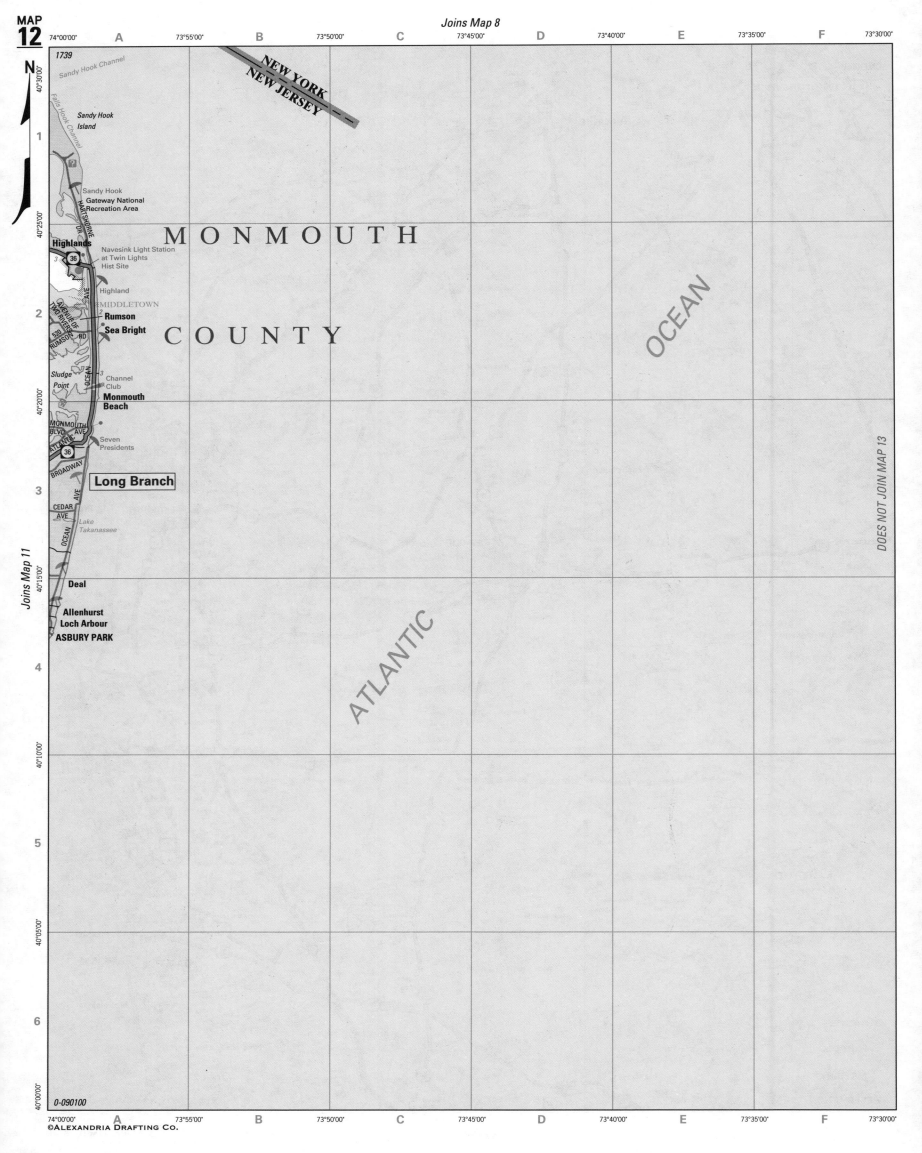

MAP

12

N

1739

Sandy Hook Channel

Falls Hook Channel

Sandy Hook
Island

Sandy Hook
Gateway National
Recreation Area

HARTSHORNE DR.

74°00'00"   A   73°55'00"   B   73°50'00"   C   73°45'00"   D   73°40'00"   E   73°35'00"   F   73°30'00"

40°30'00"

40°25'00"

40°20'00"

40°15'00"

40°10'00"

40°05'00"

40°00'00"

NEW YORK
NEW JERSEY

M O N M O U T H

C O U N T Y

O C E A N

Highlands

3   36

Navesink Light Station
at Twin Lights
Hist Site

Highland

MIDDLETOWN

Rumson

Sea Bright

AVENUE OF
TWO RIVERS

520

RUMSON   RD

OCEAN   AVE

Sludge
Point

3   Channel
 Club

**Monmouth
Beach**

MONMOUTH
BLVD

ATLANTIC   AVE

36

Seven
Presidents

BROADWAY

Long Branch

CEDAR
AVE

OCEAN   AVE

Lake
Takanassee

Deal

**Allenhurst
Loch Arbour
ASBURY PARK**

ATLANTIC

Joins Map 11

DOES NOT JOIN MAP 13

1

2

3

4

5

6

0-090100

74°00'00"   A   73°55'00"   B   73°50'00"   C   73°45'00"   D   73°40'00"   E   73°35'00"   F   73°30'00"

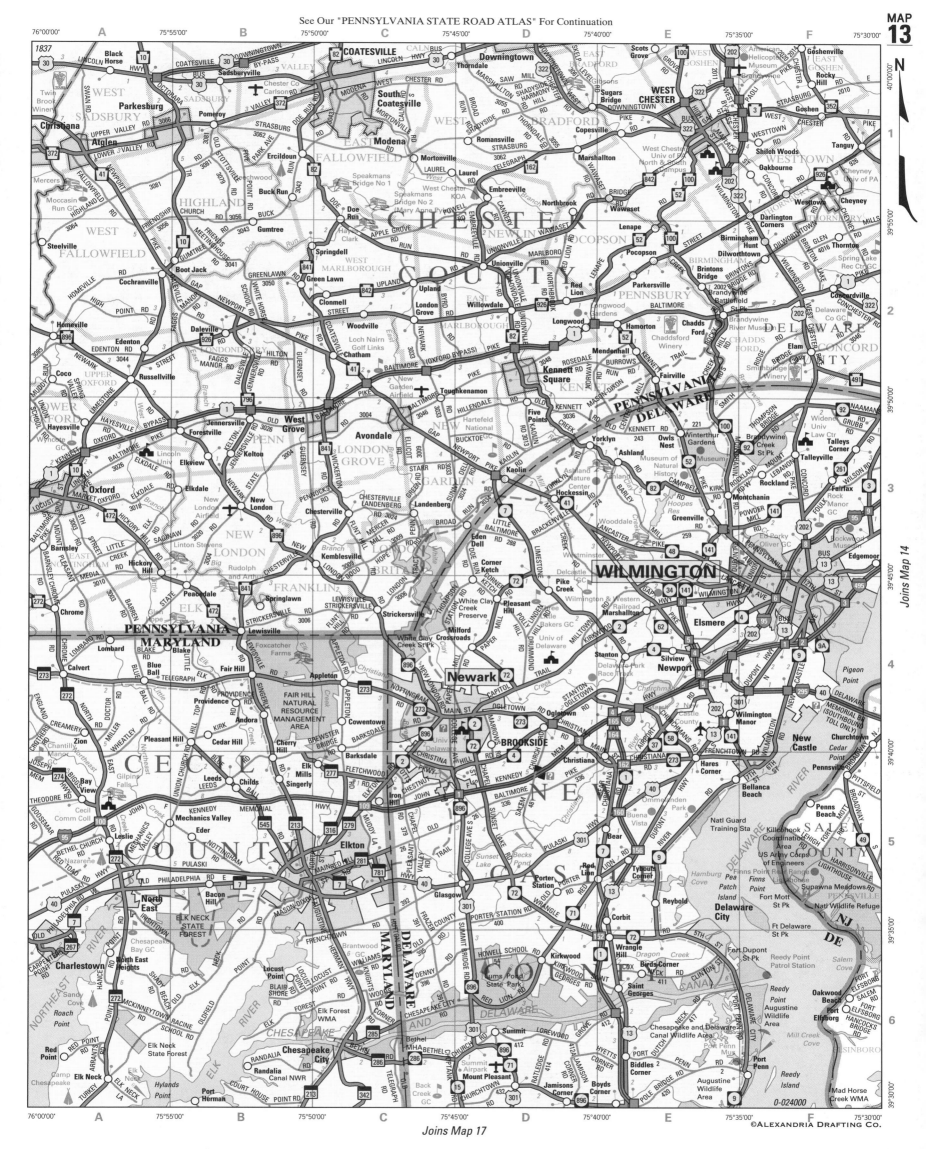

MAP 14
N
Joins Map 9

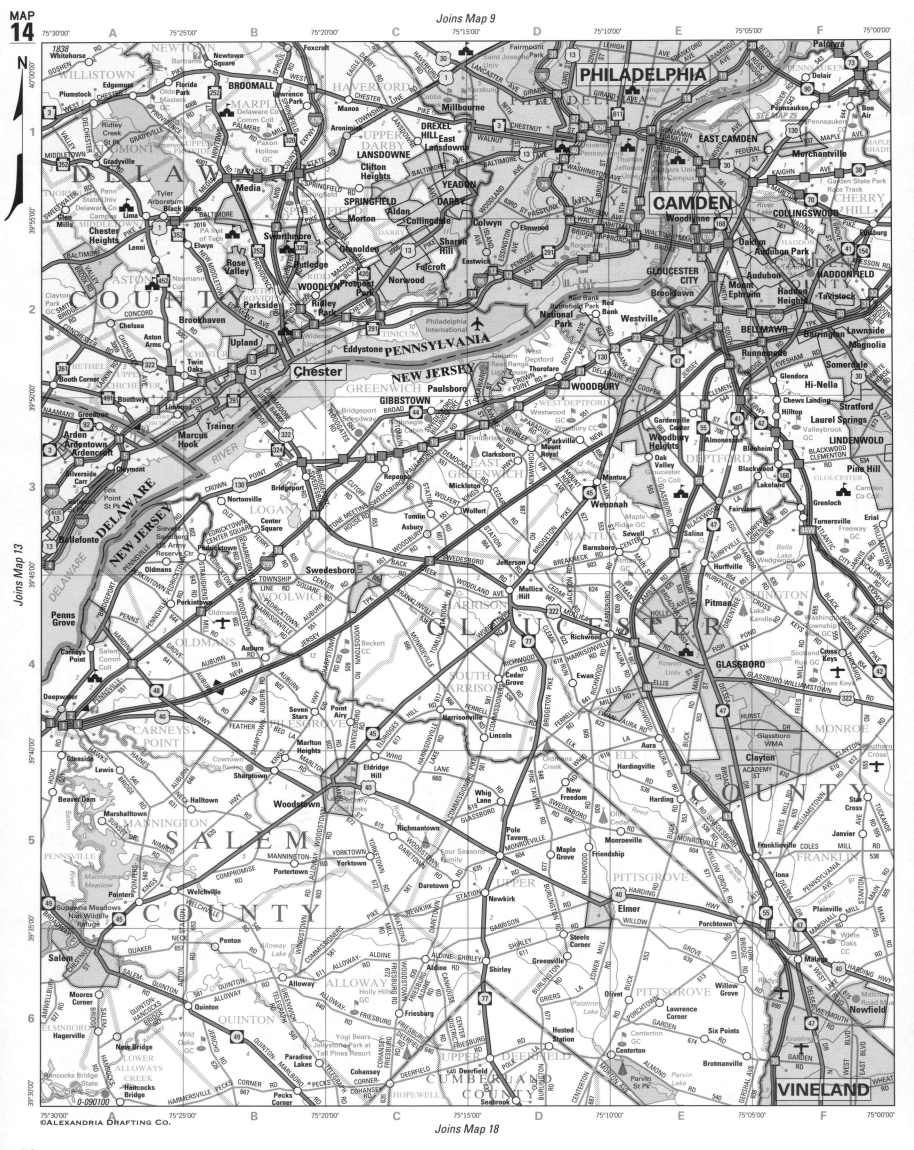

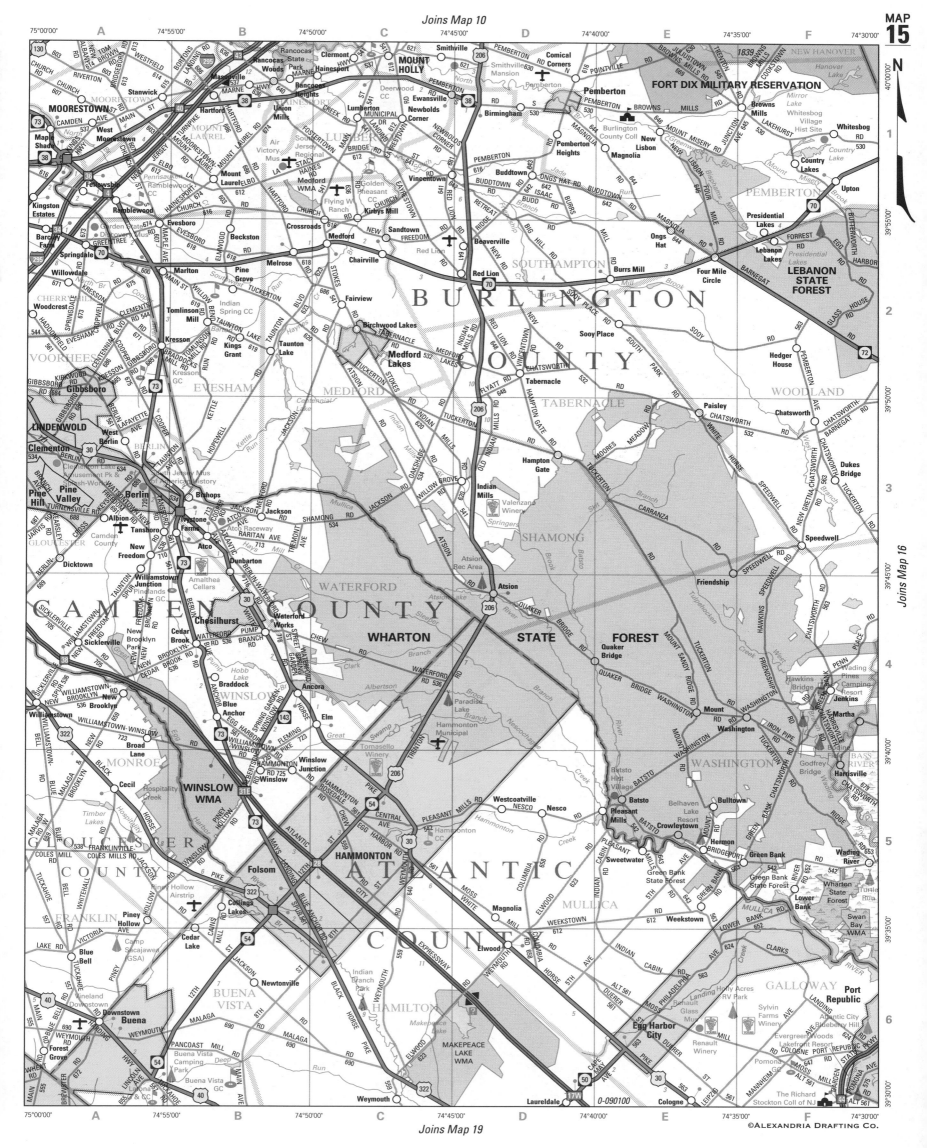

MAP
15

N

©Alexandria Drafting Co.

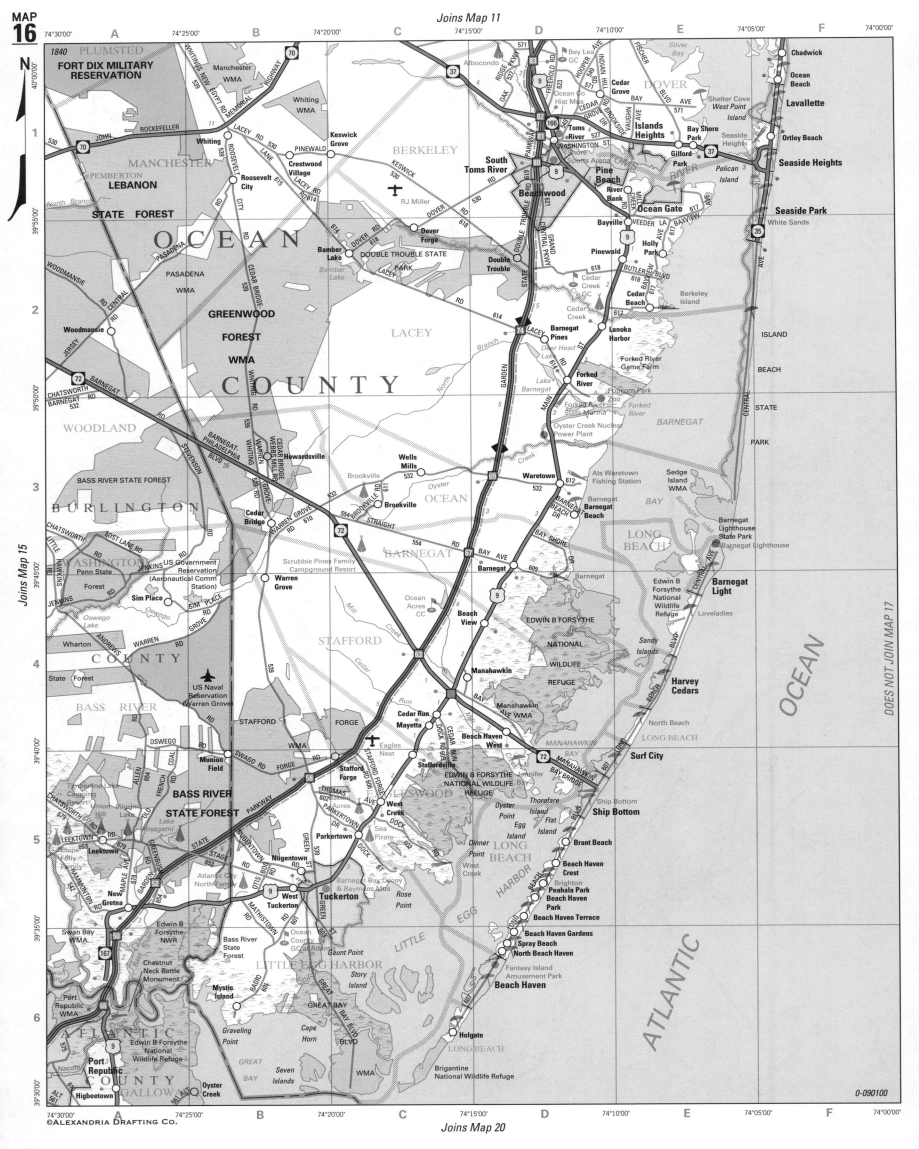

MAP 16

Joins Map 11

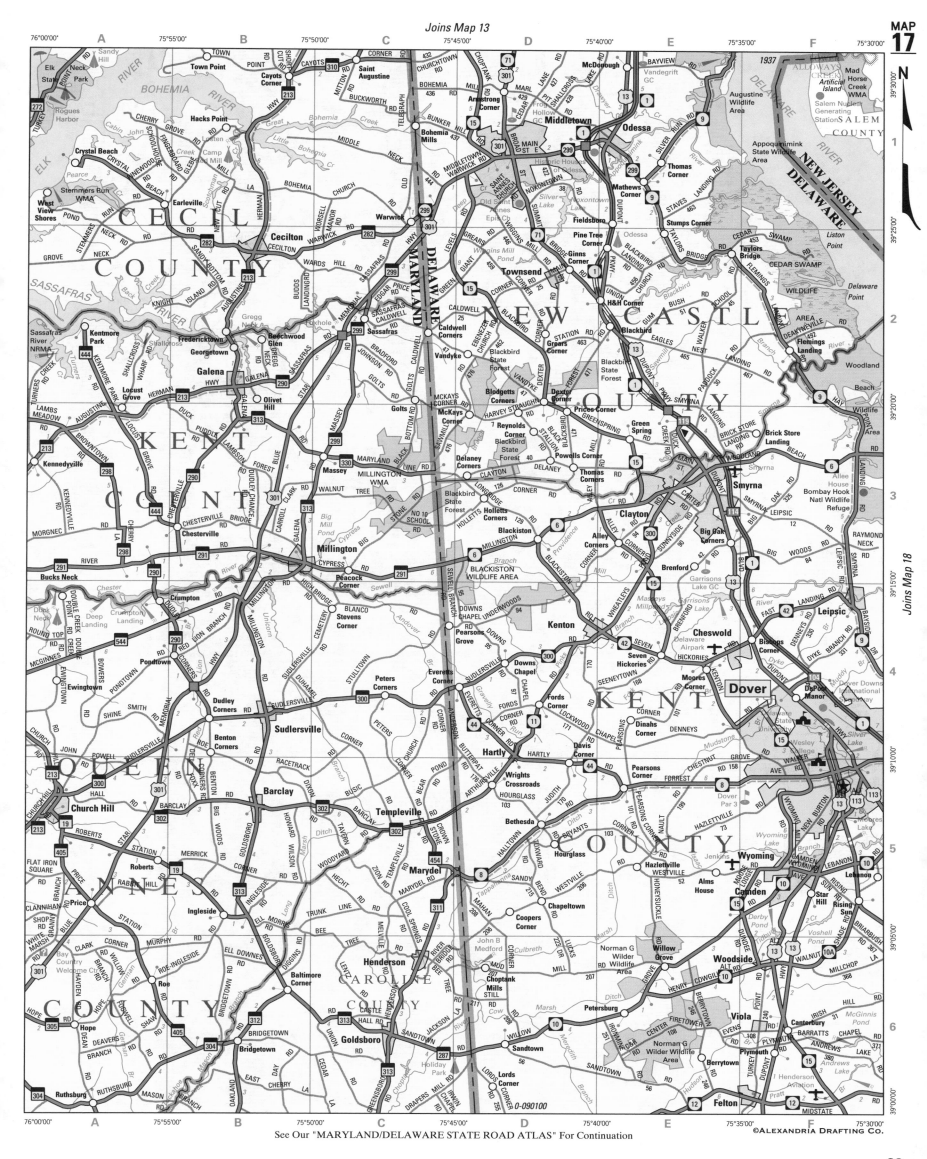

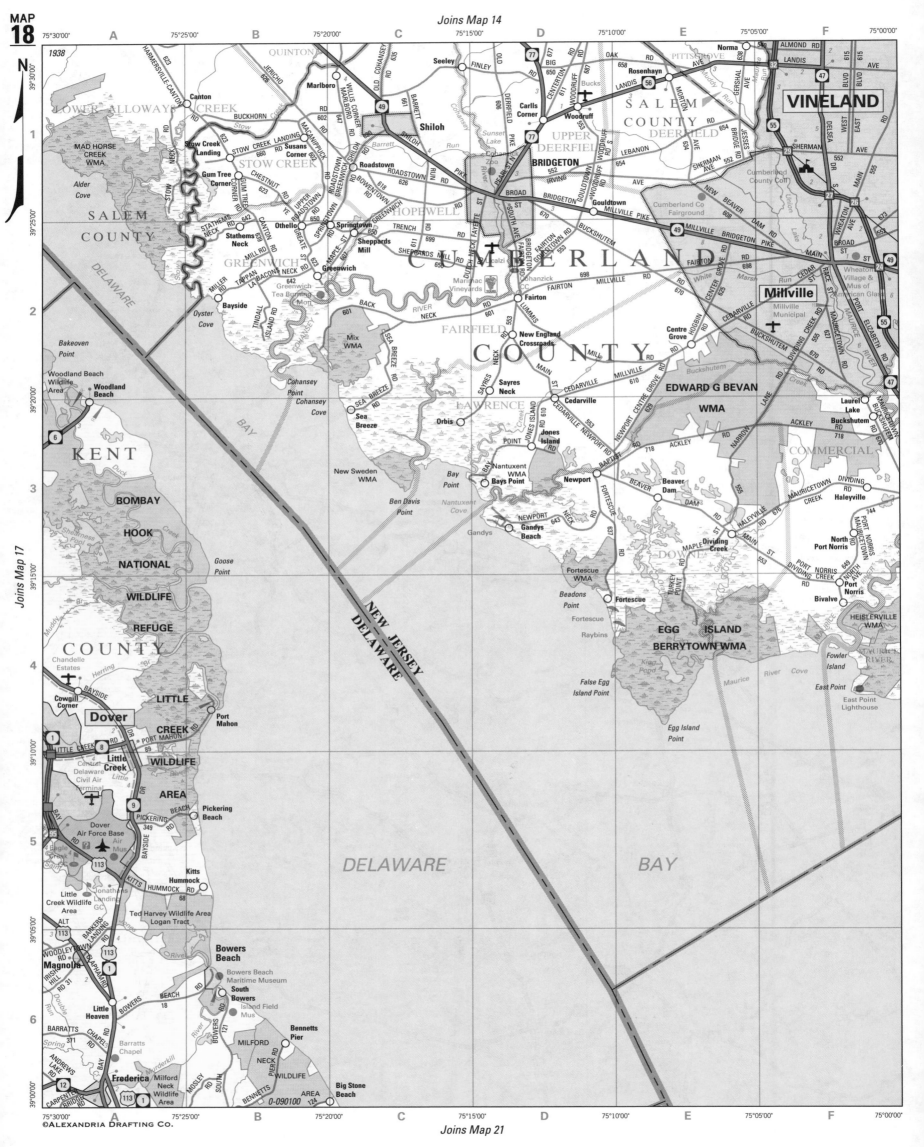

MAP
18
Joins Map 14

1938

N

75°30'00" A 75°25'00" B 75°20'00" C 75°15'00" D 75°10'00" E 75°05'00" F 75°00'00"

QUINTONE

LOWER ALLOWAYS CREEK

MAD HORSE CREEK WMA

Canton

Marlboro

Seeley Finley OLD Big Centerton Bucks Rosenhayn Norma

Carlls Corner Woodruff

SALEM COUNTY DEERFIELD **VINELAND**

Shiloh

Stow Creek Landing Susans Corner STOW CREEK Roadstown ROADSTOWN BRIDGETON

UPPER DEERFIELD

Woodruff

Gum Tree Corner CHESTNUT

Stathems Neck

Othello Springtown

GREENWICH Sheppards Mill

Bayside Greenwich TRENCH

CUMBERLAND Gouldtown

Cumberland Co Fairground

Sherman

Cumberland County Coll

SALEM COUNTY

DELAWARE

Bakeoven Point

Woodland Beach Wildlife Area Woodland Beach

Oyster Cove

KENT COUNTY

BOMBAY

HOOK

NATIONAL

WILDLIFE

REFUGE

COUNTY

Chandelle Estates

Cowgill Corner BAYSIDE

Dover

LITTLE

CREEK

Port Mahon

WILDLIFE

AREA

Dover Air Force Base

Pickering Beach

Kitts Hummock

Little Creek Wildlife Area

Ted Harvey Wildlife Area Logan Tract

Magnolia

Little Heaven

Bowers Beach

Bowers Beach Maritime Museum

South Bowers Island Field Mus

Barratts Chapel

ANDREWS LAKE RD

Frederica Milford Neck Wildlife Area MILFORD Bennetts Pier

Big Stone Beach

0-090100

Fairton LUMMIS

FAIRFIELD

New England Crossroads Sayres Sayres Neck

LAWRENCE Orbis

Cedarville Jones Island

NEW SWEDEN WMA

Bay Point

Ben Davis Point

Nantuxent Cove

Nantuxent WMA Bays Point

Newport

NEWPORT NECK

Gandys Gandys Beach

Beadons Point

Fortescue WMA

Fortescue Raybins

False Egg Island Point

Egg Island Point

Centre Grove

EDWARD G BEVAN

WMA

COMMERCIAL

Laurel Lake Buckshutem

Beaver Dam

Haleyville

DOWNE

Dividing Creek

North Port Norris

Port Norris

Bivalve

EGG ISLAND

BERRYTOWN WMA

Kian Pond

Maurice River Cove

HEISLERVILLE WMA

Fowler Island

East Point

East Point Lighthouse

Millville Municipal

Millville

NEW

JERSEY

DELAWARE

DELAWARE BAY

75°30'00" A 75°25'00" B 75°20'00" C 75°15'00" D 75°10'00" E 75°05'00" F 75°00'00"

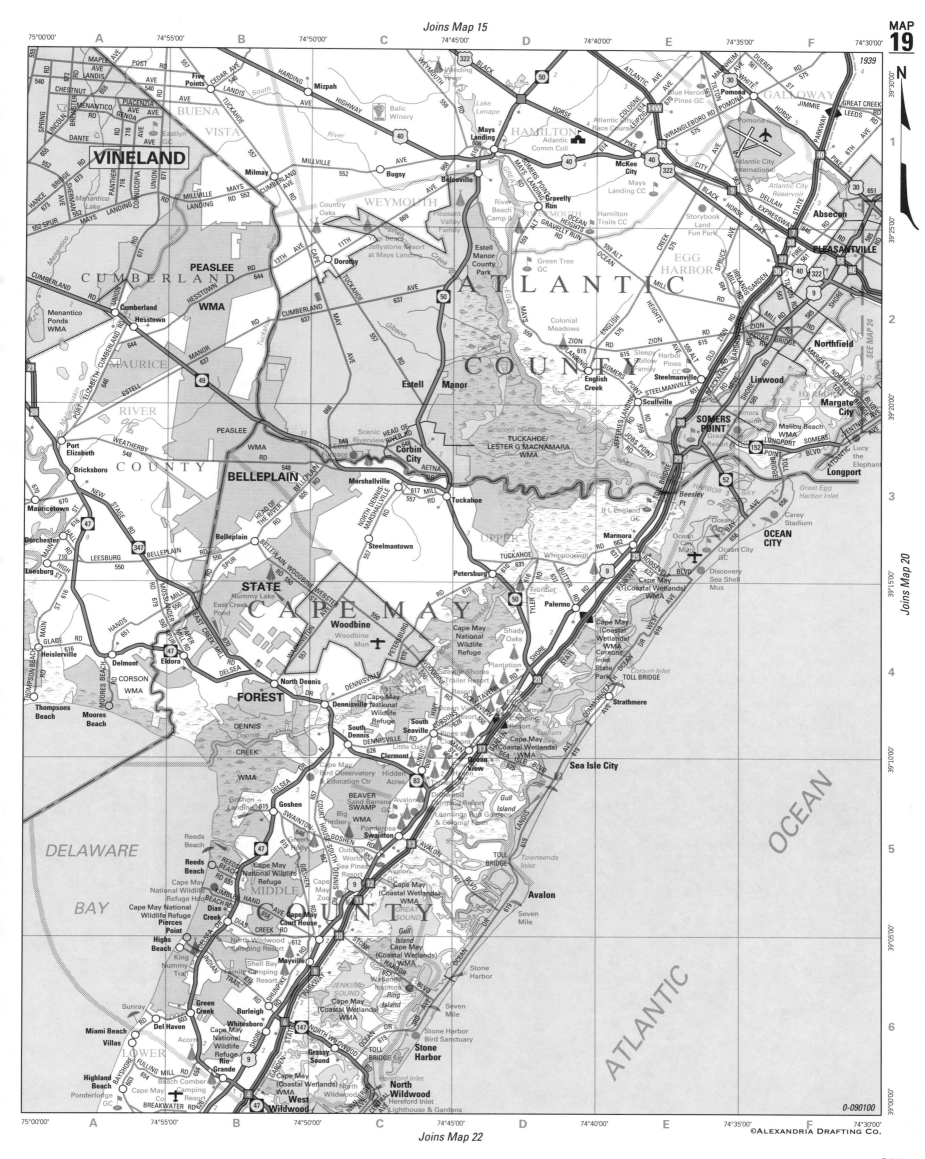

MAP
20
Joins Map 16

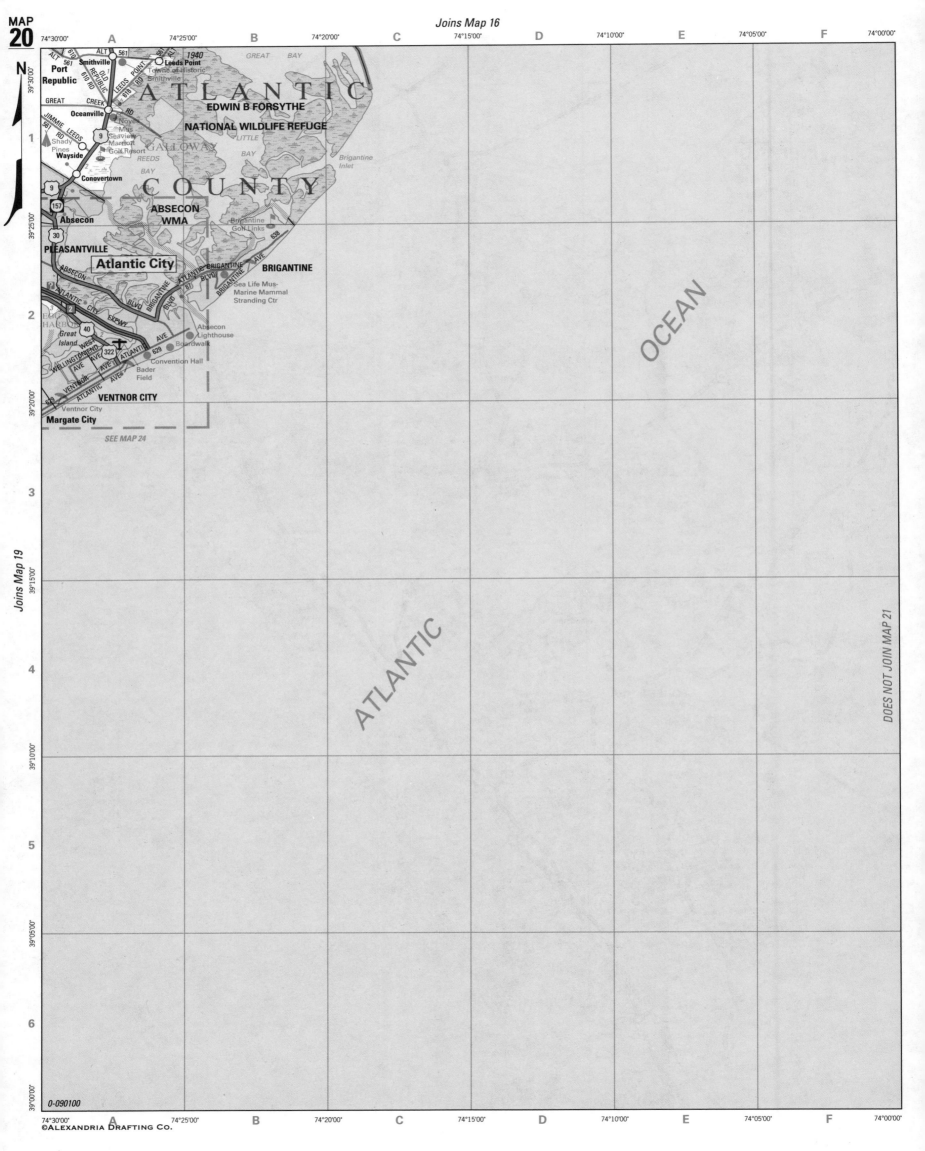

©Alexandria Drafting Co.

0-090100

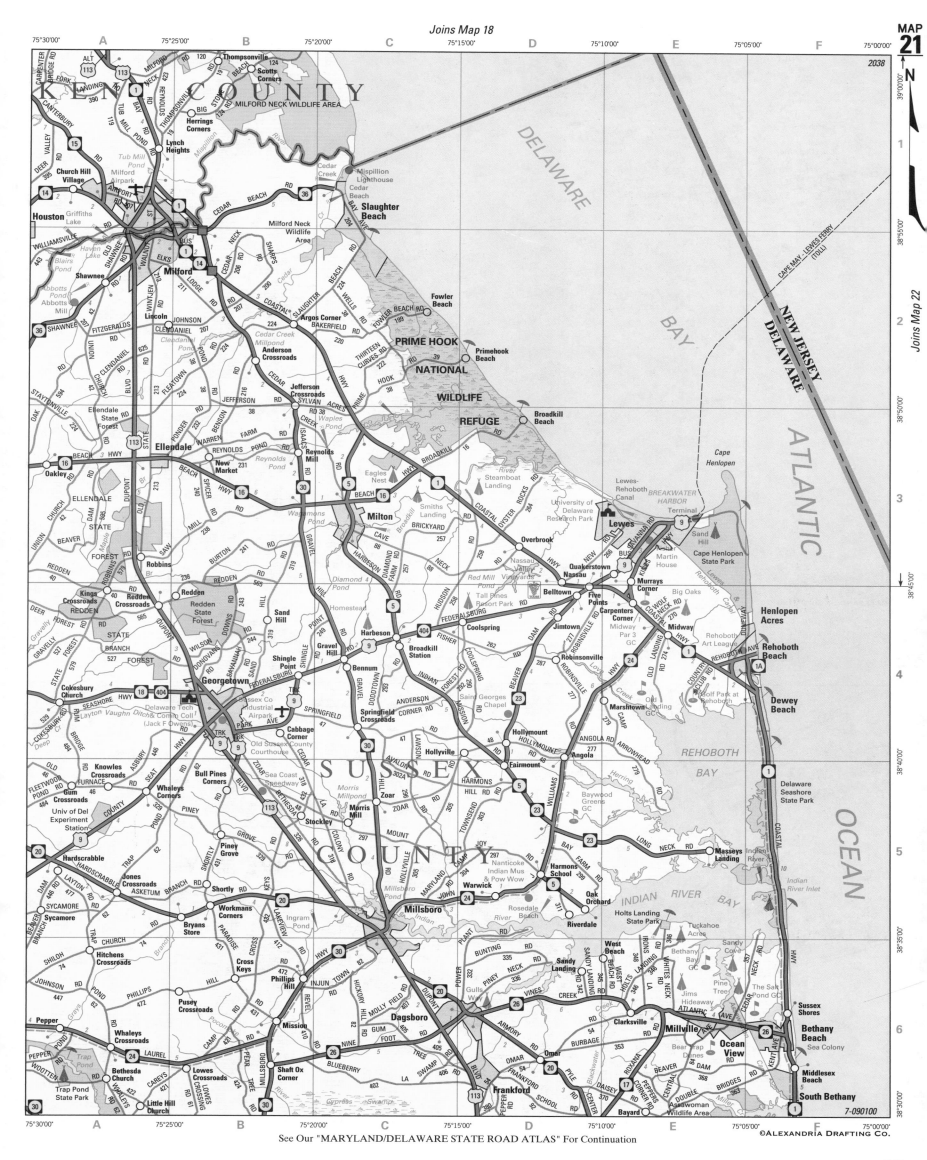

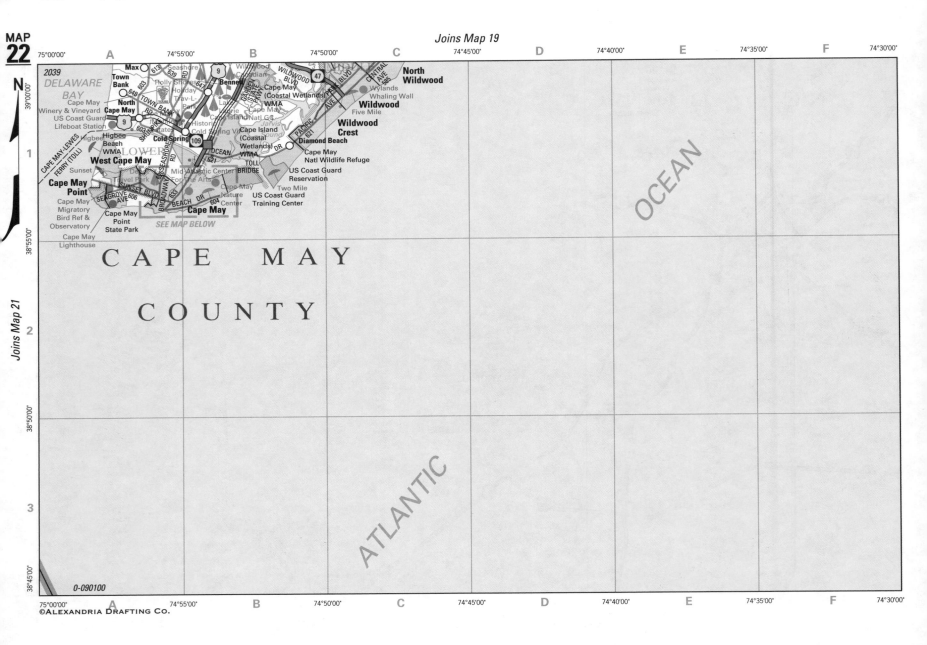

MAP
22

CAPE MAY

COUNTY

Joins Map 21

ATLANTIC

©ALEXANDRIA DRAFTING CO.

MAP
23

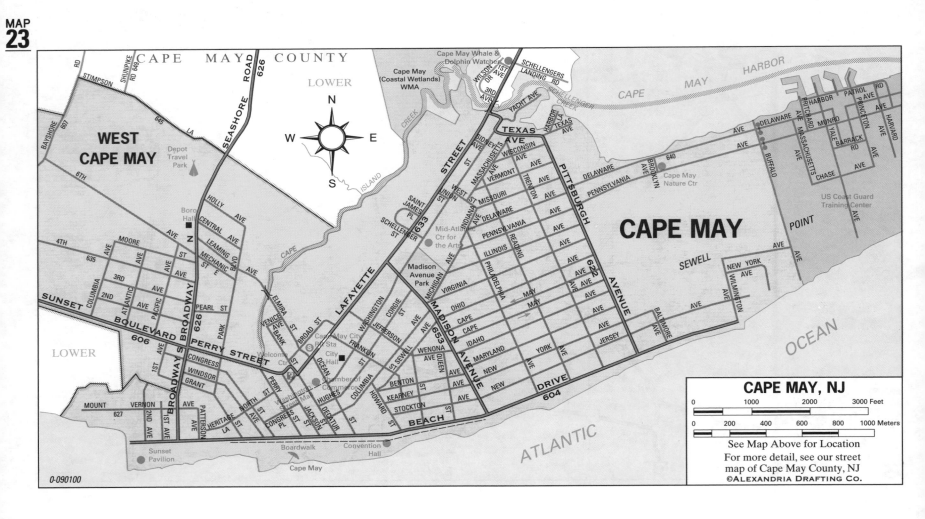

WEST
CAPE MAY

CAPE MAY

CAPE MAY, NJ

| 0 | 1000 | 2000 | 3000 Feet |

| 0 | 200 | 400 | 600 | 800 | 1000 Meters |

See Map Above for Location
For more detail, see our street
map of Cape May County, NJ
©ALEXANDRIA DRAFTING CO.

38

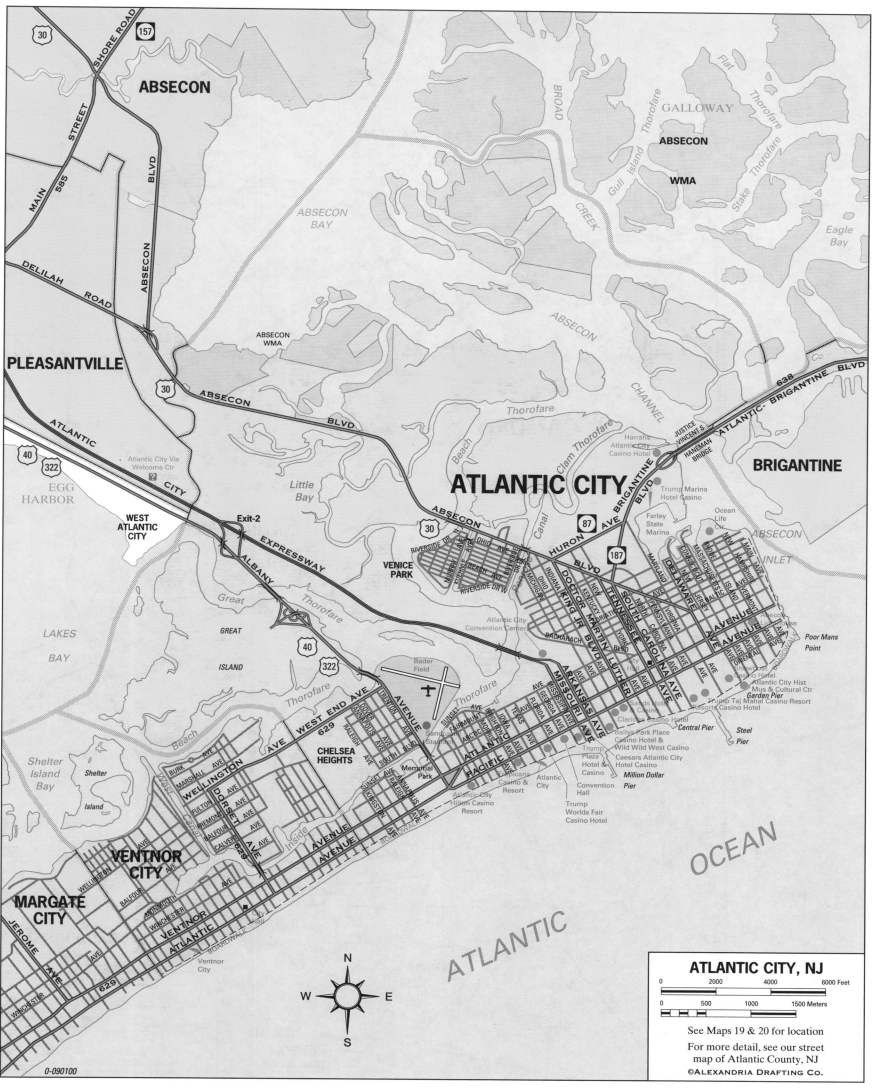

MAP
24

ABSECON

PLEASANTVILLE

GALLOWAY

ABSECON
WMA

Eagle
Bay

ABSECON BAY

ABSECON
WMA

Little
Bay

ATLANTIC CITY

BRIGANTINE

Harrahs
Atlantic City
Casino Hotel

JUSTICE
VINCENT S.
HANEMAN
BRIDGE

ATLANTIC-BRIGANTINE BLVD

Trump Marina
Hotel Casino

EGG
HARBOR

WEST
ATLANTIC CITY

Atlantic City Vis
Welcome Ctr

Exit-2

VENICE
PARK

Farley
State
Marina

Ocean
Life
Ctr

ABSECON
INLET

Poor Mans
Point

LAKES
BAY

GREAT
ISLAND

Atlantic City
Convention Center

Bader
Field

Atlantic City Hist
Mus & Cultural Ctr

Garden Pier

Trump Taj Mahal Casino Resort

Resorts Casino Hotel

Shelter
Island
Bay

Shelter
Island

CHELSEA
HEIGHTS

Memorial
Park

Sands Hotel
Casino

Claridge Casino Hotel

Central Pier

Steel
Pier

Ballys Park Place
Casino Hotel &
Wild Wild West Casino

Caesars Atlantic City
Hotel Casino

Million Dollar
Pier

Trump
Plaza
Hotel &
Casino

Tropicana
Casino &
Resort

Atlantic
City

Convention
Hall

Atlantic City
Hilton Casino
Resort

Trump
Worlds Fair
Casino Hotel

OCEAN

VENTNOR
CITY

MARGATE
CITY

Ventnor
City

ATLANTIC

ATLANTIC CITY, NJ

0   2000   4000   6000 Feet

0   500   1000   1500 Meters

See Maps 19 & 20 for location

For more detail, see our street
map of Atlantic County, NJ

©Alexandria Drafting Co.

0-090100

39

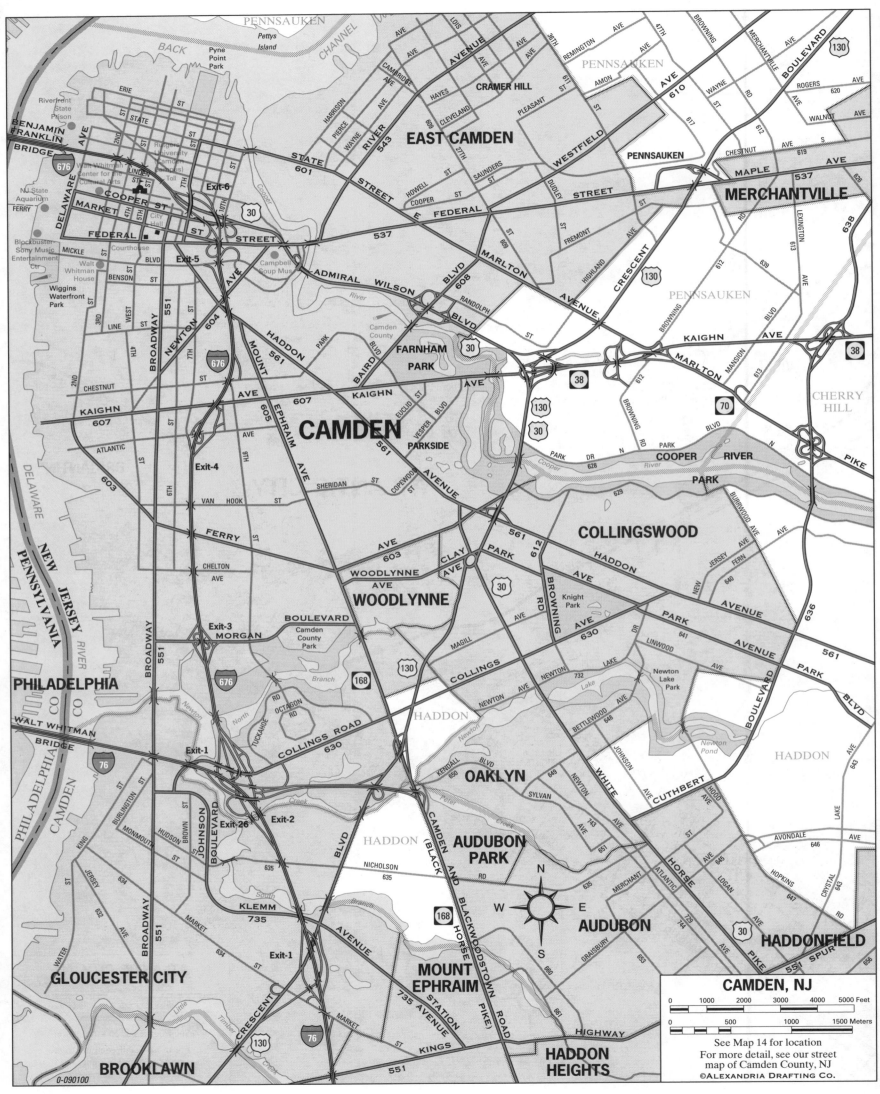

MAP
25

PENNSAUKEN

Pettys
Island

BACK

PENNSAUKEN CHANNEL

Pyne
Point
Park

Riverfront
State
Prison

CRAMER HILL

PENNSAUKEN

BROWNING

BOULEVARD 130

ROGERS AVE 620

WALNUT

ERIE ST

STATE ST

2ND ST

Walt Whitman
Center for the
Cultural Arts

BENJAMIN
FRANKLIN
BRIDGE

676

Rutgers University
(Camden campus)

Exit-6

EAST CAMDEN

WESTFIELD

PENNSAUKEN

CHESTNUT AVE 619

MAPLE 537 AVE

MERCHANTVILLE

LINDEN ST

COOPER ST

30

STATE STREET 601

537

E FEDERAL

MARLTON

608

CRESCENT 130

638

LEXINGTON 613

NJ State
Aquarium

FERRY

MARKET 4TH 5TH ST

FEDERAL

City
Hall

STREET

Campbell
Soup Mus

537

130
30

PENNSAUKEN

Blockbuster
Sony Music
Entertainment
Ctr

MICKLE ST

Courthouse

Exit-5

BLVD

ADMIRAL WILSON

608

BLVD

608

38

612

612

639

Walt
Whitman
House

BENSON
ST

BROADWAY 551

NEWTON 7TH ST

604

676

HADDON 561

MOUNT EPHRAIM AVE 605

BAIRD BLVD

Camden
County
Park

FARNHAM
PARK

30

KAIGHN AVE

38

130
30

70

CHERRY
HILL

Wiggins
Waterfront
Park

3RD ST

WEST LINE ST

4TH ST

CHESTNUT ST

KAIGHN
607

ATLANTIC ST

603

AVE

607

KAIGHN

EUCLID ST

VESPER BLVD

CAMDEN

561

PARKSIDE

KAIGHN

MARLTON

MANSION

613

Cooper River

COOPER RIVER PARK

628

DELAWARE RIVER

NEW JERSEY
PENNSYLVANIA CO

Exit-4

6TH ST

9TH ST

VAN HOOK ST

SHERIDAN ST

COPEWOOD ST

AVENUE 561

629

BURRWOOD AVE

636

FERRY AVE 603

CHELTON AVE

WOODLYNNE AVE

CLAY AVE

PARK AVE

561
612

COLLINGSWOOD

HADDON AVE

NEW JERSEY AVE

FERN AVE 640

Exit-3
MORGAN

BOULEVARD

Camden
County Park

WOODLYNNE

30

BROWNING RD

Knight
Park

630

PARK AVENUE

561

636

PHILADELPHIA

BROADWAY 551

676

Branch

168

130

MAGILL AVE

COLLINGS AVE

AVE

DR

LINWOOD AVE

641

Newton
Lake
Park

PARK BOULEVARD

WALT WHITMAN
BRIDGE

76

RD

OCTAGON RD

TUCKAHOE

COLLINGS ROAD 630

North

Branch

Newton

NEWTON AVE

732

Lake

Newton
Lake Park

Newton

BETTLEWOOD AVE 648

JOHNSON AVE

Newton
Pond

HADDON

643

PHILADELPHIA
CAMDEN CO

Exit-1

Creek

KENDALL BLVD

650

OAKLYN

WHITE HORSE PIKE

SYLVAN AVE

NEWTON AVE

649

CUTHBERT

HOOD AVE

LAKE AVE

WALT WHITMAN
BRIDGE

BURLINGTON ST

BROWN ST

Exit-26

Exit-2

Creek

HADDON

AUDUBON
PARK

Peter

Creek

743

651

AVE

645

LOGAN AVE

AVONDALE AVE 646

HOPKINS

CRYSTAL 643

HADDON

JERSEY 634

MONMOUTH ST

HUDSON ST

JOHNSON BOULEVARD

635

NICHOLSON 635

CAMDEN AND BLACKWOODSTOWN ROAD

RD

N

W   E

S

635

MERCHANT AVE

ATLANTIC AVE

729

744

30

HADDONFIELD

KING ST

WATER ST

632

BROADWAY 551

MARKET ST

KLEMM 735

Exit-1

South Branch

168

AVENUE

634

735 AVENUE

STATION

Little Timber Creek

KINGS

551

MOUNT
EPHRAIM

AUDUBON

GRAISBURY AVE

653

660

661

HIGHWAY

551 SPUR

GLOUCESTER CITY

130

76

BROOKLAWN

HADDON
HEIGHTS

0-090100

CAMDEN, NJ

| 0 | 1000 | 2000 | 3000 | 4000 | 5000 Feet |

| 0 | 500 | 1000 | 1500 Meters |

See Map 14 for location
For more detail, see our street
map of Camden County, NJ
©Alexandria Drafting Co.

40

MAP
26

HARRISON

NEWARK

KEARNY

HOBOKEN

JERSEY CITY

LINCOLN PARK

Saint Peters College

Hudson Co Comm Coll

City Univ of New Jersey

Dead Sailors Point

NEWARK BAY BRIDGE

NEWARK BAY

Hudson County Park

Veterans Memorial Stadium & Park

City Park

City Hall

BAYONNE

Military Ocean Terminal Bayonne (US Army)

Constable Hook

BAYONNE BRIDGE

KILL VAN KULL

HUDSON COUNTY
RICHMOND COUNTY

STATEN ISLAND

NEW YORK

NEW JERSEY
NEW YORK

US Army Reserve

Liberty State Park

LIBERTY STATE PARK

Liberty Science Center

Liberty Harbor RV Park

Department of Defense

Visitors Center

Ellis Island

Immigration Mus

Ellis Island National Monument

Liberty Island

Statue of Liberty National Monument

LIBERTY HARBOR

Caven Point

NORTH RIVER

UPPER
NEW YORK
BAY

HUDSON COUNTY
KINGS COUNTY

NEW JERSEY
NEW YORK

Holland Tunnel Bus

Hoboken Terminal

City Hall

Journal Sq Transportation Ctr

N
W   E
S

JERSEY CITY, NJ

| 0 | 2000 | 4000 | 6000 | 8000 Feet |

| 0 | 500 | 1000 | 1500 | 2000 Meters |

See Map 7 for Location
For more detail, see our atlas of
Union Co., Hudson Co., and Essex Co.
©Alexandria Drafting Co.

0-090100

MAP
27

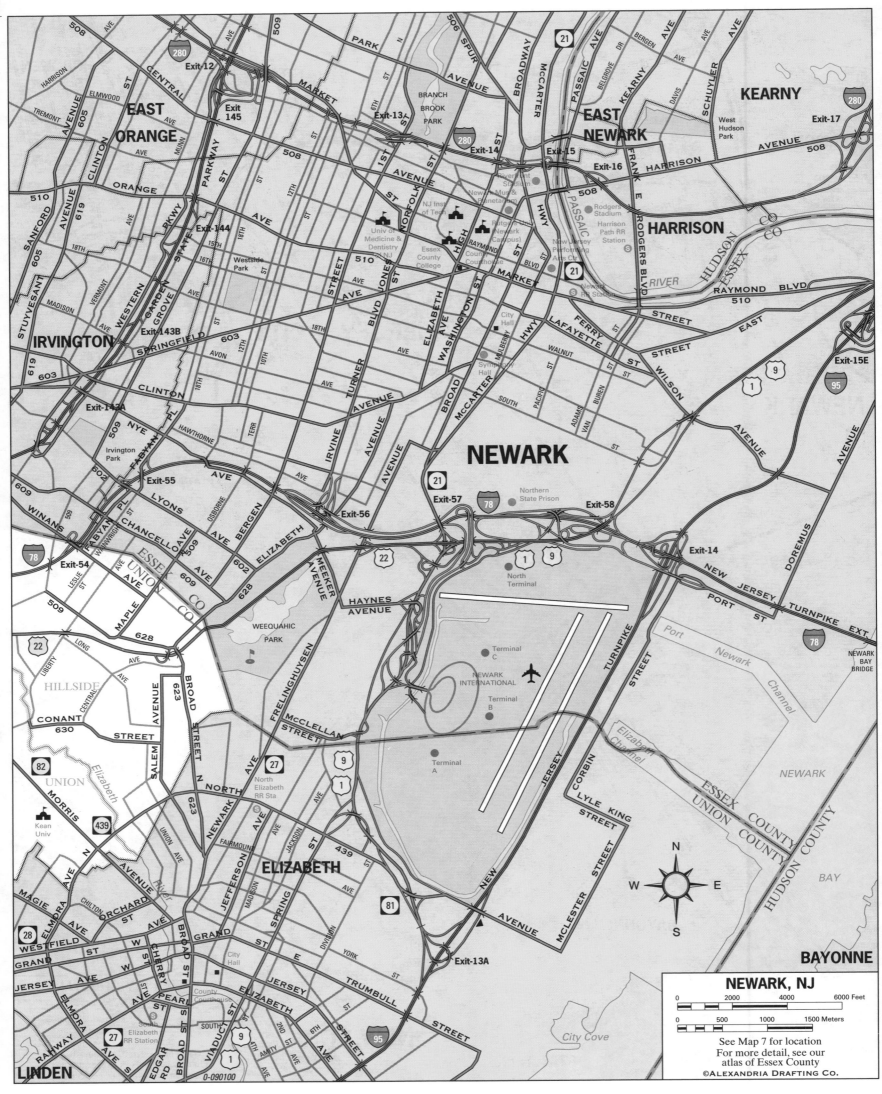

NEWARK, NJ

| 0 | 2000 | 4000 | 6000 Feet |

| 0 | 500 | 1000 | 1500 Meters |

See Map 7 for location
For more detail, see our
atlas of Essex County
©Alexandria Drafting Co.

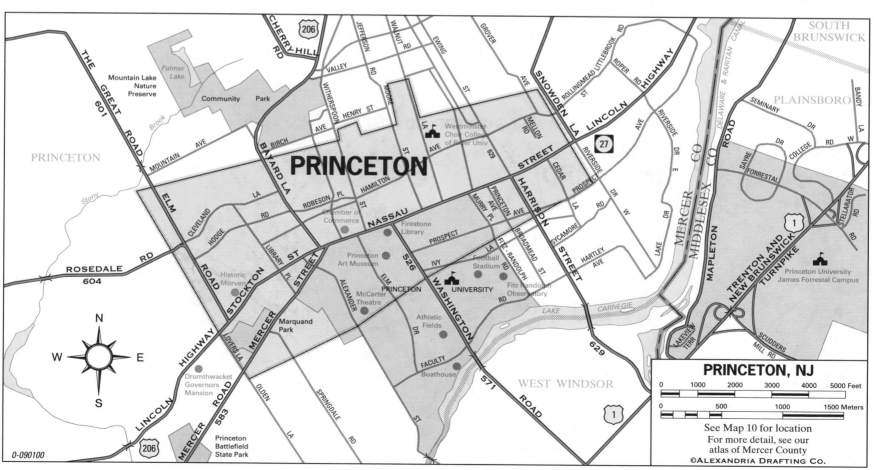

MAP
28

NEW BRUNSWICK, NJ

0 1000 2000 3000 4000 5000 Feet

0 500 1000 1500 Meters

See Maps 7 & 11 for location
For more detail, see our
atlas of Middlesex County
©Alexandria Drafting Co.

Rutgers Univ
New Brunswick
(Busch Campus)

18

EASTON

527

OAKLAND AVE
BLAKE AVE

FRANKLIN BLVD

PINE GROVE AVE

HIGHLAND

BUCCLEUCH PARK

SOMERSET CO

FRANKLIN

SOMERSET

514

BAIER AVE

HAMILTON

HENRY ST

AMBROSE ST

BROOKLINE AVE

DOUGLAS AVE

27

QUENTIN AVE

AVENUE 693

JERSEY

91

NEW
BRUNSWICK

JOYCE

5TH ST

KILMER

LORETO

MAY

LIVINGSTON

LEE

26

CLEREMONT PL

LINWOOD PL

AVE

HEDGES ST

NASSAU ST

NORTH BRUNSWICK

CHROME ST

0-090100

LANDING LANE
BRIDGE

JOHN LYNCH SR MEMORIAL

WEBER

COLLEGE AVE

HUNTINGTON ST

WYCKOFF ST

STONE ST

COURTLAND ST

BISHOP

Rutgers Univ
New Brunswick
(College Ave Campus)

GEORGE

SOMERSET STREET

STREET

STREET

FRENCH

WELTON ST

HALE ST

HANDY ST

SUYDAM ST

AVENUE

SANDFORD ST

HOWARD ST

THROOP

AVE

FULTON ST

WARD ST

ELLEN ST

REMSEN ST

COMMERCIAL AVE

ST

NICHOL AVE

Jane Voorhees
Zimmerli
Art Mus

City Hall
BAYARD ST
State
Theatre
NEW ST

New
Brunswick
Cultural Ctr

171

172

RD

Rutgers Univ
New Brunswick
(Cook/Douglas Campus)

RYDERS LA

CLIFTON AVE

JOHNSON
COUNTY PARK

CEDAR DR

RIVER

RARITAN

RIVER

PARKWAY

DONALDSON COUNTY PARK

18

LAWRENCE

Rutgers
Display
Gardens

1

HIGHLAND
PARK

5TH ST

HAMLIN RD

CLEVELAND AVE

2ND AVE

LINCOLN AVE

6TH AVE

RARITAN

1ST AVE S
2ND AVE S
ADELAIDE AVE

3RD AVE
4TH AVE
BENNER ST

5TH AVE S

7TH AVE S

MANSFIELD AVE

9TH AVE S

11TH AVE S

VALENTINE

CROWELLS RD

8TH

WOODBRIDGE

EDISON

27

SUTTONS LA

PLAINFIELD AVE

514

AVE

SILVER LAKE AVE

EDISON

SILVER
LAKE

TURNPIKE

N
W   E
S

BROOK

JERSEY

TURNPIKE

PATTON DR

MYRON PL

GAGE RD

Toll

NEW

Exit-9

NJ Turnpike
Administration
Area

SCHOOL AVE

AINSWORTH

GATES

MITCHELL

HOUSE AVE

WESTON PL

EDGEBORO RD

EAST
BRUNSWICK

18

MAP
29

PRINCETON, NJ

0 1000 2000 3000 4000 5000 Feet

0 500 1000 1500 Meters

See Map 10 for location
For more detail, see our
atlas of Mercer County
©Alexandria Drafting Co.

CHERRY HILL RD

206

THE GREAT ROAD 601

Mountain Lake
Nature
Preserve

Palmer Lake

Community Park

Brook

PRINCETON

ROSEDALE RD

604

MOUNTAIN AVE

CLEVELAND

ELM

HODGE RD

LA

RD

STOCKTON

MERCER

LINCOLN HIGHWAY

583

OLDEN LA

206

Princeton
Battlefield
State Park

JEFFERSON

WALNUT ST

VALLEY RD

WITHERSPOON ST

HENRY ST

BIRCH AVE

AVE

BAYARD LA

PRINCETON

ROBESON PL

HAMILTON

NASSAU

Chamber of
Commerce

LIBRARY PL

Historic
Morven

Princeton
Art Museum

ST

Firestone
Library

Marquand
Park

McCarter
Theatre

Drumthwacket
Governors
Mansion

N
W   E
S

EWING ST

MOORE ST

ST

GROVER AVE

529

Westminster
Choir College
of Rider Univ

PROSPECT

526

ELM

PRINCETON

ALEXANDER

PRINCETON AVE

MURRY PL

IVY LA

UNIVERSITY

WASHINGTON

571

FACULTY RD

Athletic
Fields

Football
Stadium

Princeton
University

Fitz Randolph
Observatory

Faculty
Boathouse

LAKE

ROLLINGMEAD

LITTLEBROOK RD

ROPER RD

MELLON

SNOWDEN LA

CEDAR LA

HARRISON STREET

RIVERSIDE DR E

PROSPECT AVE

BROADMEAD

FITZ-RANDOLPH RD

SYCAMORE AVE

HARTLEY AVE

LINCOLN

27

629

LAKE DR

CARNEGIE

MERCER CO

MIDDLESEX CO

DELAWARE & RARITAN CANAL

SEMINARY

MAPLETON RD

TRENTON AND
NEW BRUNSWICK
TURNPIKE

LAKEVIEW TERR

SCUDDERS
MILL RD

SOUTH
BRUNSWICK

PLAINSBORO

BANDY LA

DR

SAYRE DR

FORRESTAL

COLLEGE RD W

STELLARATOR RD

1

Princeton University
James Forrestal Campus

WEST WINDSOR

0-090100

MAP
30

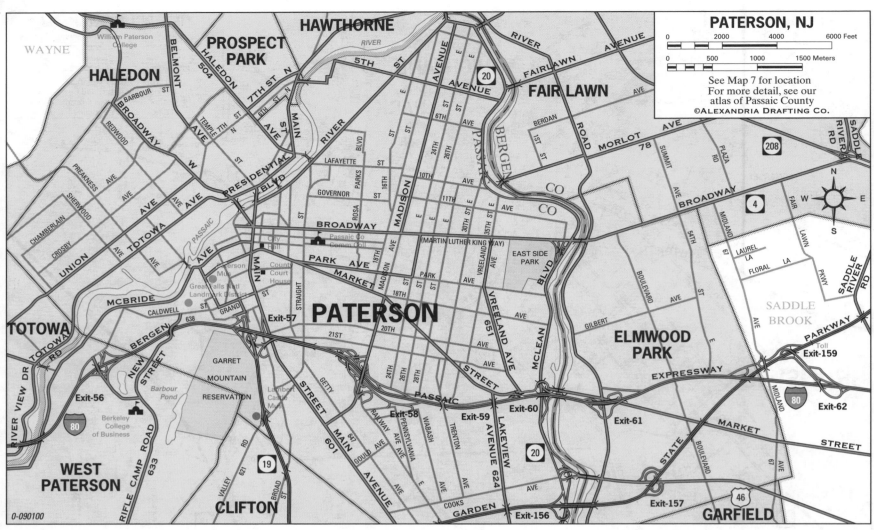

MAP
31

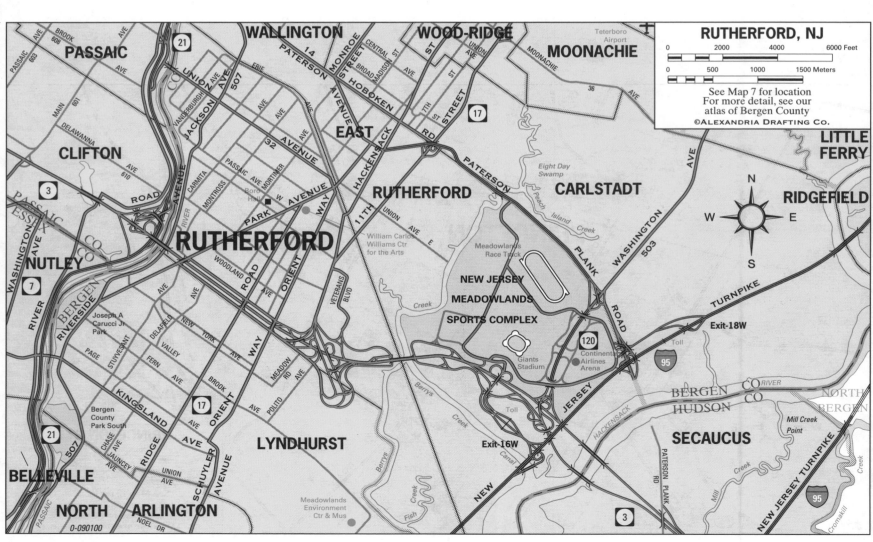

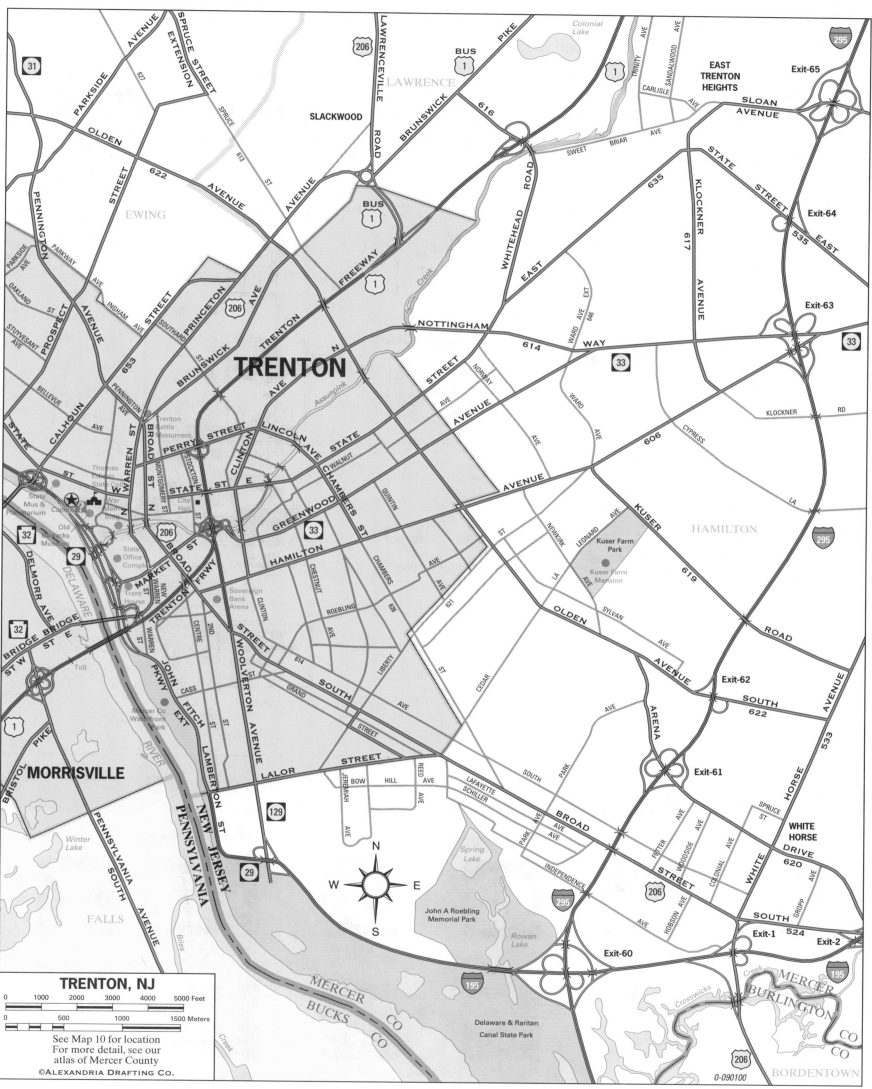

MAP
32

TRENTON, NJ

0 1000 2000 3000 4000 5000 Feet

0 500 1000 1500 Meters

See Map 10 for location
For more detail, see our
atlas of Mercer County

©ALEXANDRIA DRAFTING CO.

0-090100

Regulatory Signs

STOP

YIELD

DO NOT
ENTER

NO LEFT
TURN

NO RIGHT
TURN

NO U
TURN

LEFT TURN
ONLY

LEFT OR
THROUGH

RIGHT TURN
ONLY

RIGHT OR
THROUGH

KEEP
RIGHT

KEEP
LEFT

NO TRUCKS

2-WAY LEFT
TURN LANE

NO
BICYCLES

NO
PARKING

NO
PEDESTRIANS

NO
HITCHHIKING

RESTRICTED
LANE

ONE WAY
TRAFFIC

TOW AWAY
ZONE

TRUCK
WEIGHT
LIMIT

RESERVED
PARKING FOR
HANDICAPPED

DIVIDED
HIGHWAY

RAILROAD
CROSSING

Service Signs

HOSPITAL

GAS

FOOD

ACCESS FOR
HANDICAPPED

CAMPING
(TRAILER)

INFORMATION

REST
AREA

LODGING

PHONE

DIESEL

CAMPING
(TENT)

TRAILER
SANITARY
STATION

Index

NAME	TERR	MAP	GRID
Conashaugh	Pke	2	B3
Concordville	Del	13	F2
Congers	Rck	4	A5
Conovertown	At	20	A1
Conshohocken	Mnt	9	C6
Convent Station	Mrr	7	A3
Cookstown	Bur	10	F6
Cool Spring	Sux	21	D4
Coolbaugh	Mnr	1	E6
Cooper	Mom	11	E2
Coopers Corner	Ket	17	D5
Coopersburg	Leh	5	A6
Coopersville	War	5	E4
Copesville	Che	13	D1
Coplay	Leh	5	A4
Copper Hill	Hnt	10	B1
Corbin City	At	19	C3
Corbit	NC	13	E5
Corner Ketch	NC	13	D3
Cornville	Sal	14	C5
Cornwall-On-Hudson	Orn	3	F1
Cornwall-On-Hudson	Orn	4	A1
Cornwell Heights	Buk	10	A6
Cortez	Lak	1	A1
Cos Cob	Ffd	4	E6
Country Lakes	Bur	15	F1
Coveville	Mnr	1	C4
Cowentown	Cec	13	C4
Cowgill Corner	Ket	18	A4
Crafts	Put	4	D2
Cragmere Park	Brg	3	E5
Craigville	Orn	3	C2
Cranbury	Mid	10	F3
Cranbury Station	Mid	11	A3
Cranford	Uni	7	C5
Cream Ridge	Mom	10	F5
Creamery	Mnt	9	A4
Cresco	Mnr	1	C5
Cresskill	Brg	8	A1
Crestwood Village	Oc	16	B1
Crofts Corners	Put	4	B2
Crompond	Wch	4	B3
Cross Keys	Buk	9	E2
Cross Keys	Gle	14	F4
Cross Keys	Sux	21	B6
Cross River	Wch	4	E3
Cross Roads	Nth	5	B3
Crossroads	Bur	15	B2
Crosswicks	Mnt	9	E5
Croton	Hnt	6	A6
Croton Falls	Wch	4	D2
Croton-On-Hudson	Wch	4	B4
Crotonville	Wch	4	B4
Crowleytown	Bur	15	E5
Crugers	Wch	4	A4
Crumpton	Ken	17	B4
Crystal Beach	Cec	17	A1
Crystal Run	Orn	3	B1
Cuddebackville	Orn	2	E1
Culvers Inlet	Ssx	2	C4
Cumberland	Cmb	19	A2

D

NAME	TERR	MAP	GRID
Dagsboro	Sux	21	C6
Daleville	Che	13	B2
Danboro	Buk	9	E2
Danbury	Ffd	4	F1
Dannersville	Nth	5	A4
Darby	Del	14	C1
Daretown	Sal	14	C5
Darlington	Brg	3	D6
Darlington Corners	Che	13	F1
Darmac	Put	4	D2
Davis Corner	Ket	17	D4
Dayton	Mid	10	F2
Deacons	Bur	10	C6
Deal	Mom	11	F3
Deal	Mom	12	A4
Deans Corners	Put	4	E2
Deepwater	Sal	14	A4
Deerfield	Cmb	14	C6
Deforest Corners	Put	4	F1
Del Haven	CM	19	A6
Delair	CaC	14	F1
Delanco	Bur	10	A6
Delaney Corners	NC	17	D3
Delaware	War	5	F2
Delaware City	NC	13	E5
Delaware Water Gap	Mnr	5	D1
Delmont	Cmb	19	A4
Delphi	Mnt	9	A3
Demarest	Brg	8	A1
Denniston	Orn	3	E1
Dennisville	CM	19	C4
Denton	Orn	3	B2
Denville	Mrr	7	A2
Devon	Che	9	A6
Dewey Beach	Sux	21	F4
Dexter Corner	NC	17	D2
Diamond Beach	CM	22	B1
Dias Creek	CM	19	B5
Dicktown	CaC	15	A3
Dillingersville	Leh	9	A1
Dilworthtown	Del	13	E2
Dinahs Corner	Ket	17	E4
Dingmans Ferry	Pke	2	B4
Dividing Creek	Cmb	18	E3
Dobbs Ferry	Wch	4	B6
Doe Run	Che	13	C2
Dolington	Buk	10	A3
Dorchester	Cmb	19	A3
Dorothy	At	19	C2
Double Trouble	Oc	16	D2
Dover	Ket	17	E4
Dover	Ket	18	A4
Dover	Mrr	6	F2
Dover Forge	Oc	16	C2
Downingtown	Che	13	D1
Downs Chapel	Ket	17	D6
Downstown	Gle	15	A6
Doylestown	Buk	9	E3
Dresher	Mnt	9	D5
Drewville Heights	Put	4	E2
Drexel Hill	Del	14	C1
Drinker	Lak	1	A2
Dublin	Buk	9	D2
Dudley Corners	QA	17	B4
Dukes Bridge	Bur	15	F3
Dumont	Brg	8	A1
Dunbarton	CaC	15	B3
Dunellen	Mid	7	A5
DuPont Manor	Ket	17	F4
Durham Furnace	Buk	5	D6
Durham Mill	Buk	5	D6
Durland	Orn	3	C3
Durlandville	Orn	3	A2
Dutch Hollow	Orn	3	B3
Dutch Neck	Mer	10	E3
Dyerstown	Buk	9	E2
Dykemans	Put	4	E1

E

NAME	TERR	MAP	GRID
Eagle Valley	Orn	3	D5
Eagleville	Mnt	9	A5
Earleville	Cec	17	B1
Earlington	Mnt	9	B3
East Bangor	Nth	5	D2
East Camden	CaC	14	E1
East Freehold	Mom	11	C3
East Greenville	Mnt	9	A1
East Hanover	Mrr	7	B3
East Hills	Nsu	8	E3
East Lansdowne	Del	14	C1
East Meadow	Nsu	8	F4
East Millstone	Hnt	6	F6
East Norwich	Nsu	8	F2
East Orange	Esx	7	D3
East Riverton	Bur	10	A6
East Rockaway	Nsu	8	D5
East Rutherford	Brg	7	E3
East Sterling	Wyn	1	B3
East Stroudsburg	Mnr	1	D6
East Stroudsburg	Mnr	5	D1
East Swiftwater	Mnr	1	C5
East Trenton Heights	Mer	10	D3
East Williston	Nsu	8	E3
East Woods	Wch	4	F4
Eastlawn Gardens	Nth	5	C4
Easton	Nth	5	D4
Eastview	Wch	4	C6
Eatontown	Mom	11	F3
Echo Lake	Mnr	1	F6
Echo Lake	Pas	3	B6
Eddystone	Del	14	C2
Edelman	Nth	5	C3
Eden	Orn	3	A3
Eden Dell	Che	13	D3
Edenton	Che	13	A2
Edenville	Orn	3	A3
Eder	Cec	13	B5
Edge Hill	Mnt	9	D5
Edgemere	Pke	2	A3
Edgemont	Del	14	A1
Edgemoor	NC	13	F3
Edgewater	Brg	8	A3
Edinburg	Mer	10	E3
Edison	Buk	9	E3
Edison	Mid	7	B6
Effort	Mnr	5	A1
Egg Harbor City	At	15	E6
Eilers Corner	Mer	10	F4
Elam	Del	13	F2
Eldora	CM	19	A4
Eldridge Hill	Sal	14	C5
Eldridge Park	Mer	10	C3
Elephant	Buk	9	D1
Elizabeth	Uni	7	D5
Elk Mills	Cec	13	B5
Elk Neck	Cec	13	A6
Elkdale	Che	13	B3
Elkton	Cec	13	C5
Elkview	Che	13	B3
Ellendale	Sux	21	A3
Ellisburg	CaC	14	F2
Ellisdale	Mom	10	F5
Elm	CaC	15	C4
Elmdale	Lak	1	A2
Elmer	Sal	14	E5
Elmont	Nsu	8	D4
Elmsford	Wch	4	C6
Elmwood	Ph	14	D2
Elmwood Park	Brg	7	E2
Elsmere	NC	13	E4
Elwood	At	15	D6
Elwyn	Del	14	B2
Embreeville	Che	13	D1
Emerson	Brg	7	F1
Emerson	Brg	8	A1
Emmaus	Leh	5	A6
Englewood	Brg	8	A2
Englewood Cliffs	Brg	8	A2
English Creek	At	19	D2
Englishtown	Mom	11	B3
Ercildoun	Che	13	B1
Erial	CaC	14	F3
Erwinna	Buk	5	F6
Espanong	Mrr	6	E1
Essex Fells	Esx	7	C3
Estell Manor	At	19	C2
Eureka	Buk	9	D4
Evansburg	Mnt	9	A4
Everetts Corner	Ket	17	C4
Everittstown	Hnt	5	F6
Evesboro	Bur	15	A2
Ewan	Gle	14	D4
Ewansville	Bur	15	C1
Ewingtown	QA	17	A4
Ewingville	Mer	10	C3

F

NAME	TERR	MAP	GRID
Fahnestock Corners	Put	4	B1
Fair Haven	Mom	11	F2
Fair Hill	Cec	13	B4
Fair Lawn	Brg	7	E1
Fairfax	NC	13	F3
Fairfield	Esx	7	C2
Fairless Hills	Buk	10	B4
Fairmount	Hnt	6	C4
Fairmount	Sux	21	D5
Fairton	Cmb	18	D2
Fairview	Brg	8	A3
Fairview	Bur	10	F6
Fairview	Bur	15	C2
Fairview	Gle	14	E3
Fairview Village	Mnt	9	B4
Fairville	Che	13	E2
Fallsington	Buk	10	B4
Fanwood	Uni	7	B5
Far Hills	Sms	6	E4
Fardale	Brg	3	D6
Farmersville	Nth	5	C5
Farmingdale	Mom	11	D4
Farmingdale	Orn	3	C2
Farmington	Leh	5	A5
Feasterville	Buk	9	F5
Fellowship	Bur	15	A1
Felton	Ket	17	E6
Fenwick	Sal	14	B5
Ferndale	Buk	5	D6
Ferrel	Gle	14	D4
Field Corners	Put	4	E1
Fieldsboro	Bur	10	C5
Fieldsboro	NC	17	D1
Finchville	Orn	2	F1
Finderne	Sms	6	E6
Finesville	Hnt	5	E5
Finland	Buk	9	A2
Finnegans Corners	Orn	3	B2
Firthcliffe	Orn	3	F1
Firthcliffe Heights	Orn	3	F1
Fitzwatertown	Mnt	9	E5
Five Points	At	19	B1
Five Points	Che	13	D3
Five Points	Nth	5	E2
Five Points	Ssx	2	B5
Five Points	Sux	21	D4
Flagtown	Sms	6	D6
Flanders	Mrr	6	D2
Flatbrookville	Ssx	2	A5
Flemings Landing	NC	17	F2
Flemington	Hnt	6	B6
Flemington	Hnt	10	B1
Flemington Junction	Hnt	6	B6
Flicksville	Nth	5	D2
Floral Park	Nsu	8	D4
Florham Park	Mrr	7	B3
Florida	Orn	3	B3
Florida Park	Del	14	A1
Flourtown	Mnt	9	D5
Flower Hill	Nsu	8	D3
Folcroft	Del	14	C2
Folsom	At	15	B5
Fords	Mid	7	C6
Fords Corner	Ket	17	D4
Forest Grove	Buk	9	F3
Forest Grove	Gle	15	A6
Forestville	Che	13	B3
Forked River	Oc	16	D2
Fort Elfsborg	Sal	13	F6
Fort Lee	Brg	8	A2
Fort Montgomery	Orn	4	A2
Fort Plains	Mom	11	D4
Fort Washington	Mnt	9	D5
Fortescue	Cmb	18	E4
Foul Rift	War	5	E3
Fountain Hill	Leh	5	A5
Fountainville	Buk	9	D2
Four Corners	Orn	3	C1
Four Corners	Put	4	A2
Four Mile Circle	Bur	15	E2
Fowler Beach	Sux	21	C2
Foxcroft	Del	14	B1
Foxtown Hill	Mnr	5	D1
Franconia	Mnt	9	B3
Frankford	Sux	21	D6
Franklin	Ssx	2	F5
Franklin Bay	Nsu	8	E5
Franklin Grove	War	2	A6
Franklin Lakes	Brg	3	D6
Franklin Lakes	Brg	7	D1
Franklin Park	Mid	10	F1
Franklin Square	Nsu	8	D4
Franklinville	Gle	14	F5
Frederica	Ket	18	A6
Fredericktown	Ken	17	B2
Fredon	Ssx	2	C6
Freehold	Mom	11	C3
Freemansburg	Nth	5	C5
Freeport	Nsu	8	E5
Freewood Acres	Mom	11	D4
Frenchtown	Hnt	5	F6
Freneau	Mom	11	C2
Fricks	Buk	9	C3
Friedensville	Leh	5	B6
Friendship	Bur	15	E4
Friendship	Sal	14	D5
Friesburg	Sal	14	C6
Fullerton	Leh	5	A5
Furlong	Buk	9	E3

G

NAME	TERR	MAP	GRID
Galena	Ken	17	B2
Gandys Beach	Cmb	18	D3
Garden City	Nsu	8	D4
Gardenville	Buk	9	E2
Gardenville Center	Gle	14	E3
Gardnerville	Orn	3	A2
Garfield	Brg	7	E2
Garrett Hill	Mnt	9	C6
Garrison	Put	4	A2
Garwood	Uni	7	C5
Gauff Hill	Leh	5	B5
Georgetown	Bur	10	E6
Georgetown	Ken	17	B2
Georgetown	Nth	5	C4
Georgetown	Sux	21	B4
Georgia	Mom	11	C4
Geryville	Buk	9	A2
Gibbsboro	CaC	15	A2
Gibbstown	Gle	14	C3
Gilbert	Mnr	5	A1
Gilbert Corners	Put	4	B2
Gilford Park	Oc	16	E1
Gillette	Mrr	7	A4
Ginns Corner	NC	17	D2
Girarde	Orn	3	D1
Gladwyne	Mnt	9	C6
Glasgow	NC	13	C5
Glassboro	Gle	14	E4
Glasser	Ssx	6	E1
Glen Cove	Nsu	8	E2
Glen Gardner	Hnt	6	A4
Glen Mills	Del	14	A1
Glen Ridge	Esx	7	D3
Glen Rock	Brg	7	E1
Glen Spey	Slv	2	C1
Glendola	Mom	11	E4
Glendon	Nth	5	D5
Glendora	CaC	14	F2
Glenolden	Del	14	C2
Glenside	Mnt	9	E5
Glenside	Sal	14	A5
Glenville	Ffd	4	E6
Glenwood	Ssx	3	A4
Glenwood Landing	Nsu	8	D3
Gloucester City	CaC	14	E2
Godeffroy	Orn	2	E1
Goldens Bridge	Wch	4	E3
Goldsboro	Crl	17	C6
Golts	Ken	17	C3
Gordons Corners	Mom	11	C3
Goshen	CM	19	B5
Goshen	Che	13	F1
Goshen	Orn	3	C2
Goshenville	Che	13	F1
Gouldsboro	Pke	1	A4
Gouldtown	Cmb	18	D1
Gradyville	Del	14	A1
Graham	Wch	4	B5
Grand View Heights	Mnt	9	C5
Grand View-On-Hudson	Rck	4	B6
Grandville	Mnr	5	B1
Granite Springs	Wch	4	C3
Grant Corner	Wch	4	E3
Grassy Sound	CM	19	C6
Graterford	Mnt	9	A4
Gravel Hill	Sux	21	C4
Gravelly Run	At	19	D1
Gravity	Wyn	1	B1
Grears Corner	NC	17	D2
Great Meadows	War	6	A2
Great Neck	Nsu	8	D3
Greeley	Pke	2	A1
Green Bank	Bur	15	F5
Green Creek	CM	19	B6
Green Grove	Mom	11	F4
Green Lane	Mnt	9	A2
Green Lawn	Che	13	B2
Green Spring	NC	17	E3
Green Village	Mrr	7	A4
Greendell	Ssx	6	C1
Greentown	Pke	1	C3
Greentree	Che	9	A6
Greentree	NC	14	A3
Greenville	NC	13	E3
Greenville	Oc	11	D5
Greenville	Orn	2	E2
Greenville	Sal	14	D6
Greenville	Wch	8	C1
Greenwich	Cmb	18	B2
Greenwich	Ffd	4	E6
Greenwood Lake	Orn	3	C4
Grenloch	CaC	14	F3
Griggstown	Sms	10	E1
Grove Hill	Pke	1	E2
Gruvertown	Nth	5	E3
Gulph Mills	Mnt	9	B6
Gum Crossroads	Sux	21	A5
Gum Tree Corner	Cmb	18	B1
Gumtree	Che	13	B2
Guttenberg	Hud	7	F3
Guttenberg	Hud	8	A3
Gwynedd	Mnt	9	C4

H

NAME	TERR	MAP	GRID
H & H Corner	NC	17	E2
Haags Mill	Wyn	1	B3
Hackensack	Brg	7	F2
Hackettstown	War	6	B2
Hacks Point	Cec	17	B1
Haddon Heights	CaC	14	F2
Haddonfield	CaC	14	F2
Hagersville	Buk	9	D2
Hagerville	Sal	14	A6
Haines Corners	Put	4	E1
Hainesburg	War	5	F1
Hainesport	Bur	15	C1
Hainesville	Ssx	2	C3
Haledon	Pas	7	D1
Haleyville	Cmb	18	F3
Halltown	Sal	14	B5
Halsey	Ssx	2	C5
Hamburg	Ssx	2	F5
Hamden	Hnt	6	B5
Hamilton Square	Mer	10	E4
Hamlin	Wyn	1	B2
Hammonton	At	15	C5
Hamorton	Che	13	E2
Hampton	Hnt	6	A4
Hampton Gate	Bur	15	D3
Hamptonburgh	Orn	3	C1
Hancocks Bridge	Sal	14	A6
Handsome Eddy	Slv	2	B1
Hanover	Mrr	7	B3
Hanoverville	Nth	5	B4
Harbeson	Sux	21	C4
Harbourton	Mer	10	B2
Harding	Gle	14	E5
Hardingville	Gle	14	E5
Hardscrabble	Sux	21	A5
Hardwick	War	2	A6
Hardwick Center	War	2	A6
Hares Corner	NC	13	E5
Harleysville	Mnt	9	B3
Harlingen	Sms	10	E1
Harmons School	Sux	21	D5
Harmonville	Mnt	9	C5
Harmony	War	5	E4
Harmonyvale	Ssx	2	E5
Harriman	Orn	3	D3
Harrington Park	Brg	8	A1
Harrison	Hud	7	E4
Harrison	Wch	4	D6
Harrison	Wch	8	D1
Harrisonville	Gle	14	C4
Harrisville	Bur	15	F5
Harrow	Buk	9	D1
Hartford	Bur	15	B1
Hartly	Ket	17	D4
Hartsville	Buk	9	E4
Harvey Cedars	Oc	16	E4
Hasbrouck Heights	Brg	7	E2
Hastings-on-Hudson	Wch	4	B6
Hastings-on-Hudson	Wch	8	B1
Hatboro	Mnt	9	E4
Hatfield	Mnt	9	C3
Haverstraw	Rck	4	A4
Haviland Hollow	Put	4	F1
Hawley	Wyn	1	D1
Haworth	Brg	8	A1
Hawthorne	Pas	7	E1
Hawthorne	Wch	4	C5
Hayesville	Che	13	A3
Hazen	War	5	F3
Hazlettville	Ket	17	E5
Headquarters	Hnt	10	A1
Hecktown	Nth	5	B4
Hedding	Bur	10	C5
Hedger House	Bur	15	F2
Heislerville	Cmb	19	A4
Hellertown	Nth	5	C6
Helmetta	Mid	11	A2
Hemlock Grove	Pke	1	C3
Hempstead	Nsu	8	E4
Henderson	Crl	17	C6
Henlopen Acres	Sux	21	F4
Henryville	Mnr	1	C5
Herbertsville	Oc	11	E5
Hermon	Bur	15	E5
Herrings Corners	Ket	21	B1
Hesstown	Cmb	19	A2
Hewlett Bay Park	Nsu	8	D5
Hewlett Harbor	Nsu	8	D5
Hi-Nella	CaC	14	F2
Hibernia	Mrr	7	A1
Hickory Hill	Che	13	A3
Hickory Tree	Mrr	7	A4
Hicksville	Nsu	8	F3
Higbeetown	At	16	A6
High Bridge	Hnt	6	B4
High Ridge	Ffd	4	F5
Highland Beach	CM	19	A6
Highland Falls	Orn	4	A2
Highland Lakes	Ssx	3	A4
Highland Mills	Orn	3	E2
Highland Park	Buk	9	C2
Highland Park	Mid	7	A6
Highland Park	Mid	11	A1
Highland Park	Nth	5	C5
Highlands	Mom	12	A2
Highs Beach	CM	19	A6
Hightstown	Mer	10	F3
Hill Gallows	Buk	5	D6
Hillburn	Brg	3	D5
Hillcrest	Rck	3	F5
Hillsdale	Brg	3	F6
Hillsdale	Mom	11	D2
Hillside	Uni	7	D4
Hilltop	CaC	14	F3
Hilltown	Buk	9	C3
Hinkletown	Buk	9	E2
Hitchens Crossroads	Sux	21	A6
Ho-Ho-Kus	Brg	3	E6
Ho-Ho-Kus	Brg	7	E1
Hoboken	Hud	7	F4
Hockessin	NC	13	D3
Hoffmans	Hnt	6	B4
Holgate	Oc	16	C6
Holicong	Buk	9	F2
Holland	Buk	10	A4
Holland	Hnt	5	D6
Holletts Corners	Ket	17	D3

NAME	TERR	MAP	GRID
Hollisterville	Wyn	1	A2
Holly Park	Oc	16	E2
Hollymount	Sux	21	D4
Hollyville	Sux	21	C4
Holmansville	Oc	11	C5
Holmdel	Mom	11	D2
Holmeson	Mom	11	A4
Homeville	Che	13	A2
Hopatcong	Ssx	6	D1
Hope	QA	17	A6
Hope	War	6	A2
Hopewell	Mer	10	C2
Hopkins Corners	Put	4	D2
Hornerstown	Mom	10	F5
Horseshoe Hill	Wch	4	E4
Horsham	Mnt	9	E3
Hosensack	Leh	9	A1
Hourglass	Ket	17	D5
Houseman Corners	Put	4	C2
Houston	Ket	21	A1
Howardsville	Oc	16	B3
Howell	Orn	3	B2
Howells	Orn	3	A1
Howellville	Che	9	A6
Howertown	Nth	5	A4
Hughesville	War	5	D5
Huguenot	Orn	2	E2
Hulmeville	Buk	10	A5
Huntsburg	Ssx	6	B1
Huntsville	Ssx	6	C1
Hurdtown	Ssx	6	E1
Hurffville	Gle	14	E3
Husted Station	Cmb	14	D6
Hutchinson	War	5	E3
Hyson	Oc	11	C5

I

NAME	TERR	MAP	GRID
Imlaystown	Mom	10	F5
Indian Mills	Bur	15	D3
Indian Park	Orn	3	C4
Ingleside	QA	17	B5
Interlaken	Mom	11	F4
Inwood	Nsu	8	C5
Iona	Gle	14	F5
Iron Hill	Cec	13	C5
Ironia	Mrr	6	E2
Irvington	Esx	7	C4
Irvington	Wch	4	B6
Iselin	Mid	7	C6
Island Park	Nsu	8	D5
Islands Heights	Oc	16	E1
Ivyland	Buk	9	E4
Ivystone Farms	CaC	15	B3

J

NAME	TERR	MAP	GRID
Jackson	CaC	15	B3
Jackson Mills	Oc	11	C5
Jacksonville	Buk	9	F4
Jacksonville	Bur	10	C6
Jacksonville	Nth	5	A4
Jacobstown	Bur	10	E6
Jamaica	Que	8	C4
Jamesburg	Mid	11	A2
Jamison	Buk	9	E3
Jamisons Corner	NC	13	D6
Janvier	Gle	14	F5
Jefferson	Gle	14	D3
Jefferson Crossroads	Sux	21	B2
Jefferson Valley	Wch	4	C2
Jeffersonville	Mnt	9	B5
Jenkins	Bur	15	F4
Jenkintown	Mnt	9	E5
Jennersville	Che	13	B3
Jericho	Nsu	8	F3
Jericho	Wyn	1	B3
Jersey City	Hud	7	E4
Jerseyville	Mom	11	D4
Jimtown	Sux	21	D4
Jobstown	Bur	10	D6
Johnson	Orn	2	F2
Johnsonburg	War	6	B1
Johnsonville	Nth	5	E2
Johnsville	Buk	9	F4
Jones Crossroads	Sux	21	A5
Jones Island	Cmb	18	D3
Jones Point	Orn	4	A3
Juliustown	Bur	10	D6
Jutland	Hnt	6	A5

K

NAME	TERR	MAP	GRID
Kaolin	Che	13	D3
Katonah	Wch	4	D3
Keansburg	Mom	11	E1
Kearny	Hud	7	E3
Keasbey	Mid	7	B6
Keelersville	Buk	9	D1
Kellers Church	Buk	9	D1
Kelton	Che	13	B3
Kemblesville	Che	13	C3
Kendall Park	Mid	10	F1
Kenilworth	Uni	7	C4
Kennedy Mills	War	5	E5
Kennedyville	Ken	17	A3
Kennett Square	Che	13	D2
Kensington	Nsu	8	C3
Kent Cliffs	Put	4	C1
Kentmore Park	Ken	17	A2
Kenton	Ket	17	D4
Kenvil	Mrr	6	E2
Keswick Grove	Oc	16	C1
Keyport	Mom	11	D1
Kimbles	Pke	1	E1
King Of Prussia	Mnt	9	B6
Kings Crossroads	Sux	21	A4
Kings Grant	Bur	15	B2
Kings Point	Nsu	8	C3
Kingston	Mid	10	E2
Kingston Estates	CaC	15	A1
Kingwood	Hnt	9	F1
Kinkora	Bur	10	D5
Kinnelon	Mrr	3	B6
Kinnelon	Mrr	7	B1
Kintnersville	Buk	5	D6
Kirbys Mill	Bur	15	C1
Kirkwood	NC	13	D6
Kiryas Joel	Orn	3	E2
Kitchawan	Wch	4	C4
Kitts Hummock	Ket	18	B5
Klecknersville	Nth	5	A3
Klinesville	Hnt	6	B6
Knechts	Nth	5	C3
Knights Eddy	Slv	2	C1
Knowles Crossroads	Sux	21	A5
Kreidersville	Nth	5	A4
Kresgeville	Mnr	5	A2
Kresson	Bur	15	A2
Kresson	CaC	15	A2
Kulps Corner	Buk	9	D2
Kulpsville	Mnt	9	B4
Kunkletown	Mnr	5	A2

L

NAME	TERR	MAP	GRID
La Anna	Pke	1	C4
La Grange	Orn	3	C1
Lackawaxen	Pke	2	A1
Lafayette	Ssx	2	D5
Lafayette Hill	Mnt	9	C5
Lahaska	Buk	9	F2
Lake Ariel	Wyn	1	B1
Lake Carmel	Put	4	D1
Lake Hiawatha	Mrr	7	B2
Lake Lincolndale	Wch	4	D2
Lake Mohawk	Ssx	2	E6
Lake Nasawa	Buk	9	C3
Lake Peekskill	Put	4	B2
Lake Purdys	Wch	4	D3
Lake Success	Nsu	8	D3
Lake Telemark	Mrr	7	A1
Lakehurst	Oc	11	B6
Lakeland	CaC	14	F3
Lakeville	Orn	3	C4
Lakeville	Wyn	1	C1
Lakewood	Oc	11	D5
Lambertville	Hnt	10	A2
Lamington	Hnt	6	D5
Lanark	Leh	5	A6
Landenberg	Che	13	C3
Landing	Ssx	6	D2
Langhorne	Buk	10	A4
Langhorne Manor	Buk	10	A5
Langhorne Terrace	Buk	10	A4
Lanoka Harbor	Oc	16	D2
Lansdale	Mnt	9	C4
Lansdowne	Del	14	C1
Larchmont	Wch	8	D1
Larisons Corner	Hnt	10	B1
Lattingtown	Nsu	8	E2
Laurel	Che	13	D1
Laurel Lakes	Cmb	18	F2
Laurel Springs	CaC	14	F3
Laureldale	At	15	D6
Laurelton	Oc	11	E6
Laurence Harbor	Mid	11	D1
Lavallette	Oc	16	F1
Laverock	Mnt	9	D5
Lawnside	CaC	14	F2
Lawrence	Nsu	8	D5
Lawrence Corner	Sal	14	E6
Lawrence Park	Del	14	B1
Lawrenceville	Mer	10	C3
Layton	Ssx	2	B4
Lebanon	Hnt	6	C5
Lebanon	Ket	17	F5
Lebanon	Orn	3	D2
Lebanon Lakes	Bur	15	F2
Lederach	Mnt	9	B3
Ledgedale	Wyn	1	B2
Ledgewood	Mrr	6	D2
Leeds	Cec	13	B5
Leeds Point	At	20	A1
Leektown	Bur	16	A5
Leesburg	Cmb	19	A3
Lehigh	Lak	1	A3
Leipsic	Ket	17	F4
Leisure Village	Oc	11	D6
Leisure Village West	Oc	11	C6
Leithsville	Nth	5	B6
Lenape	Che	13	E2
Lenni	Del	14	A2
Leonardo	Mom	11	F1
Leonia	Brg	8	A2
Leopard	Che	9	A6
Leslie	Cec	13	A5
Levittown	Buk	10	B5
Levittown	Nsu	8	F4
Lewes	Sux	21	E3
Lewis	Sal	14	A5
Lewisboro	Wch	4	F4
Lewisburg	Ssx	2	E4
Lewisville	Che	13	B4
Liberty Corner	Sms	6	F4
Liberty Corners	Orn	2	F3
Libertyville	Ssx	2	C4
Lido Beach	Nsu	8	E6
Lima	Del	14	A1
Limeport	Leh	5	A6
Lincoln	Gle	14	D3
Lincoln	Sux	21	A2
Lincoln Park	Mrr	7	C1
Lincolndale	Wch	4	D3
Lincroft	Mom	11	E3
Linden	Uni	7	D5
Lindenwold	CaC	14	F3
Lindenwold	CaC	15	A3
Line Lexington	Buk	9	C3
Linvale	Hnt	10	B2
Linwood	At	19	F2
Linwood	Del	14	A3
Little Britain	Orn	3	E1
Little Brook	Hnt	6	B4
Little Chapel	Wyn	1	B1
Little Creek	Ket	18	A5
Little Falls	Pas	7	D2
Little Ferry	Brg	7	F2
Little Heaven	Ket	18	A6
Little Hill Church	Sux	21	A6
Little Silver	Mom	11	F2
Little Summit	Mnr	1	A5
Little York	Hnt	5	F5
Little York	Orn	3	A3
Littleton	Mrr	7	A2
Livingston	Esx	7	C3
Loch Arbour	Mom	11	F4
Loch Arbour	Mom	12	A4
Locktown	Hnt	10	A1
Lockwood	Ssx	6	D1
Locust Grove	Ken	17	A2
Locust Grove	Nsu	8	F3
Locust Point	Cec	13	B6
Locust Valley	Nsu	8	E2
Lodi	Brg	7	E2
Logtown	Orn	2	E2
Lombard	Cec	13	A4
London Grove	Che	13	D2
Long Beach	Nsu	8	D6
Long Branch	Mom	12	A3
Long Bridge	War	6	B2
Long Pond	Mnr	1	A6
Long Ridge	Ffd	4	E5
Long Valley	Mrr	6	C3
Longport	At	19	F3
Longwood	Che	13	D2
Lords Corner	Ket	17	D6
Lords Valley	Pke	1	F2
Loux Corner	Buk	9	D2
Lower Bank	Bur	15	F5
Lower Harmony	War	5	E4
Lower Tannersville	Mnr	1	C6
Lowes Crossroads	Sux	21	B6
Lumberton	Bur	15	C1
Lumberville	Buk	9	F2
Lumberville	Slv	2	C1
Lynbrook	Nsu	8	D5
Lynch Heights	Ket	21	A1
Lyndhurst	Brg	7	E3
Lyonsville	Mrr	7	A1

M

NAME	TERR	MAP	GRID
Macopin	Pas	3	B6
Madison	Mrr	7	A3
Madisonville	Lak	1	A2
Magnolia	At	15	D5
Magnolia	Bur	15	E1
Magnolia	CaC	14	F2
Magnolia	Ket	18	A6
Mahopac	Put	4	D2
Mahopac Falls	Put	4	C2
Mahopac Mines	Put	4	C2
Mahwah	Brg	3	E5
Mainland	Mnt	9	B3
Malaga	Gle	14	F6
Malverne	Nsu	8	D4
Mamaroneck	Wch	8	D1
Manahawkin	Oc	16	D4
Manalapan	Mom	11	B3
Manasquan	Mom	11	F5
Manhasset	Nsu	8	D3
Manhattan	NYC	7	F4
Manhattan	NYC	8	A4
Manoa	Del	14	C1
Manorhaven	Nsu	8	D2
Mansfield	Bur	10	D5
Mantoloking	Oc	11	F6
Mantua	Gle	14	D3
Manunka Chunk	War	5	F2
Manville	Sms	6	E6
Maple Glen	Mnt	9	D4
Maple Grove	Sal	14	D5
Maple Shade	Bur	15	A1
Maple Shade	CaC	14	F1
Maplewood	Esx	7	C4
Maplewood	Wyn	1	A1
Marcella	Mrr	7	A1
Marcus Hook	Del	14	B3
Margate City	At	19	F2
Margate City	At	20	A3
Marksboro	War	6	A1
Marlboro	Cmb	18	B1
Marlboro	Mom	11	D3
Marlton	Bur	15	B2
Marlton Heights	Sal	14	B4
Marmora	CM	19	E3
Marshalls Corner	Mer	10	C2
Marshalls Creek	Mnr	1	E6
Marshallton	NC	13	D4
Marshalltown	Sal	14	A5
Marshallville	CM	19	C3
Marshtown	Sux	21	E4
Martha	Bur	15	F4
Martins Creek	Nth	5	D3
Martinsville	Sms	6	E5
Marydel	Crl	17	C5
Masonville	Bur	15	B1
Maspeth	Que	8	B4
Massey	Ken	17	C3
Masseys Landing	Sux	21	E5
Matamoras	Pke	2	D2
Matawan	Mid	11	C2
Mathews Corner	NC	17	E1
Matthews	Mom	11	C5
Mauricetown	Cmb	19	A3
Max	CM	22	A1
Maybrook	Orn	3	D1
Mayetta	Oc	16	C4
Mays Landing	At	19	D1
Mayville	CM	19	B6
Maywood	Brg	7	F2
McAfee	Ssx	2	F4
McDonough	NC	17	D1
McIlhaney	Mnr	5	B1
McKays Corner	NC	17	C3
McKee City	CM	19	E1
McKeel Corners	Put	4	B1
McMichaels	Mnr	5	A1
Meadowbrook	Mnt	9	F5
Meadowbrook	Orn	3	E1
Meadowbrook Village	Oc	11	B5
Meads Corners	Put	4	C1
Mechanics Valley	Cec	13	B5
Mechanicsville	Buk	9	E2
Medford	Bur	15	C2
Medford Lakes	Bur	15	C2
Media	Del	14	B1
Meisertown	Mnr	1	C6
Melrose	Bur	15	B2
Mendenhall	Che	13	D2
Mendham	Mrr	6	E3
Menlo Park	Mid	7	B6
Mercerville	Mer	10	D4
Merchantville	CaC	14	F1
Meriden	Mrr	7	A1
Merrick	Nsu	8	F5
Merwinsburg	Mnr	5	A1
Metedeconk	Oc	11	E6
Metuchen	Mid	7	B6
Meyersville	Mrr	7	A4
Miami Beach	CM	19	A6
Mianus	Ffd	4	E6
Michigan Corners	Orn	3	B1
Mickleton	Gle	14	C3
Middle Valley	Mrr	6	C3
Middlesex	Mid	7	A6
Middlesex	Sms	6	F6
Middlesex Beach	Sux	21	F6
Middletown	NC	17	D1
Middletown	Nth	5	B5
Middletown	Orn	3	A1
Middletown	Ssx	6	F1
Middleville	Ssx	2	B6
Midland Park	Brg	3	E6
Midland Park	Brg	7	E1
Midway	Sux	21	E4
Milford	Hnt	5	F6
Milford	Pke	2	C2
Milford	Sux	21	A2
Milford Crossroads	NC	13	C4
Milford Square	Buk	9	B1
Mill Brook	Mrr	6	F2
Mill Neck	Nsu	8	F2
Millbourne	Ph	14	C1
Millbrook	War	2	A6
Millburn	Esx	7	C4
Miller Creek	Orn	3	B3
Miller Manor	Nth	5	A4
Millhurst	Mom	11	B4
Millington	Ken	17	C3
Millington	Mrr	6	F4
Millrift	Pke	2	C2
Millsboro	Sux	21	C5
Millsburg	Orn	2	F2
Millstone	Sms	6	E6
Millstone	Sms	10	E1
Milltown	Mid	11	A1
Milltown	Mrr	6	D3
Milltown	Put	4	F2
Millville	Cmb	18	F2
Millville	Ssx	2	C3
Millville	Sux	21	E6
Millwood	Wch	4	C4
Milmay	At	19	B1
Milton	Mrr	2	F6
Milton	Sux	21	C3
Mine Hill	Mrr	6	E2
Mineola	Nsu	8	D4
Minisink Ford	Slv	2	A1
Mission	Sux	21	B6
Mizpah	At	19	C1
Modena	Che	13	C1
Moe	Pas	3	B5
Mohegan Lake	Wch	4	B3
Mongaup	Slv	2	C1
Monmouth	Mom	12	A2
Monmouth Junction	Mid	10	F2
Monroe	Orn	3	D3
Monroe	Ssx	2	E5
Monroeville	Sal	14	D5
Monsey	Rck	3	E5
Mont Clare	Mnt	9	A5
Montague	Ssx	2	C3
Montana	War	5	F3
Montchanin	NC	13	E3
Montclair	Esx	7	D3
Montebello	Rck	3	E5
Montgomery	Sms	10	D1
Montgomery Square	Mnt	9	D4
Montgomeryville	Mnt	9	D4
Montrose	Wch	4	A3
Montvale	Brg	3	F6
Montville	Mrr	7	B1
Moonachie	Brg	7	F2
Moores Beach	Cmb	19	A4
Moores Corner	Ket	17	E4
Moores Corner	Sal	14	A6
Moorestown	Bur	15	A1
Moorestown	Nth	5	B3
Morganville	Mom	11	D2
Morris Mill	Sux	21	C5
Morris Plains	Mrr	7	A3
Morristown	Mrr	7	A3
Morrisville	Buk	10	C4
Morton	Del	14	C1
Mortonville	Che	13	C1
Mount	Bur	15	E4
Mount Airy	Hnt	10	B2
Mount Arlington	Mrr	6	E2
Mount Bethel	Nth	5	E2
Mount Cobb	Lak	1	A1
Mount Ephraim	CaC	14	E2
Mount Freedom	Mrr	6	E3
Mount Holly	Bur	15	C1
Mount Hope	Mrr	6	F1
Mount Hope	Orn	2	F1
Mount Ivy	Rck	3	F4
Mount Joy	Hnt	5	D5
Mount Kisco	Wch	4	D4
Mount Laurel	Bur	15	B1
Mount Pleasant	Hnt	5	F6
Mount Pleasant	NC	13	D6
Mount Pleasant	Nth	5	E3
Mount Pocono	Mnr	1	B5
Mount Rose	Mer	10	D2
Mount Royal	Gle	14	D3
Mount Vernon	Wch	8	B2
Mount Zion	Mnr	1	D6
Mountain House	Orn	3	D2
Mountain Lakes	Mrr	7	A2
Mountain Lodge	Orn	3	E2
Mountain View	Pas	7	C1
Mountainhome	Mnr	1	C4
Mountainside	Uni	7	B4
Mountainville	Hnt	6	C4
Mountainville	Orn	3	F2
Mozart	Buk	9	F3
Mullica Hill	Gle	14	D4
Munion Field	Bur	16	B5
Munsey Park	Nsu	8	D3
Murray Hill	Uni	7	B4
Murrays Corner	Sux	21	E3
Muttontown	Nsu	8	F3
Myers Grove	Orn	2	E1
Myrtle Grove	Ssx	2	C5
Mystic Island	Oc	16	B6

N

NAME	TERR	MAP	GRID
Naceville	Buk	9	B2
Nanuet	Rck	3	F5
Narbeth	Mnt	9	C6
Nassau	Sux	21	D3
National Park	Gle	14	D2
Naughright	Mrr	6	C3
Nauraushaun	Rck	4	A6
Navesink	Mom	11	F2
Nazareth	Nth	5	B4
Neelytown	Orn	3	C1
Nelson Corners	Put	4	A2
Nelsonville	Put	4	A1
Neola	Mnr	5	B1
Neptune City	Mom	11	F4
Nesco	At	15	D5
Neshaminy	Buk	9	D4
Neshaminy Woods	Buk	10	A5
Neshanic	Sms	10	D1
Neshanic Station	Sms	6	C6
Netcong	Mrr	6	D2
New Bridge	Sal	14	A6
New Britain	Buk	9	D3
New Brooklyn	Gle	15	A4
New Brunswick	Mid	11	A1
New Castle	NC	13	F4
New City	Rck	4	A5
New City Park	Rck	4	A5
New Egypt	Oc	10	F6
New England Crossroads	Cmb	18	D2
New Freedom	CaC	15	A3
New Freedom	Sal	14	D5
New Gretna	Bur	16	A5
New Hampton	Hnt	6	A4
New Hampton	Orn	3	A2
New Hempstead	Rck	3	F5
New Hope	Buk	10	A2
New Hyde Park	Nsu	8	D4
New Lisbon	Bur	15	E1
New London	Che	13	B3
New Market	Sux	21	B3
New Milford	Brg	7	F1
New Milford	Orn	3	B4
New Monmouth	Mom	11	F1
New Providence	Uni	7	B4
New Rochelle	Wch	8	C2
New Russia	Ssx	2	F6
New Sharon	Mer	10	F4
New Square	Rck	3	F5
New Vernon	Mrr	7	A4
New Village	War	5	F4
New Windsor	Orn	3	F1
New York	Kng	8	B6
New York	NYC	7	F6
New York	NYC	8	B6
Newark	Esx	7	D4
Newark	NC	13	C4
Newbolds Corner	Bur	15	C1
Newburg	Nth	5	C4
Newburgh	Orn	3	F1
Newfield	Ffd	4	F5
Newfield	Gle	14	F6
Newfoundland	Pas	3	A6
Newfoundland	Wyn	1	B3
Newkirk	Sal	14	D5
Newport	Cmb	18	D3
Newport	NC	13	E4
Newport	Orn	3	A3
Newton	Ssx	2	D6

NAME	TERR	MAP	GRID
Newtonville	At	15	B6
Newtown	Buk	10	A4
Newtown Square	Del	14	B1
Nixon	Mid	7	B6
Norma	Sal	18	E1
Normandy Beach	Oc	11	F6
Normanock	Ssx	2	C4
Norristown	Mnt	9	B5
North Arlington	Brg	7	E3
North Beach Haven	Oc	16	D6
North Bellmore	Nsu	8	F4
North Branch	Sms	6	D5
North Caldwell	Esx	7	C2
North Cape May	CM	22	A1
North Catasauqua	Nth	5	A4
North Church	Ssx	2	E5
North Dennis	CM	19	B4
North East	Cec	13	A5
North East Heights	Cec	13	A6
North Greenwich	Ffd	4	D5
North Haledon	Pas	7	D1
North Highland	Put	4	B1
North Hills	Nsu	8	D3
North Merrick	Nsu	8	F4
North Mianus	Ffd	4	F6
North Middletown	Mom	11	E1
North New Hyde Park	Nsu	8	D3
North Plainfield	Sms	7	A5
North Port Norris	Cmb	18	F3
North Salem	Wch	4	F2
North Stamford	Ffd	4	F5
North Wales	Mnt	9	C4
North Wantagh	Nsu	8	F4
North Water Gap	Mnr	1	E6
North Wildwood	CM	19	C6
North Wildwood	CM	22	C1
Northampton	Nth	5	A4
Northbrook	Che	13	D1
Northfield	At	19	F2
Northvale	Brg	4	A6
Northville	Cmb	14	D6
Nortonville	Gle	14	B3
Norwood	Brg	8	A1
Norwood	Del	14	C2
Nottingham	Buk	10	A5
Nugentown	Oc	16	B5
Nutley	Esx	7	E3
Nyack	Rck	4	B5

O

NAME	TERR	MAP	GRID
Oak Grove	Mnr	1	E6
Oak Orchard	Sux	21	D5
Oak Park	Mnt	9	C3
Oak Ridge	Pas	3	A6
Oak Tree	Mid	7	B6
Oak Valley	Gle	14	E3
Oakbourne	Che	13	F1
Oakbrook	Rck	3	F5
Oakhurst	Mom	11	F3
Oakland	Brg	3	C6
Oakley	Sux	21	A3
Oaklyn	CaC	14	E2
Oaks	Mnt	9	A5
Oakwood Beach	Sal	13	F6
Ocean Beach	Oc	16	F1
Ocean City	CM	19	F3
Ocean Gate	Oc	16	E1
Ocean View	CM	19	D5
Ocean View	Sux	21	E6
Oceanport	Mom	11	F3
Oceanside	Nsu	8	E5
Oceanville	At	20	A1
Odessa	NC	17	E1
Ogdensburg	Ssx	2	E6
Ogletown	NC	13	D4
Old Brookville	Nsu	8	E3
Old Greenwich	Ffd	4	F6
Old Tappan	Brg	4	A6
Old Westbury	Nsu	8	E3
Oldmans	Sal	14	A3
Oldwick	Hnt	6	C4
Olivet	Sal	14	D6
Olivet Hill	Ken	17	B2
Omar	Sux	21	D6
Ongs Hat	Bur	15	E2
Oradell	Brg	7	F1
Orange	Esx	7	D3
Orangeburg	Rck	4	A6
Orchard View	Bur	10	B6
Oreland	Mnt	9	D5
Orrs Mill	Orn	3	F1
Ortley Beach	Oc	16	F1
Osbornville	Oc	11	E6
Oscawana	Wch	4	A4
Oscawana Corners	Put	4	B2
Ossining	Wch	4	B5
Othello	Cmb	18	B2
Otisville	Orn	2	F1
Otter Kill	Orn	3	C2
Ottsville	Buk	9	E1
Overbrook	Sux	21	D3
Owens	Ssx	2	F3
Owls Nest	NC	13	E3
Oxford	Che	13	A3
Oxford	War	5	F3
Oxford	War	6	A3
Oyster Bay	Nsu	8	F2
Oyster Bay Cove	Nsu	8	F2
Oyster Creek	At	16	B6

P

NAME	TERR	MAP	GRID
Pailsey	Bur	15	E3
Palermo	CM	19	D4
Palisades	Rck	4	B6
Palisades Park	Brg	8	A2
Palmer Heights	Nth	5	C4
Palmyra	Bur	9	F6
Palmyra	Bur	14	F1
Palmyra	Hnt	5	F6
Panther	Pke	1	C3
Paoli	Che	9	A6
Paradise	Orn	2	E1
Paradise Lakes	Sal	14	B6
Paradise Valley	Mnr	1	C5
Paramus	Brg	7	E1
Park Ridge	Brg	3	F6
Parker	Mrr	6	C3
Parkersville	Che	13	E2
Parkertown	Oc	16	B5
Parkesburg	Che	13	A1
Parkside	Del	14	B2
Parkside	Mnr	1	C5
Parkville	Gle	14	D3
Parsippany	Mrr	7	A2
Passaic	Pas	7	E2
Paterson	Pas	7	D2
Pattenburg	Hnt	5	F5
Paulina	War	6	A1
Paulsboro	Gle	14	C2
Paupack	Pke	1	D2
Peacedale	Che	13	B4
Peacock Corner	Ken	17	C3
Peahala Park	Oc	16	D5
Peapack-Gladstone	Sms	6	D4
Pearl River	Rck	3	F6
Pearsons Corner	Ket	17	E5
Pearsons Grove	Ket	17	D4
Pecks Corner	Sal	14	B6
Pecks Pond	Pke	1	E3
Pedricktown	Sal	14	B3
Peekskill	Wch	4	A3
Pelham	Wch	8	C2
Pelham Manor	Wch	8	C2
Pellettown	Ssx	2	D5
Pemberton	Bur	15	D1
Pemberton Heights	Bur	15	D1
Pemberwick	Ffd	4	E6
Pen Argyl	Nth	5	D2
Penn Square	Mnt	9	C5
Penndel	Buk	10	A5
Pennington	Mer	10	C3
Penns Beach	Sal	13	F5
Penns Grove	Sal	14	A4
Penns Park	Bur	10	A3
Pennsauken	CaC	14	F1
Pennsburg	Mnt	9	A2
Pennsville	Sal	13	F5
Penton	Sal	14	B6
Penwell	War	6	B3
Pepper	Sux	21	A6
Pequest	War	6	A2
Perkasie	Buk	9	C2
Perkintown	Sal	14	A4
Perkiomenville	Mnt	9	A3
Perrineville	Mom	11	A4
Perth Amboy	Mid	7	C6
Peters Corner	Buk	9	F2
Peters Corner	QA	17	C4
Petersburg	CM	19	D3
Petersburg	Ket	17	D6
Petersburg	Mrr	2	F6
Petersburg	War	6	B2
Petersville	Nth	5	A3
Philadelphia	Ph	9	F6
Philadelphia	Ph	10	A5
Philadelphia	Ph	14	D1
Phillips Hill	Sux	21	B6
Phillipsburg	Orn	3	B1
Phillipsburg	War	5	D4
Pickering Beach	Ket	18	B5
Pierces Point	CM	19	A5
Piermont	Rck	4	B6
Pike Creek	NC	13	D4
Pilgrim Corners	Orn	3	A1
Pine Beach	Oc	16	D1
Pine Brook	Mrr	7	B2
Pine Grove	Bur	15	B2
Pine Hill	CaC	14	F3
Pine Hill	CaC	15	A3
Pine Island	Orn	3	A3
Pine Lake Park	Oc	11	C6
Pine Tree Corner	NC	17	D2
Pine Valley	CaC	15	A3
Pineville	Buk	9	F3
Pinewald	Oc	16	D2
Piney Grove	Sux	21	B5
Piney Hollow	Gle	15	A5
Pink	Wyn	1	B1
Pinneys Corners	Ffd	4	F4
Pipersville	Buk	9	E1
Piscataway	Mid	7	A6
Pitman	Gle	14	E4
Pittstown	Hnt	6	A6
Plainfield	Uni	7	A5
Plainsboro	Mid	10	E2
Plainville	Gle	14	F5
Plandome	Nsu	8	D3
Plandome Heights	Nsu	8	D3
Plandome Manor	Nsu	8	D3
Plaza Park	Bur	10	B6
Pleasant Grove	Mrr	6	B3
Pleasant Grove	Oc	11	B5
Pleasant Hill	Cec	13	A4
Pleasant Hill	NC	13	D4
Pleasant Mills	At	15	E5
Pleasant Plains	Oc	11	D6
Pleasant Run	Hnt	6	C6
Pleasant Valley	Buk	5	C6
Pleasant Valley	War	5	F3
Pleasantville	At	19	F2
Pleasantville	At	20	A2
Pleasantville	Wch	4	C5
Pluckemin	Sms	6	E5
Plumbsock	Ssx	2	D4
Plumsteadville	Buk	9	E2
Plumstock	Che	14	A1
Plymouth	Ket	17	F6
Plymouth Meeting	Mnt	9	C5
Pocono Lake	Mnr	1	A5
Pocono Manor	Mnr	1	B5
Pocono Pines	Mnr	1	A5
Pocono Summit	Mnr	1	B5
Pocopson	Che	13	E2
Point Airy	Sal	14	C4
Point Lookout	Nsu	8	F5
Point Morris	Ssx	6	D2
Point Pleasant	Buk	9	E1
Point Pleasant	Oc	11	E6
Point Pleasant Beach	Oc	11	F6
Pointers	Sal	14	A5
Pole Tavern	Sal	14	D5
Polkville	War	5	F1
Pomeroy	Che	13	B1
Pomona	At	19	E1
Pomona	Rck	3	F4
Pompton Lakes	Pas	3	C6
Pompton Lakes	Pas	7	C1
Pompton Plains	Mrr	7	C1
Pond Eddy	Slv	2	B1
Pondtown	QA	17	A4
Pools Corner	Buk	9	E3
Poplar Bridge	Mnr	1	E6
Porchtown	Sal	14	E5
Port Chester	Ffd	4	E6
Port Chester	Ffd	8	E1
Port Colden	War	6	A3
Port Elizabeth	Cmb	19	A3
Port Herman	Cec	13	B6
Port Jervis	Orn	2	D2
Port Mahon	Ket	18	B4
Port Mercer	Mer	10	D3
Port Monmouth	Mom	11	E1
Port Murray	War	6	A3
Port Norris	Cmb	18	F4
Port Orange	Orn	2	E1
Port Penn	NC	13	F6
Port Reading	Mid	7	D6
Port Republic	At	15	F6
Port Republic	At	16	A6
Port Republic	At	20	A1
Port Warren	War	5	E4
Port Washington	Nsu	8	D3
Port Washington North	Nsu	8	D2
Porter Station	NC	13	D5
Porters Lake	Pke	1	F4
Portertown	Sal	14	B5
Portland	Nth	5	E1
Postville	Pas	3	B5
Potterstown	Hnt	6	C5
Pottersville	Sms	6	D4
Pound Ridge	Wch	4	F4
Powells Corners	NC	17	D3
Powerville	Mrr	7	A1
Presidential Lakes	Bur	15	F1
Price	QA	17	A5
Prices Corner	NC	17	D3
Primehook Beach	Sux	21	D2
Princeton	Mer	10	D2
Promised Land	Pke	1	D3
Prospect Hill	Orn	2	E1
Prospect Park	Del	14	C2
Prospect Park	Nth	5	C4
Prospect Park	Pas	7	D1
Prospect Plains	Mid	11	A3
Prospectville	Mnt	9	D4
Prospertown	Oc	11	A5
Providence	Cec	13	B4
Pullentown	Mom	10	F4
Purchase	Wch	4	D6
Purdys	Wch	4	E3
Purdys Station	Wch	4	E3
Pusey Crossroads	Sux	21	B6
Putnam Lake	Put	4	F1
Putnam Valley	Put	4	B2
Pymble	Del	14	B1

Q

NAME	TERR	MAP	GRID
Quaker Bridge	Bur	15	E4
Quaker Ridge	Ffd	4	D5
Quakerstown	Sux	21	D3
Quakertown	Buk	9	B1
Quakertown	Hnt	6	A6
Quarryville	Ssx	2	F4
Queens	Que	8	C4
Quicktown	Lak	1	A2
Quinton	Sal	14	B6

R

NAME	TERR	MAP	GRID
Rahns	Mnt	9	A4
Rahway	Uni	7	C5
Ralston	Mrr	6	E3
Ramapo	Rck	3	E5
Ramblewood	Bur	15	A1
Ramsey	Brg	3	E6
Ramseyburg	War	5	F2
Rancocas	Bur	10	B6
Rancocas Heights	Bur	15	B1
Rancocas Woods	Bur	15	B1
Randalia	Cec	13	B6
Raritan	Sms	6	E6
Raubsville	Nth	5	D5
Raven Rock	Hnt	9	F2
Raymond	Sms	6	E5
Readington	Hnt	6	C6
Reaville	Hnt	10	C1
Red Bank	Mom	11	E2
Red Hill	Mnt	9	A2
Red Lion	Bur	15	D2
Red Lion	Che	13	D2
Red Lion	NC	13	D5
Red Oak	Lak	1	A1
Red Point	Cec	13	A6
Redden	Sux	21	B4
Redden Crossroads	Sux	21	A4
Redington	Nth	5	C5
Reeders	Mnr	1	B6
Reeds Beach	CM	19	B5
Rehoboth Beach	Sux	21	F4
Reliance	Mnt	9	B3
Repaupo	Gle	14	C3
Resica Falls	Mnr	1	E5
Revere	Buk	5	E6
Reybold	NC	13	E5
Reynolds Corner	NC	17	D3
Reynolds Mill	Sux	21	B3
Rich Hill	Buk	9	C2
Richboro	Buk	9	F4
Richlandtown	Buk	9	C1
Richmantown	Sal	14	D5
Richmond	Nth	5	E2
Richwood	Gle	14	D4
Ridgebury	Ffd	4	F2
Ridgebury	Orn	3	A2
Ridgefield	Brg	7	F3
Ridgefield	Brg	8	A3
Ridgefield Park	Brg	7	F2
Ridgeway	Ffd	4	E6
Ridgeway	Oc	11	C6
Ridgewood	Brg	7	E1
Ridley Park	Del	14	B2
Riegelsville	Buk	5	D5
Ringoes	Hnt	10	B1
Ringwood	Pas	3	C5
Rio	Orn	2	D1
Rio Grande	CM	19	B6
Rising Sun	Ket	17	F5
River Bank	Oc	16	D1
River Edge	Brg	7	F1
River Vale	Brg	3	F6
Riverdale	Mrr	7	C1
Riverdale	Sux	21	D5
Riverside	Bur	10	A6
Riverside	Ffd	4	E6
Riversville	Ffd	4	D6
Riverton	Bur	9	F6
Riviera Beach	Oc	11	E5
Roadstown	Cmb	18	C1
Robbins	Sux	21	A3
Robbinsville	Mer	10	E4
Roberts	QA	17	A5
Robertsville	Mom	11	C2
Robinsville	Sux	21	D4
Rock Tavern	Orn	3	D1
Rockaway	Mrr	6	F2
Rockland	NC	13	F3
Rockledge	Mnt	9	E5
Rockleigh	Brg	4	A6
Rockport	War	6	B2
Rocktown	Hnt	10	B2
Rockville	Orn	3	A1
Rockville Centre	Nsu	8	E4
Rocky Hill	Che	13	F1
Rocky Hill	Orn	3	B4
Rocky Hill	Sms	10	E2
Roe	QA	17	A6
Roe Park	Wch	4	B3
Roebling	Bur	10	C5
Romansville	Che	13	D1
Roosevelt	Mom	11	A4
Roosevelt	Nsu	8	E4
Roosevelt City	Oc	16	B1
Rose Valley	Del	14	B2
Rosedale	Mer	10	C2
Roseland	Esx	7	C3
Roselle	Uni	7	C5
Roselle Park	Uni	7	C4
Rosemont	Hnt	10	A1
Rosenhayn	Cmb	18	E1
Roses Point	Orn	2	E1
Roseto	Nth	5	D2
Roslyn	Nsu	8	E3
Roslyn Estates	Nsu	8	D3
Roslyn Harbor	Nsu	8	E3
Roslyn Heights	Nsu	8	E3
Ross Corner	Ssx	2	D5
Round Hill	Ffd	4	E5
Round Top	Sms	6	F5
Rowland	Pke	1	F1
Roxbury	War	5	E3
Roys	Ssx	2	E4
Rumson	Mom	11	F2
Rumson	Mom	12	A2
Runnemede	CaC	14	F2
Russellville	Che	13	A2
Rutherford	Brg	7	E3
Ruthsburg	QA	17	A6
Rutledge	Del	14	B2
Rye	Wch	8	D1
Rye Brook	Wch	4	D6
Rye Brook	Wch	8	D1

S

NAME	TERR	MAP	GRID
Saco	Lak	1	A1
Saddle River	Brg	3	E6
Saddle Rock	Nsu	8	C3
Sadsburyville	Che	13	B1
Saint Augustine	Cec	17	C1
Saint Davids	Del	9	B6
Saint Georges	NC	13	E6
Saint Nicholas Village	Hnt	6	B3
Salem	Sal	14	A6
Salem Center	Wch	4	E3
Salford	Mnt	9	A3
Salfordville	Mnt	9	A3
Salina	Gle	14	E3
Salisbury Mills	Orn	3	E1
Sally	Pas	7	D1
Sand Brook	Hnt	10	B1
Sand Hill	Sux	21	B4
Sandhill	Mnr	5	C1
Sands Point	Nsu	8	D2
Sandtown	Bur	15	C2
Sandtown	Ket	17	D6
Sandts Eddy	Nth	5	D3
Sandy Landing	Sux	21	D6
Sandyville	Pke	1	F5
Sarles Corners	Wch	4	E4
Sassafras	Ken	17	C2
Sayres Neck	Cmb	18	D2
Sayreville	Mid	7	C6
Sayreville	Mid	11	C1
Scarsdale	Wch	4	C6
Scarsdale	Wch	8	C1
Schoenersville	Nth	5	A4
Schooleys Mountain	Mrr	6	C3
Schwenksville	Mnt	9	A3
Sciota	Mnr	5	C1
Scobeyville	Mom	11	E3
Scotch Plains	Uni	7	B5
Scotchtown	Orn	3	B1
Scotrun	Mnr	1	C6
Scots Grove	Che	13	E1
Scotts Corners	Ket	21	B1
Scotts Corners	Wch	4	F4
Scudders Falls	Mer	10	B3
Scullville	At	19	E2
Sea Breeze	Cmb	18	C3
Sea Bright	Mom	12	A2
Sea Cliff	Nsu	8	E2
Sea Girt	Mom	11	F5
Sea Isle City	CM	19	D5
Seabrook	Cmb	14	D6
Sears Corners	Put	4	F1
Seaside Heights	Oc	16	F1
Seaside Park	Oc	16	F1
Secaucus	Hud	7	E3
Secor Corners	Put	4	D2
Seeley	Cmb	18	C1
Seidersville	Nth	5	B5
Sellecks Corners	Ffd	4	F4
Sellersville	Buk	9	C2
Sergeantsville	Hnt	10	A1
Seven Hickories	Ket	17	E4
Seven Stars	Oc	11	D6
Seven Stars	Sal	14	B4
Sewaren	Mid	7	C6
Sewell	Gle	14	E3
Shaft Ox Corner	Sux	21	B6
Shahola Falls	Pke	2	A2
Sharon Hill	Del	14	C2
Sharptown	Sal	14	B5
Shawnee	Mnr	1	E6
Shawnee	Sux	21	A2
Shelly	Buk	9	B1
Shenorock	Wch	4	D3
Sheppards Mill	Cmb	18	C2
Shiloh	Cmb	18	C1
Shiloh Woods	Che	13	F1
Shin Hollow	Orn	2	E2
Shingle Point	Sux	21	B4
Ship Bottom	Oc	16	D5
Shirley	Sal	14	D6
Shoemakers	Mnr	1	F6
Shohola	Pke	2	B1
Shohola Falls	Pke	2	A2
Shore Acres	Oc	11	E6
Short Hills	Esx	7	C4
Shortly	Sux	21	B5
Shrewsbury	Mom	11	F3
Shrewsbury Road	Mom	10	F4
Shrub Oak	Wch	4	B3
Sicklerville	CaC	15	A4
Sidney	Hnt	6	A5
Siloam	Mom	11	B4
Silverdale	Buk	9	C2
Silverside Carr	NC	14	A3
Silverton	Oc	11	E6
Silview	NC	13	E4
Sim Place	Bur	16	A4
Singerly	Cec	13	B5
Six Points	Sal	14	E6
Skillman	Sms	10	D1
Skippack	Mnt	9	B4
Skytop	Mnr	1	C4
Slackwood	Mer	10	C3
Slate Hill	Orn	3	A2
Slateford	Nth	5	E1
Slaughter Beach	Sux	21	C1
Sleepy Hollow	Wch	4	B5
Sloatsburg	Rck	3	D4
Smith Corners	Orn	2	E2
Smithburg	Mom	11	B4
Smiths Mills	Pas	3	B6
Smithville	At	20	A1
Smithville	Bur	15	C1
Smoke Rise	Mrr	3	B6
Smyrna	Ket	17	E3
Snufftown	Orn	3	A3
Snydersville	Mnr	5	C1
Sodom	Put	4	E2
Solebury	Buk	9	F2
Somerdale	CaC	14	F2
Somers	Wch	4	D3
Somers Point	At	19	E3
Somerset	Mid	11	A1
Somerville	Sms	6	E6
Sooy Place	Bur	15	D2
Souderton	Mnt	9	C3
Sourland	Sms	10	D1
South Amboy	Mid	11	C1
South Belmar	Mom	11	F4
South Bethany	Sux	21	F6
South Bound Brook	Sms	6	F6
South Bowers	Ket	18	B6
South Branch	Sms	6	D6
South Centerville	Orn	2	F2

NAME	TERR	MAP	GRID
South Coatesville	Che	13	C1
South Dennis	CM	19	C4
South Lakewood	Oc	11	C6
South Nyack	Rck	4	B6
South Orange	Esx	7	C3
South Plainfield	Mid	7	A6
South River	Mid	11	B1
South Salem	Wch	4	F3
South Seaville	CM	19	C4
South Sterling	Wyn	1	B3
South Toms River	Oc	16	D1
Southampton	Buk	9	F4
Southard	Mom	11	D5
Southfields	Orn	3	D4
Sparrow Bush	Orn	2	D2
Sparta	Ssx	2	E6
Speedwell	Bur	15	F3
Spinnerstown	Buk	9	A1
Spotswood	Mid	11	B2
Spray Beach	Oc	16	D6
Spring House	Mnt	9	D4
Spring Lake	Mom	11	F5
Spring Lake Heights	Mom	11	E5
Spring Mills	Hnt	5	E5
Spring Mount	Mnt	9	A3
Spring Valley	Rck	3	F5
Springdale	CaC	15	A2
Springdale	Ffd	4	F5
Springdale	Ssx	2	C6
Springdell	Che	13	C2
Springfield	Del	14	C1
Springfield	Uni	7	B4
Springfield Crossroads	Sux	21	C4
Springlawn	Che	13	B4
Springtown	Buk	5	C6
Springtown	Bur	10	B6
Springtown	Cmb	18	C2
Springtown	War	5	E5
Squankum	Mom	11	D5
Stafford Forge	Oc	16	C5
Staffordville	Oc	16	C5
Stamford	Ffd	4	F5
Stanhope	Ssx	6	D1
Stanton	Hnt	6	B6
Stanton	NC	13	D4
Stanton Station	Hnt	6	B6
Stanwich	Ffd	4	E5
Stanwick	Bur	15	A1
Star Cross	Gle	14	F5
Star Hill	Ket	17	F5
Staten Island	Rmd	7	D5
Stathems Neck	Cmb	18	B2
Steel City	Nth	5	C5
Steelmantown	CM	19	C3
Steelmanville	At	19	E2
Steels Corner	Sal	14	D6
Steelville	Che	13	A2
Steinbeck Corners	Put	4	E1
Steinsburg	Buk	9	A1
Stephensburg	War	6	B3
Sterling	Wyn	1	B2
Sterling Forest	Orn	3	C4
Stevens	Bur	10	C5
Stevens Corners	QA	17	C4
Stewart Manor	Nsu	8	D4
Stewartsville	War	5	E4
Stillwater	Put	4	C2
Stillwater	Ssx	2	B6
Stirling	Mrr	7	A4
Stockertown	Nth	5	D3
Stockholm	Ssx	2	F6
Stockley	Sux	21	B5
Stockton	Hnt	10	A2
Stone Church	Nth	5	E2
Stone Harbor	CM	19	C6
Stone Tavern	Mom	11	A4
Stony Ford	Orn	3	C1
Stony Point	Rck	3	F4
Stony Point	Rck	4	A4
Stormville	Mnr	5	C1
Stow Creek Landing	Cmb	18	B1
Strafford	Che	9	A6
Stratford	CaC	14	F3
Strathmere	CM	19	E4
Strickersville	Che	13	C4
Stroudsburg	Mnr	5	D1
Stumps Corner	NC	17	E1
Succasunna	Mrr	6	D2
Sudlersville	QA	17	B4
Suffern	Rck	3	E5
Sugar Loaf	Orn	3	C3
Sugars Bridge	Che	13	E1
Summit	NC	13	D6
Summit	Uni	7	B4
Summit Lawn	Leh	5	A6
Sumneytown	Mnt	9	A3
Surf City	Oc	16	E5
Susans Corner	Cmb	18	B1
Sussex	Ssx	2	E4
Sussex Mills	Ssx	2	D6
Sussex Shores	Sux	21	F6
Swainton	CM	19	C5
Swarthmore	Del	14	B2
Swartswood	Ssx	2	B5
Swedeland	Mnt	9	B6
Swedesboro	Gle	14	B3
Swedesburg	Mnt	9	C5
Sweetman	Mom	11	B4
Sweetwater	At	15	E5
Swiftwater	Mnr	1	C5
Swinesburg	Hnt	5	F5
Sycamore	Sux	21	A5
Sykesville	Bur	10	E6
Syosset	Nsu	8	F3

T

NAME	TERR	MAP	GRID
Tabernacle	Bur	15	D2
Tadmor	Nth	5	B4
Tafton	Pke	1	D2
Talleys Corner	NC	13	F3
Talleyville	NC	13	F2
Tamiment	Pke	1	F5
Tanguy	Che	13	F1
Tannersville	Mnr	1	C6
Tansboro	CaC	15	A3
Tappan	Rck	4	A6
Taraton	Bur	10	D6
Tarrytown	Wch	4	B6
Tatamy	Nth	5	C4
Taunton Lake	Bur	15	B2
Tavistock	CaC	14	F2
Taylor Corners	Ffd	4	F1
Taylor Mills	Mom	11	B3
Taylors Bridge	NC	17	F2
Taylortown	Mrr	7	B1
Telford	Buk	9	B3
Telford	Mnt	9	B3
Templeville	QA	17	C5
Tenafly	Brg	8	A2
Tennent	Mom	11	C3
Teterboro	Brg	7	F2
Thiells	Rck	3	F4
Thomas Corner	NC	17	E1
Thomas Corners	NC	17	D3
Thomaston	Nsu	8	D3
Thompkins Corner	Put	4	C2
Thompsons Beach	Cmb	19	A4
Thompsonville	Ket	21	B1
Thorndale	Che	13	D1
Thornton	Del	13	F2
Thornwood	Wch	4	C5
Thorofare	Gle	14	D2
Three Bridges	Hnt	6	C6
Tierneys Corner	Ssx	6	E1
Tilly Foster	Put	4	E1
Timbuctoo	Bur	10	C6
Tinicum	Buk	9	B1
Tinton Falls	Mom	11	E3
Titicus	Ffd	4	F3
Titusville	Mer	10	B3
Tobyhanna	Mnr	1	B4
Tomkins Cove	Rck	4	A3
Tomlin	Gle	14	C3
Tomlinson Mill	Bur	15	A2
Toms River	Oc	16	D1
Totowa	Pas	7	D2
Toughkenamon	Che	13	C2
Towaco	Mrr	7	B1
Town Bank	CM	22	A1
Town Estates	Bur	10	B6
Town Point	Cec	17	B1
Towners	Put	4	E1
Townsbury	War	6	A2
Townsend	NC	17	D2
Trainer	Del	14	B3
Tranquility	Ssx	6	C1
Trappe	Mnt	9	A4
Trenton	Mer	10	C4
Tresslarville	Wyn	1	A1
Trevose	Buk	10	A5
Trooper	Mnt	9	A5
Troy Hills	Mrr	7	B2
Trumbauersville	Buk	9	B1
Tuckahoe	CM	19	D3
Tuckahoe	Wch	8	C1
Tuckerton	Oc	16	B5
Tullytown	Buk	10	C5
Turnersville	Gle	14	F3
Turnersville	Lak	1	A3
Tuttles Corner	Ssx	2	C4
Tuxedo Park	Orn	3	D4
Twin Lakes	Pke	2	A2
Twin Oaks	Del	14	A2
Tybouts Corner	NC	13	E5
Tylersport	Mnt	9	B2

U

NAME	TERR	MAP	GRID
Uhlerstown	Buk	5	E6
Union	Uni	7	C4
Union Beach	Mom	11	D1
Union City	Hud	7	F3
Uniontown	War	5	E4
Unionville	Buk	9	C3
Unionville	Bur	10	C6
Unionville	Che	13	D2
Unionville	Orn	2	F3
University Gardens	Nsu	8	C3
Upland	Che	13	C2
Upland	Del	14	B2
Upper Black Eddy	Buk	5	E6
Upper Brookville	Nsu	8	F2
Upper Darby	Del	14	C1
Upper Greenwood Lake	Pas	3	B4
Upper Macopin	Pas	3	B5
Upper Mongaup	Orn	2	C1
Upper Mongaup	Slv	2	C1
Upper Nyack	Rck	4	A5
Upper Saddle River	Brg	3	E6
Upton	Bur	15	F1
Uswick	Wyn	1	D1
Uttertown	Pas	3	B5

V

NAME	TERR	MAP	GRID
Vails Gate	Orn	3	F1
Valhalla	Wch	4	C6
Valley Cottage	Rck	4	A5
Valley Forge	Che	9	A5
Valley Stream	Nsu	8	D4
Van Cortlandtville	Wch	4	B4
Vanderburg	Mom	11	D3
Vandyke	NC	17	C2
Vanhiseville	Oc	11	B5
Varden	Wyn	1	B1
Ventnor City	At	20	A2
Vera Cruz	Leh	5	A6
Vernfield	Mnt	9	B3
Vernon	Ssx	3	A4
Verona	Esx	7	C3
Verplanck	Wch	4	A3
Victory Gardens	Mrr	6	F2
Vienna	War	6	B2
Villanova	Del	9	B6
Villas	CM	19	A6
Vincentown	Bur	15	C1
Vineland	Cmb	14	F6
Vineland	Cmb	18	F1
Vineland	Cmb	19	A1
Viola	Ket	17	E6
Viola	Rck	3	E5

W

NAME	TERR	MAP	GRID
Wading River	Bur	15	F5
Wagnersville	Nth	5	C5
Waldwick	Brg	3	E6
Walker Lake	Pke	2	A1
Wall	Mom	11	F5
Wallenpaupack Mills	Wyn	1	A2
Wallington	Brg	7	E2
Walnut Valley	War	5	F1
Walpack Center	Ssx	2	B5
Walton Park	Orn	3	E3
Wanaque	Pas	3	C6
Wantagh	Nsu	8	F4
Waretown	Oc	16	D3
Warminster	Buk	9	E4
Warnertown	Mnr	1	A5
Warren Glen	War	5	E5
Warren Grove	Oc	16	B4
Warrenville	War	6	B2
Warrington	Buk	9	E4
Warrington	War	5	F1
Warwick	Cec	17	C1
Warwick	Orn	3	B3
Warwick	Sux	21	D5
Washington	Bur	15	E4
Washington	War	6	A3
Washington Crossing	Buk	10	B3
Washington Crossing	Mer	10	B3
Washington Valley	Mrr	6	F3
Washingtonville	Orn	3	D1
Watchung	Sms	7	A5
Waterford Works	CaC	15	B4
Waterloo Mills	Orn	2	E3
Wawaset	Che	13	E1
Wawayanda	Ssx	3	A4
Wayne	Del	9	B6
Wayne	Pas	7	C1
Wayside	At	20	A1
Wayside	Mom	11	F3
Weaversville	Nth	5	A4
Weekstown	At	15	E5
Weir Lake	Mnr	5	B2
Welchville	Sal	14	B5
Wells Mills	Oc	16	C3
Wenonah	Gle	14	D3
Wertsville	Hnt	10	C1
Wescoatville	At	15	D5
Wesley Hills	Rck	3	E5
West Beach	Sux	21	E6
West Berlin	CaC	15	A3
West Caldwell	Esx	7	C2
West Cape May	CM	22	A1
West Chester	Che	13	E1
West Conshohocken	Mnt	9	C6
West Cornwall	Orn	3	E1
West Creek	Oc	16	C5
West Easton	Nth	5	C5
West Freehold	Mom	11	C4
West Grove	Che	13	B3
West Haverstraw	Rck	3	F4
West Haverstraw	Rck	4	A4
West Hempstead	Nsu	8	E4
West Long Branch	Mom	11	F3
West Mahopac	Put	4	C2
West Mantoloking	Oc	11	F6
West Milford	Pas	3	B5
West Moorestown	Bur	15	A1
West New York	Hud	7	F3
West Nyack	Rck	4	A5
West Orange	Esx	7	C3
West Paterson	Pas	7	D2
West Pen Argyl	Nth	5	C2
West Point	Mnt	9	C4
West Trenton	Mer	10	C3
West Tuckerton	Oc	16	B5
West View Shores	Cec	17	A1
West Wildwood	CM	19	B6
Westbrookville	Orn	2	F1
Westbury	Nsu	8	E3
Westfield	Uni	7	B5
Westgate Hills	Nth	5	B5
Westmont	CaC	14	F2
Westtown	Che	13	F1
Westtown	Orn	2	F2
Westville	Gle	14	E2
Westwood	Brg	7	F1
Weymouth	At	15	C6
Whaleys Corners	Sux	21	A5
Whaleys Crossroads	Sux	21	A6
Wharton	Mrr	6	E2
Whig Lane	Sal	14	D5
Whippany	Mrr	7	B3
White Horse	Buk	9	C2
White Horse	Mer	10	D4
White Plains	Wch	4	C6
White Plains	Wch	8	C1
Whitehall	Leh	5	A5
Whitehorse	Che	14	A1
Whitehouse	Hnt	6	C5
Whitehouse Station	Hnt	6	C5
Whitemarsh	Mnt	9	D5
Whitesbog	Bur	15	F1
Whitesboro	CM	19	B6
Whitesville	Oc	11	C6
Whiting	Oc	16	B1
Wickatunk	Mom	11	C2
Wickham Knolls	Orn	3	C3
Wilcox	Orn	3	A3
Wildwood	CM	22	C1
Wildwood Crest	CM	22	C1
Williamstown	Gle	15	A4
Williamstown Junction	CaC	15	A4
Williston Park	Nsu	8	E3
Willow Brook	Ssx	3	B4
Willow Grove	Ket	17	E6
Willow Grove	Mnt	9	E5
Willow Grove	Sal	14	E6
Willowdale	CaC	15	B5
Willowdale	Che	13	D2
Wilmington	NC	13	E3
Wilmington Manor	NC	13	E4
Wilson	Nth	5	D4
Wilsonville	Wyn	1	D1
Wind Gap	Nth	5	C2
Windmill Farm	Wch	8	B4
Windsor	Mer	10	F4
Winslow	CaC	15	B5
Winslow Junction	CaC	15	B5
Wiscasset	Mnr	1	B5
Wisner	Orn	3	B3
Wolfert	Gle	14	C3
Wood-Ridge	Brg	7	F2
Woodbine	CM	19	C4
Woodbourne	Buk	10	B4
Woodbourne	Ssx	2	D4
Woodbridge	Mid	7	C6
Woodbury	Gle	14	D2
Woodbury	Gle	14	D3
Woodbury	Orn	3	E2
Woodbury Heights	Gle	14	E3
Woodcliff Lake	Brg	3	F6
Woodcrest	CaC	15	A2
Wooddale	Mnr	1	D6
Woodglen	Hnt	6	B4
Woodland Beach	Ket	18	A2
Woodlyn	Del	14	B2
Woodlynne	CaC	14	E1
Woodmansie	Bur	16	A2
Woodmere	Nsu	8	D5
Woodport	Mrr	6	E1
Woodridge	Brg	7	E2
Woodruff	Cmb	18	D1
Woodruffs Gap	Ssx	2	E6
Woods Tavern	Hnt	6	E6
Woodside	Buk	10	B4
Woodside	Ket	17	E6
Woodstown	Sal	14	C5
Woodsville	Mer	10	C2
Woodville	Che	13	C2
Worcester	Mnt	9	B4
Workmans Corners	Sux	21	B5
Wormansville	Buk	9	E1
Worthington	Wch	4	C6
Woxall	Mnt	9	A3
Wrangle Hill	NC	13	E6
Wrights Crossroads	Ket	17	D5
Wrightstown	Buk	10	A3
Wrightstown	Bur	10	E6
Wrightsville	Mom	10	F4
Wyckoff	Brg	3	D6
Wyckoff Mills	Mom	11	C4
Wycombe	Buk	9	F3
Wykertown	Ssx	2	D4
Wyola	Del	9	A6
Wyoming	Ket	17	F5

Y

NAME	TERR	MAP	GRID
Yardley	Buk	10	B4
Yardville	Mer	10	E4
Yeadon	Del	14	C1
Yellow Frame	War	6	B1
Yonkers	Wch	8	B1
Yorklyn	NC	13	E3
Yorktown	Sal	14	C5
Yorktown	Wch	4	C3
Yorktown Heights	Wch	4	C3
Youngsville	Nth	5	A3

Z

NAME	TERR	MAP	GRID
Zarephath	Sms	6	F6
Zieglerville	Mnt	9	A3
Zion	Cec	13	A4
Zion	Sms	10	D1
Zionhill	Buk	9	B1
Zionsville	Leh	9	A1
Zoar	Sux	21	C5

Airports

NAME	TERR	MAP	GRID
Aeroflex Andover	Ssx	2	D6
Alexandria Field	Hnt	5	F5
Allaire	Mom	11	E4
Atlantic City Intl	At	19	E1
Bader Field	At	20	A2
Blairstown	War	6	A1
Brandywine	Che	13	F1
Bucks	Cmb	18	D1
Buehl Field	Buk	10	B4
Camden Co	CaC	15	A3
Cape May Co	CM	19	A6
Central Delaware Civil Air Terminal	Ket	18	A5
Central Jersey Reg	Sms	6	E6
Chandelle Estates	Ket	18	A4
Chester Co Carlson	Che	13	B1
Cross Keys	Gle	14	F4
Delaware Airpark	Ket	17	E4
Dover AFB	Ket	18	A5
Doylestown	Buk	9	E2
Eagles Nest	Oc	16	C4
Easton	Nth	5	D4
Essex Co	Esx	7	C2
Flying Dollar	Mnr	1	C4
Flying W Ranch	Bur	15	C1
Greenwood Lake	Pas	3	B5
Hackettstown	War	6	B3
Hammonton Mun	At	15	C4
Henderson Aviation	Ket	17	F6
Jenkins	Ket	17	E5
John F Kennedy Intl	Que	8	C5
Kroelinger	Cmb	14	F6
La Guardia Intl	Que	8	B3
Lakehurst Naval Air Engineering Ctr	Oc	11	B6
Lakewood	Oc	11	D6
Lehigh Valley Intl	Leh	5	A5
Licalzi	Cmb	18	D2
Lincoln Pk	Mrr	7	C1
Linden	Uni	7	D5
Mahopac	Put	4	C2
Marlboro	Mom	11	C2
McGuire AFB	Bur	10	E6
Mercer Co	Mer	10	C3
Milford Airpark	Ket	21	A1
Millville Mun	Cmb	18	F2
Morristown Mun	Mrr	7	A3
New Castle Co	NC	13	E4
New Garden Airfield	Che	13	C2
New London Airfield	Che	13	B3
Newark Intl	Esx	7	E4
Newton	Ssx	2	C6
Northeast Philadelphia	Ph	9	F5
Ocean City Mun	CM	19	E3
Old Bridge	Mid	11	B2
Oldmans	Sal	14	B4
Pemberton	Bur	15	D1
Pennridge	Buk	9	C2
Perkiomen Valley	Mnt	9	A4
Philadelphia Intl	Del	14	C2
Piney Hollow Airstrip	Gle	15	A5
Pocono Mountains Mun	Mnr	1	B5
Princeton	Sms	10	D2
Quakertown	Buk	9	B1
Queen City	Al	5	A6
Randall	Orn	3	A1
Red Lion	Bur	15	C2
Red Wing	Bur	10	D6
RJ Miller	Oc	16	C1
Rudys	Cmb	14	F6
Sky Manor	Hnt	6	A6
Smyrna	Ket	17	F3
Solberg-Hunterdon	Hnt	6	D5
Somerset	Sms	6	D5
South Jersey Reg	Bur	15	B1
Southern Cross	Gle	14	F4
Spring Hill Airpark	Wyn	1	A2
Stewart Intl	Orn	3	E1
Stroudsburg Pocono	Mnr	1	D6
Summit Airpark	NC	13	D6
Sussex	Ssx	2	E4
Sussex Co Ind Airpark	Sux	21	B4
Teterboro	Brg	7	F2
Trenton-Robbinsville	Mer	10	E4
Trinca	Ssx	6	C1
Twin Pine	Mer	10	C3
US Naval Air Station Willow Grove	Mnt	9	E4
US Naval Resv (Warren Grove)	Bur	16	B4
Van Sant	Buk	9	E1
Vineland Downstown	Gle	15	A6
Warwick Mun	Orn	3	C3
Westchester Co	Wch	4	D6
Wings Field	Mnt	9	C5
Woodbine Mun	CM	19	C4

Beaches

NAME	TERR	MAP	GRID
Allenhurst	Mom	12	A4
Asbury Pk	Mom	11	F4
Atlantic Beach	Nsu	8	D6
Atlantic City	At	20	A2
Avon-By-The-Sea	Mom	11	F4
Barnegat	Oc	16	D3
Barnegat Light	Oc	16	E3
Bay Head	Oc	11	F6
Bayshore Waterfront Pk	Mom	11	E1
Beach Haven	Oc	16	D6
Beach Haven Crest	Oc	16	D5
Beach Haven Gardens	Oc	16	D6
Beach Haven Pk	Oc	16	D5
Beach Haven Terrace	Oc	16	D5
Beesley Pt	CM	19	E3
Belmar	Mom	11	F4
Bradley Beach	Mom	11	F4
Brant Beach	Oc	16	D5
Brick	Oc	11	F6
Brigantine	At	20	B2

NAME	TERR	MAP	GRID
Brighton	Oc	16	D5
Broadkill	Sux	21	D3
Cape Henlopen St Pk	Sux	21	F3
Cape May	CM	22	B1
Coney Is	Kng	8	A6
Deal	Mom	12	A3
Delaware Seashore St Pk	Sux	21	F4
Dewey	Sux	21	F4
Elk Neck St Pk	Cec	17	A1
Five Mile	CM	22	C1
Fortescue	Cmb	18	D4
Gandys	Cmb	18	C3
Harvey Cedars	Oc	16	E4
Higbee	CM	22	A1
Highland	Mom	12	A2
Holgate	Oc	16	C6
Holts Ldg St Pk	Sux	21	E5
Indian River Inlet	Sux	21	F5
Island Beach St Pk	Oc	16	E2
Island Heights	Oc	16	E1
Jennifer Bay	Oc	16	D5
Jones	Nsu	8	F5
Keansburg	Mom	11	E1
Lavallette	Oc	16	F1
Lido Beach	Nsu	8	E5
Long Beach	Nsu	8	D6
Long Br	Mom	12	A3
Longport	At	19	F3
Loveladies	Oc	16	E4
Manasquan	Mom	11	F5
North Beach	Oc	16	E4
North Beach Haven	Oc	16	D6
Ocean Beach	Oc	16	F1
Ocean City	CM	19	F3
Ocean Gate	Oc	16	E1
Ocean Grove	Mom	11	F4
Orchard	Brx	8	C2
Ortley Beach	Oc	16	F1
Peahala Pk	Oc	16	D5
Point Pleasant Beach	Oc	11	F5
Primehook	Sux	21	D2
Raybins	Cmb	18	D4
Reeds Beach	CM	19	B5
Rehoboth	Sux	21	F4
Rockaway	Que	8	B6
Sandy Hook	Mom	11	F1
Sandy Hook	Mom	12	A1
Sea Bright	Mom	12	A2
Sea Colony	Sux	21	F6
Sea Girt	Mom	11	F5
Sea Isle City	CM	19	D5
Seaside Heights	Oc	16	F1
Seaside Pk	Oc	16	F1
Seven Mile	CM	19	C6
Seven Mile	CM	19	D5
Seven Presidents	Mom	12	A3
Shelter Cove	Oc	16	E1
Ship Bottom	Oc	16	D5
Short	Nsu	8	F6
Silver Lake	Ket	17	F4
Slaughter	Sux	21	C2
South Belmar	Mom	11	F5
Spray Beach	Oc	16	D6
Spring Lake	Mom	11	F5
Sunray	CM	19	A6
Sunset	CM	22	A1
Surf City	Oc	16	E5
Trap Pond St Pk	Sux	21	A6
Two Mile	CM	22	B1
Union Beach	Mom	11	D1
Ventnor City	At	20	A3
White Sands	Oc	16	F2
Windward	Oc	11	E6

Boat Ramps

NAME	TERR	MAP	GRID
Abbotts Pond	Sux	21	A2
Als Waretown Fishing Station	Oc	16	D3
Andrews Lake	Ket	17	F6
Augustine Wildlife Area	NC	17	E1
Barnegat	Oc	16	D4
Bay Shore	Sux	21	F5
Beach Haven	Oc	16	C6
Bear Wallow	Pke	1	D3
Becks Pond	NC	13	D5
Berkeley Is	Oc	16	E2
Betzwood	Mnt	9	A5
Blairs Pond	Sux	21	A2
Bowers Beach	Ket	18	B6
Budd Lake Docks Marina	Mrr	6	C2
Burley Inlet	Pke	1	D3
Bushkill	Pke	2	A5
Caffrey Rec Area	Wyn	1	D1
Canal Launch	Oc	11	F6
Cedar Beach	Sux	21	C1
Cedar Cr	Sux	21	B1
Channel Club	Mom	12	A2
Clarence Fahnestock St Pk	Put	4	B1
Crumpton Ldg	QA	17	A4
Deep Ldg	QA	17	A4
Delaware River	Buk	10	B6
Derby Pond	Ket	17	F5
Dingmans Ferry	Pke	2	B4
Duck Neck	QA	17	A4
East Creek Pond	CM	19	B4
Elizabeth City	Uni	7	D5
Elk Neck	Cec	13	A6
Fairview Lake	Pke	1	D2
Forge Pond	Oc	11	E6
Forked River St Marina	Oc	16	D3
Foxhole	Ken	17	B2
Frankford	Ph	9	F6
Garrisons Lake	Ket	17	E4
Goshen Landing	CM	19	B5
Gouldsboro Lake	Mnr	1	A4
Greeley Lake	Pke	1	F2
Green Lane Res Pk	Mnt	9	A2
Greenwood Lake	Pas	3	B5
Gregg Neck	Ken	17	B2
Griffiths Lake	Ket	21	A1
Havens Lake	Ket	21	A2
Holts Ldg St Pk	Sux	21	E5
Indian River	Sux	21	F5
Ingram Pond	Sux	21	B5
Island Pond	Orn	3	E3
John B Medford	Ket	17	D6
Johnson Co Pk	Mid	7	A6
Lake Kanawauke	Orn	3	E4
Lake Musconetcong	Mrr	6	D2
Lake Sebago	Rck	3	E4
Lake Shenandoah	Oc	11	D6
Lake Skannatat	Orn	3	E4
Lake Tiorati	Orn	3	F3
Lake Wallenpaupack	Wyn	1	D1
Leonardo St Marina	Mom	11	F1
Lewes-Rehoboth Canal	Sux	21	E3
Liberty St Pk	Hud	7	F4
Little Cr Wildlife Area	Ket	18	A4
Little Egg Hbr	Oc	16	D5
Losten	Cec	17	B1
Lower Lake/Dam	Pke	1	C3
Lums Pond St Pk	NC	13	D6
Main Beach	Pke	1	D3
Main Marina	Buk	9	D1
Matamoras	Pke	2	D2
Maurice River	Cmb	18	F2
Mc Ginnis Lake	Ket	17	F6
Mercer Co Central Pk	Mer	10	E3
Milford Beach	Pke	2	C3
Milton	Sux	21	C3
Moores Lake	Ket	17	F5
Neshaminy St Pk	Buk	10	B6
Newark Bay	Uni	7	D5
Newburgh	Orn	3	F1
Nockamixon St Pk	Buk	9	D1
North Wildwood	CM	19	C6
Nummy Lake	CM	19	B4
Ocean City	CM	19	E3
Old Rte 402	Pke	1	E3
Passaic River	Esx	7	C2
Picnic Area	Pke	1	F3
Raritan River	Mid	7	A6
Reeds Beach	CM	19	B5
Reynolds Pond	Sux	21	B3
Ridgefield Pt	Pke	1	D3
Rogues Hbr	Cec	17	A1
Rosedale Beach	Sux	21	D5
Sandts Eddy	Nth	5	D3
Sassafras River	Cec	17	A2
Sea Isle City	CM	19	D5
Seaside Heights	Oc	16	E1
Seaside Pk	Oc	16	F1
Shaddin Reach	QA	17	B4
Shallcross	Ken	17	A2
Shohola First	Pke	2	A2
Shohola Second	Pke	2	A2
Silver Lake	Ket	17	F4
Smithfield Beach	Mnr	1	E6
Snow Shanty	Pke	1	E3
Spruce Run St Pk	Hnt	6	A5
Stemmers Run WMA	Cec	17	A1
Stone Hbr	CM	19	D6
Tacony	Ph	9	F6
Thompson Pk	Mid	11	A2
Three Mile Run	Buk	9	C1
Tobyhanna Lake	Mnr	1	B4
Tub Mill Pond	Ket	21	A1
Turner Cr	Ken	17	A2
Upper Black Eddy	Buk	5	E6
Waples Pond	Sux	21	C3
Welch Lake	Rck	3	E4
West Cr	Oc	16	C5
West Deptford	Gle	14	D2
West Essex Pk	Esx	7	C2
White Dear	Pke	1	E2
Woodland Beach	Ket	18	A3
Yardley	Buk	10	B3
Zane Grey	Pke	2	A1

Campsites

NAME	TERR	MAP	GRID
Acorn	CM	19	B6
Albocondo	Oc	16	C1
Allaire St Pk	Mom	11	E4
Anthony Wayne	Orn	3	F3
Atlantic City Blueberry Hill	At	15	F6
Atlantic City North Family	Oc	16	B5
Atsion Rec Area	Bur	15	D3
Avalon	CM	19	C5
Bakers Acres	Oc	16	C5
Bass River St Forest	Bur	16	A5
Beach Comber Camping Resort	CM	19	B6
Beaver Hill	Ssx	2	E5
Beaver Pond	Rck	3	E4
Beaver Valley	Buk	9	E1
Beechwood	Che	13	B1
Belhaven Lake Resort	Bur	15	E5
Belleplain St Forest	CM	19	B3
Big Oaks	Sux	21	E4
Big Timber	CM	19	C5
Bodine Field	Bur	15	F4
Brookville	Oc	16	C3
Buena Vista Camping Pk	At	15	B6
Bulls Is Rec Area	Hnt	9	F2
Butterfly Camping Resort	Oc	11	C5
Camp Carr	Hnt	6	B5
Camp Chesapeake	Cec	13	A6
Camp Red Mill	Cec	17	B1
Camp Sacajawea (GSA)	Gle	15	A6
Camp Taylor	War	5	E1
Campgaw Mtn Co Resv	Brg	3	D6
Cape Is	CM	22	B1
Cape May Mobile Ests	CM	22	A1
Cedar Cr	Oc	16	D2
Cedar Ridge	Ssx	2	C3
Cheesequake St Pk	Mid	11	C1
Chips Folly Family	Bur	16	A5
Clarence Fahnestock St Pk	Put	4	B1
Colonial Meadows	At	19	D2
Colonial Woods	Buk	5	E6
Columbia Valley	Ssx	6	D1
Country Oaks	At	19	C1
Cranberry Run	Mnr	1	C6
Deer Wood	Buk	9	E1
Delaware River Family	War	5	E2
Delaware Seashore St Pk	Sux	21	F5
Delaware Water Gap KOA	Mnr	1	F6
Depot Travel Pk	CM	22	A1
Doe Run	Buk	9	E1
Driftstone on the Delaware	Nth	5	E2
Driftwood Camping Resort	CM	19	C5
Duck Neck	QA	17	A4
Eagles Nest	Sux	21	C3
Echo Farm	CM	19	D4
Elk Neck St Pk	Cec	17	A1
Elks-Brox	Orn	2	D2
Evergreen Lake	Nth	5	B3
Evergreen Woods Lakefront Resort	At	15	F6
Fla-Net Pk	Mrr	6	D2
Four Seasons Family	Sal	14	C5
Fox Wood Family	Mnr	1	E6
Frontier	CM	19	D4
Godfrey Bridge	Bur	15	F5
Green Holly	CM	19	B5
Green Valley Beach Family	Ssx	2	C6
Gulls Way	Sux	21	D6
Harmony Ridge	Ssx	2	C4
Hawkins Bridge	Bur	15	F4
Hemlock	Mnr	1	B5
Hidden Acres	CM	19	C5
High Pt St Pk	Ssx	2	D3
Holiday Pk	Crl	17	C6
Holly Acres RV Pk	At	15	E6
Holly shores Holiday Trav-L-Pk	CM	22	A1
Homestead	Sux	21	C4
Hospitality Cr	Gle	15	A5
Indian Br Pk	At	15	C6
Indian River Bay	Sux	21	E5
Indian Rock RV Resort & Family Campground	Oc	11	B5
Jenny Jump St Forest	War	6	A2
Jims Hideaway	Sux	21	E6
Jugtown Mtn	Hnt	5	F5
Kens Wood	Pke	1	F5
King Nummy Tr	CM	19	B6
Kymers Camping Resort	Ssx	2	D4
Lake Kandle	Gle	14	E4
Lake Laurie	CM	22	B1
Lake Sebago Beach	Rck	3	E4
Laurel Pond RV & Campground Resort	Mom	11	A5
Lebanon St Forest	Bur	15	F2
Little Oaks	CM	19	C4
Lums Pond St Pk	NC	13	D6
Mahlon Dickerson Resv	Mrr	6	F1
Maple Lake	Oc	11	C6
Mount Pocono	Mnr	1	B5
Mountain View	Hnt	5	E5
Mountain Vista	Mnr	1	D6
Nazarene	Cec	13	A5
North Wildwood Camping Resort	CM	19	B6
Ocean View Resort	CM	19	C4
Odessa	NC	17	E2
Old Cedar	Sal	14	E5
Oldmans Cr	Sal	14	D5
Otter Lake	Mnr	1	E5
Outdoor World Sea Pines Resort	CM	19	C5
Panther Lake Camping Resort	Ssx	6	D1
Paradise Lake	At	15	D4
Parvin St Pk	Sal	14	E6
Pilgrim Lake	Bur	16	A5
Pine Cone	Mom	11	C4
Pine Haven	CM	19	D5
Pine Tree	Sux	21	E6
Plantation	CM	19	D4
Pleasant Acres Farm	Ssx	2	E3
Pleasant Valley Family	At	19	C1
Pocono Vacation Pk	Mnr	5	C1
Pomona	At	19	F1
Ponderosa	CM	19	C5
Quaker Woods	Buk	9	B1
Resort	CM	19	D4
River Beach	Pke	2	C3
River Beach Camp II	At	19	D1
Round Valley Rec Area	Hnt	6	B5
Sand Hill	Sux	21	E3
Sandy Cove	Cec	13	A6
Sandy Cove	Cec	17	A6
Sandy Cove	Sux	21	E6
Sandy Hill	Cec	17	A1
Scenic Riverview	CM	19	C3
Scrubbie Pines Family Campground Resort	Oc	16	B3
Sea Grove Camping Resort	CM	19	D4
Sea Pirate	Oc	16	C5
Seashore	CM	22	A1
Seaville Shores Trailer Resort	CM	19	C4
Shady Acres	Nth	5	E2
Shady Oaks	CM	19	D4
Shady Pines	At	20	A1
Shellbay Family Camping Resort	CM	19	B6
Shippekonk	Ssx	2	D2
Silver Mine Lake	Orn	3	F3
Silver Valley	Mnr	5	C1
Sleepy Hollow Family	At	19	E2
Smiths Ldg	Sux	21	C3
Spring Mtn	Mnt	9	A4
Spruce Run Rec Area	Hnt	6	A5
Steamboat Ldg	Sux	21	D3
Stephens St Pk	Mrr	6	C2
Stokes St Forest	Ssx	2	C4
Surf & Stream	Oc	11	D6
Swartswood St Pk	Ssx	2	C6
Tall Pines Resort Pk	Sux	21	D4
Tamerlane	CM	19	D5
Timberland Lake	Oc	11	A5
Timberlane	Gle	14	D3
Timberline Lake Camping Resort	Bur	16	A5
Tip Tam RV Pk Camping Resort	Oc	11	C5
Tobys Hide Away	Oc	11	C5
Trap Pond St Pk	Sux	21	A6
Triplebrook Family Camping Resort	War	5	F1
Tuckahoe Acres	Sux	21	E5
Turkey Swamp	Mom	11	C4
Turtle Run	Bur	15	F5
Union Hill	Bur	16	A5
Voorhees St Pk	Hnt	6	B4
Wading Pines Camping Resort	Bur	15	F4
Washington Crossing St Pk	Hnt	10	B3
Wawayanda St Pk	Pas	3	A4
West Chester KOA	Che	13	C1
Whippoorwill	CM	19	D3
Wildwood Canadian	CM	22	B1
Winding River	At	19	C1
Worthington St Forest	War	1	E6
Worthington St Forest	War	5	E1
WT Family	Mnr	1	A6
Yogi Bears Jellystone Pk at Tall Pines Resort	Sal	14	C6
Yogi Bears Jellystone Resort at Mays Ldg	At	19	C2

Colleges & Universities

NAME	TERR	MAP	GRID
Academy & Coll of Saint Elizabeth	Mrr	7	A3
Academy of The New Church	Mnt	9	E5
Adelphi Univ	Nsu	8	D4
Allentown Coll of Saint Francis de Sales	Leh	5	B6
Alma White Coll	Sms	6	F6
Atlantic Comm Coll	At	19	D1
Beaver Coll	Mnt	9	D6
Bergen Comm Coll	Brg	7	E1
Berkeley Coll of Bus	Pas	7	D2
Bloomfield Coll	Esx	7	D3
Brookdale Comm Coll	Mom	11	E2
Bryn Mawr Coll	Mnt	9	C6
Bucks Co Comm Coll	Buk	10	A4
Burlington Co Coll	Bur	15	E1
Cabrini Coll	Del	9	B6
Caldwell Coll	Esx	7	C3
Camden Co Coll	CaC	14	F3
Cecil Comm Coll	Cec	13	A5
Centenary Coll	War	6	B2
Chestnut Hill Coll	Ph	9	D5
Cheyney Univ of Pennsylvania	Del	13	F1
City Univ of New Jersey	Hud	7	E4
City Univ of New York Bronx Comm Coll	Brx	8	B2
City Univ of New York Brooklyn Coll	Kng	8	A5
City Univ of New York City Coll & Medical Sch	NYC	8	A3
City Univ of New York Coll of Staten Is	Rmd	7	E5
City Univ of New York Hunter Coll	NYC	8	A3
City Univ of New York Kingsborough Comm Coll	Kng	8	A6
City Univ of New York Lehmann Coll	Brx	8	A2
City Univ of New York Medgar Evers Coll	Kng	8	A5
City Univ of New York Queens Coll & Law Sch	Que	8	C4
City Univ of New York Queensborough Comm Coll	Que	8	C3
City Univ of New York York Coll	Que	8	C4
College of Mt Saint Vincent	Brx	8	B2
College of New Jersey	Mer	10	C3
College of New Rochelle	Wch	8	C1
Columbia Univ	NYC	8	A3
County Coll of Morris	Mrr	6	F2
Cumberland Co Coll	Cmb	18	E1
Delaware Co Comm Coll	Del	14	B1
Delaware St Univ	Ket	17	F4
Delaware Tech & Comm Coll (Jack F Owens Campus)	Sux	21	A4
Delaware Valley Coll	Buk	9	D3
Drew Univ	Mrr	7	A3
East Stroudsburg Univ of Pennsylvania	Mnr	5	D1
Eastern Coll	Del	9	B6
Eastern Pilgrim Coll	Al	5	A5
Essex Co Coll	Esx	7	D4
Fairleigh Dickenson Univ Edward Williams Coll	Brg	7	F2
Fairleigh Dickenson Univ Teaneck-Hackensack Campus	Brg	7	F2
Fairleigh Dickinson Univ Florham-Madison Campus	Mrr	7	A3
Faith Theol Seminary	Mnt	9	E6
Felician Coll	Brg	7	E2
Fordham Univ Main Campus	Brx	8	B2
Georgian Court Coll	Oc	11	C5
Gloucester Co Coll	Gle	14	E3
Gratz Coll	Mnt	9	E6
Gwynedd Mercy Coll	Mnt	9	D4
Harcum Coll	Mnt	9	C6
Haverford Coll	Del	9	C6
Hofstra Univ	Nsu	8	E4
Holy Family Coll	Ph	10	A6
Hudson Co Comm Coll	Hud	7	F4
Iona Coll	Wch	8	C1
Kean Univ	Uni	7	C4
Lafayette Coll	Nth	5	D4
LaSalle Univ	Ph	9	E6
Lehigh Univ (South Mtn Campus)	Bt	5	B5
Lincoln Univ	Che	13	A3
Long Is Univ Brooklyn	Kng	8	A4
Long Is Univ C W Post Ctr	Nsu	8	E3
Lutheran Theol Seminary	Ph	9	D6
Manhattan Coll	Brx	8	A2
Manhattanville Coll	Wch	4	D6
Manor Jr Coll	Mnt	9	E5
Marymount Coll	Wch	4	B6
Mercer Co Comm Coll	Mer	10	E3
Middlesex Co Coll	Mid	7	B6
Molloy Coll	Nsu	8	E4
Monmouth Univ	Mom	11	F3
Montclair St Univ	Esx	7	D2
Montgomery Co Comm Coll	Mnt	9	C4
Moravian Coll	Bt	5	B5
Nassau Comm Coll	Nsu	8	E4
Neumann Coll	Del	14	A2
New Jersey Inst of Tech	Esx	7	D3
New York Inst of Tech	Nsu	8	E3
New York Univ	NYC	8	A4
Northampton Co Area Comm Coll	Nth	5	B4
Northeastern Bible Coll	Esx	7	C2
Northeastern Christian Jr Coll	Mnt	9	C6
Ocean Co Coll & Planetarium	Oc	11	D6
Orange Co Comm Coll	Orn	3	A1
Pace Univ Pleasantville-Briarcliff	Wch	4	C5
Pace Univ White PLains	Wch	4	C6
Passaic Co Comm Coll	Pas	7	D1
Penn St Univ (Delaware Co Campus)	Del	14	A1
Penn St Univ Abington-Ogontz Campus	Mnt	9	E5

NAME	TERR	MAP	GRID
Pennsylvania Inst of Tech	Del	14	B2
Philadelphia Coll of Bible	Buk	10	B5
Polytechnic Univ	Kng	8	A4
Princeton Univ	Mer	10	E2
Princeton Univ (James Forrestal Campus)	Mid	10	E2
Rabbinical Coll of America	Mrr	6	F3
Ramapo Coll of New Jersey	Brg	3	D5
Raritan Valley Comm Coll	Sms	6	D5
Rider Univ	Mer	10	C3
Rockefeller Univ	NYC	8	A3
Rockland Comm Coll	Rck	3	F5
Rosemont Coll	Mnt	9	C6
Rowan Univ	Gle	14	E4
Rutgers Univ (Camden Campus)	CaC	14	E1
Rutgers Univ (New Brunswick Campus)	Mid	7	A6
Rutgers Univ Newark Campus	Esx	7	E4
Saint Johns Univ	Que	8	C4
Saint Josephs Univ	Mnt	14	D1
Saint Peters Coll	Hud	7	E4
Saint Thomas Aquinas Coll	Rck	4	B6
Salem Comm Coll	Gle	14	A4
Sarah Lawrence Coll	Wch	8	C1
Seton Hall Univ	Esx	7	D4
State Univ of New York Coll at Old Westbury	Nsu	8	F3
State Univ of New York Health Science Ctr	Kng	8	A5
State Univ of New York Maritime Coll	Brx	8	C3
State Univ of New York Purchase	Wch	4	D6
Stevens Inst of Tech	Hud	7	F3
Sussex Co Comm Coll	Ssx	2	C6
Swarthmore Coll	Del	14	B2
Temple Univ	Ph	14	E1
Temple Univ (Tyler Sch of Fine Arts)	Mnt	9	E6
The American Coll	Mnt	9	B6
The Richard Stockton Coll of New Jersey	At	15	F6
Thomas Jefferson Univ	Ph	14	E1
Union Co Coll	Uni	7	C4
University of Delaware	NC	13	C4
University of Delaware	NC	13	D4
University of Delaware Experiment Station	Sux	21	A5
University of Delaware Research Pk	Sux	21	D3
University of Medicine & Dentistry of New Jersey	Esx	7	D4
University of Pennsylvania	Ph	14	D1
Ursinus Coll	Mnt	9	A4
US Mil Acad at West Pt	Orn	3	F2
US Mil Acad at West Pt	Orn	4	A2
Villanova Univ	Del	9	B6
Wagner Coll	Rmd	7	E5
Warren Co Comm Coll	War	5	F4
Wesley Coll	Ket	17	F4
West Chester Univ of Pennsylvania (N & S Campus)	Che	13	E1
Westchester Comm Coll	Wch	4	C6
Westminster Choir Coll of Rider Univ	Mer	10	E2
Widener Univ	Del	14	B2
Widener Univ Law Ctr	NC	13	F3
William Paterson Coll	Pas	7	D1

Covered Bridges

NAME	TERR	MAP	GRID
Ashland	NC	13	E3
Bartrams	Del	14	A1
Cabin Run	Buk	9	E1
Erwinna	Buk	5	E6
Foxcatcher Farms	Cec	13	B4
Frankenfield	Buk	9	E1
Gibsons	Che	13	D1
Gilpins Falls	Cec	13	A5
Glen Hope	Che	13	A4
Green Sergeant	Hnt	10	A1
Hayes Clark	Che	13	C2
Knechts	Buk	5	C6
Knox-Valley Forge Dam	Mnt	9	A6
Kreidersville (Solts Mill)	Nth	5	A4
Linton Stevens	Che	13	B3
Loux	Buk	9	E1
Mercers	Che	13	A1
Moods	Buk	9	C2
Pine Valley	Buk	9	D3
Rudolph and Arthur	Che	13	B3
Sheards Mill	Buk	9	C1
South Perkasie	Buk	9	C2
Speakmans Bridge No 1	Che	13	C1
Speakmans Bridge No 2 (Mary Anne Pyle)	Che	13	C1
Thomas Mill	Ph	9	D6
Uhlerstown	Buk	5	E6
Van Sant	Buk	10	A3
Westminster	NC	13	D3
Wooddale	NC	13	E3

Forest & Wildlife Areas

NAME	TERR	MAP	GRID
Abram S Hewitt St Forest	Pas	3	B4
Absecon WMA	At	20	A1
Amwell Lake WMA	Hnt	10	B2
Appoquinimink St Wildlife Area	NC	17	F1
Assawoman Wildlife Area	Sux	21	E6
Assunpink Fish & WMA	Mom	10	F4
Assunpink Watershed	Mer	10	E4
Assunpink WMA	Mom	11	A4
Augustine Wildlife Area	NC	13	E6
Augustine Wildlife Area	NC	13	F6
Augustine Wildlife Area	NC	17	E1
Baldwin WMA	Mer	10	C2
Bass River St Forest	Bur	16	A3
Bass River St Forest	Bur	16	A5
Bass River St Forest	Oc	16	B6
Beaver Swamp WMA	CM	19	C5
Belleplain St Forest	CM	19	B3
Berkshire Valley WMA	Mrr	6	E1
Bethel Managed Hunting Area	Cec	13	C6
Black River WMA	Mrr	6	E3
Blackbird St Forest	NC	17	C3
Blackbird St Forest	NC	17	E2
Blackiston Wildlife Area	Ket	17	D3
Bombay Hook Natl Wildlife Ref	Ket	17	F3
Bombay Hook Natl Wildlife Ref	Ket	18	A3
Brigantine Natl Wildlife Ref	Oc	16	C6
Buckhorn St Nat Area	Pke	2	C1
Bur Green Bank St Forest	At	15	E5
Butterfly Bogs WMA	Oc	11	C5
Campgaw Mtn Co Resv	Brg	3	D6
Canal Natl Wildlife Ref	Cec	13	B6
Cape Island WMA	CM	22	B1
Cape May Bird Observatory & Education Ctr	CM	19	C5
Cape May Migratory Bird Ref & Observatory	CM	22	A1
Cape May Natl Wildlife Ref	CM	19	A5
Cape May Natl Wildlife Ref	CM	19	B5
Cape May Natl Wildlife Ref	CM	19	B6
Cape May Natl Wildlife Ref	CM	19	C4
Cape May Natl Wildlife Ref	CM	19	D4
Cape May Natl Wildlife Ref	CM	22	B1
Cape May Natl Wildlife Ref Hdq	CM	19	B5
Cape May WMA	CM	19	B6
Cape May WMA	CM	19	C5
Cape May WMA	CM	19	C6
Cape May WMA	CM	19	D4
Cape May WMA	CM	19	E3
Cape May WMA	CM	19	E4
Cape May WMA	CM	22	B1
Capoolong WMA	Hnt	6	A5
Cedar Swamp Wildlife Area	NC	17	F2
Chesapeake & Delaware Canal Wildlife Area	NC	13	E6
Clay Pit Ponds Preserve	Rmd	7	D6
Clinton WMA	Hnt	6	A4
Colliers Mills WMA	Oc	11	A5
Corson WMA	Cmb	19	A4
Delaware & Raritan Canal St Forest	Sms	6	F6
Delaware St Forest	Mnr	1	D4
Delaware St Forest	Pke	1	D2
Delaware St Forest	Pke	1	E2
Delaware St Forest	Pke	1	E3
Delaware St Forest	Pke	1	F1
Delaware St Forest	Pke	2	A2
Delaware St Forest	Pke	2	A3
Delaware St Forest	Pke	2	A5
Delaware St Forest	Pke	2	C2
Dennis Cr WMA	CM	19	B4
Doris Duke Wildlife Sanctuary	Orn	3	D3
Dryden Kuser Nat Area	Ssx	2	E2
Edward G Bevan WMA	Cmb	18	E2
Edwin B Forsythe Natl Wildlife Ref	At	16	A6
Edwin B Forsythe Natl Wildlife Ref	At	20	B1
Edwin B Forsythe Natl Wildlife Ref	Bur	16	A5
Edwin B Forsythe Natl Wildlife Ref	Oc	16	C5
Edwin B Forsythe Natl Wildlife Ref	Oc	16	D4
Egg Is Berrytown WMA	Cmb	18	E4
Elk Forest WMA	Cec	13	C6
Elk Neck St Forest	Cec	13	A6
Elk Neck St Forest	Cec	13	B5
Ellendale St Forest	Sux	21	A3
Fair Hill NRMA	Cec	13	B4
Flatbrook St WMA	Ssx	2	B4
Forked River Game Farm	Oc	16	E2
Fortescue WMA	Cmb	18	D3
Glassboro WMA	Gle	14	F4
Gravies Pt Preserve	Nsu	8	E2
Great Bay Blvd WMA	Oc	16	B6
Great Swamp Natl Wildlife Ref	Mrr	6	F4
Great Swamp Natl Wildlife Ref	Mrr	7	A4
Green Bank St Forest	At	15	E5
Greenwood Forest WMA	Bur	16	B2
Greenwood Forest WMA	Oc	16	B2
Hainesville WMA	Ssx	2	C3
Hamburg Mtn WMA	Ssx	2	F5
Heislerville WMA	Cmb	18	F4
Higbee Beach WMA	CM	22	A1
Jenny Jump St Forest	War	5	F2
Jenny Jump St Forest	War	6	A2
Ken Lockwood WMA	Hnt	6	B4
Lakota Wolf Preserve	War	5	E1
Lebanon St Forest	Bur	15	F2
Lebanon St Forest	Bur	16	A1
Lebanon St Forest	Oc	16	A1
Little Cr Wildlife Area	Ket	18	A5
Mad Horse Cr WMA	Sal	13	F6
Mad Horse Cr WMA	Sal	17	F1
Mad Horse Cr WMA	Sal	18	A1
Makepeace Lake WMA	At	15	C6
Malubu Beach WMA	At	19	F3
Manahawkin WMA	Oc	16	D4
Manasquan River WMA	Oc	11	E5
Manchester WMA	Oc	11	B6
Manchester WMA	Oc	16	B1
Manitoga Nature Ctr	Put	4	A2
Medford WMA	Bur	15	B1
Menantico Ponds WMA	Cmb	19	A2
Merrill Cr Environmental Resource Preserve	War	5	E4
Milford Neck Wildlife Area	Ket	18	A6
Milford Neck Wildlife Area	Ket	18	B6
Milford Neck Wildlife Area	Ket	21	B1
Millington WMA	Ken	17	C3
Mix WMA	Cmb	18	C2
Nantuxent WMA	Cmb	18	D3
Natural Resource Education Ctr	War	6	A3
New Sweden WMA	Cmb	18	C3
Norman G Wilder Wildlife Area	Ket	17	E6
Norvin Green St Forest	Pas	3	B5
Norvin Green St Forest	Pas	3	B6
Oyster Bay Natl Wildlife Ref	Nsu	8	F2
Pasadena WMA	Bur	16	A2
Pasadena WMA	Oc	16	A2
Peaslee WMA	CmB	19	B3
Peaslee WMA	Cmb	19	B2
Penn St Forest	Bur	16	A3
Pequest WMA	War	6	A2
Phillips Preserve	Mid	11	B2
Port Republic WMA	At	16	A6
Prime Hook Natl Wildlife Ref	Sux	21	C2
Ramapo Mtn St Forest	Pas	3	C6
Ramapo Valley Co Resv	Brg	3	D5
Redden St Forest	Sux	21	A4
Redden St Forest	Sux	21	B4
Rockport St Game Farm	War	6	B3
Roy St WMA	Ssx	2	B4
Sassafras River NRMA	Ken	17	A2
Saw Mill Cr WMA	Hud	7	E3
Scherman-Hoffman Wildlife Sanctuary	Sms	6	F4
Sedge Is WMA	Oc	16	E3
Sourland Monmouth Reserve	Sms	10	D1
Stafford Forge WMA	Oc	16	B4
State Game Lands No 38	Mnr	1	B6
State Game Lands No 38	Mnr	5	A1
State Game Lands No 56	Buk	5	E6
State Game Lands No 116	Pke	2	A1
State Game Lands No 127	Mnr	1	A4
State Game Lands No 127	Mnr	1	B4
State Game Lands No 139	Buk	9	C2
State Game Lands No 157	Buk	5	C6
State Game Lands No 157	Buk	9	D1
State Game Lands No 168	Mnr	5	A3
State Game Lands No 168	Nth	5	A3
State Game Lands No 168	Nth	5	B3
State Game Lands No 180	Pke	1	F2
State Game Lands No 180	Pke	2	A2
State Game Lands No 183	Pke	1	E1
State Game Lands No 186	Mnr	5	C1
State Game Lands No 196	Buk	9	B2
State Game Lands No 209	Pke	2	B1
State Game Lands No 221	Mnr	1	C4
State Game Lands No 300	Lak	1	A1
State Game Lands No 310	Wyn	1	A1
State Game Lands No 312	Lak	1	A4
State Game Lands No 312	Wyn	1	A4
Stemmers Run WMA	Cec	17	A1
Stillwater St Nat Area	Pke	1	F4
Stillwater St Nat Area	Pke	2	A4
Stokes St Forest	Ssx	2	B4
Stokes St Forest	Ssx	2	C3
Stokes St Forest	Ssx	2	C4
Stone Hbr Bird Sanctuary	CM	19	C6
Supawna Meadows Natl Wildlife Ref	Sal	13	F5
Supawna Meadows Natl Wildlife Ref	Sal	14	A5
Swan Bay WMA	Bur	15	F5
Swan Bay WMA	Bur	16	A6
Ted Harvey Wildlife Area Logan Tract	Ket	18	A5
Tenafly Nature Ctr	Brg	8	A1
Tillman Ravine St Nat Area	Ssx	2	B5
Tuckahoe/Lester G MacNamara WMA	At	19	D3
Tuckahoe/Lester G MacNamara WMA	CM	19	D3
Turkey Swamp WMA	Mom	11	B4
Wallkill River Natl Wildlife Ref	Ssx	2	F4
Walpack St WMA	Ssx	2	B5
Wanaque WMA	Pas	3	C5
Ward Pound Ridge Resv	Wch	4	E3
Wharton St Forest	Bur	15	C4
Wharton St Forest	Bur	15	F5
Wharton St Forest	Bur	16	A4
Wharton St Forest	CaC	15	C4
Whiting WMA	Oc	16	B1
Whittingham WMA	Ssx	2	C6
Whittingham WMA	Ssx	6	C1
William Hutcheson Mem Forest	Sms	10	F1
Winslow WMA	CaC	15	B5
Winslow WMA	Gle	15	B5
Woodland Beach Wildlife Area	Ket	17	F2
Woodland Beach Wildlife Area	Ket	18	A2
Worthington St Forest	War	1	E6
Worthington St Forest	War	5	E1

Golf Courses

NAME	TERR	MAP	GRID
Apple Mtn GC	War	5	F3
Ashbourne CC	Mnt	9	E6
Ashbrook GC	Uni	7	B5
Avalon GC	CM	19	C5
B L England GC	CM	19	E3
Back Cr GC	NC	13	C6
Ballyowen GC	Ssx	2	E5
Bay Pk GC	Nsu	8	E5
Baywood Greens GC	Sux	21	D5
Bear Trap Dunes	Sux	21	E6
Beaver Brook CC	Hnt	6	B5
Beckett CC	Gle	14	F4
Bel-Aire GC	Mom	11	E5
Bensalem CC	Buk	10	A5
Bethany Bay GC	Sux	21	E6
Bethlehem Mun GC	Nth	5	B5
Bey Lea GC	Oc	16	D1
Black Bear G & CC	Ssx	2	E5
Blair Acad GC	War	6	A1
Blue Heron Pines GC	At	19	E1
Bowling Green GC	Mrr	2	F6
Brantwood GC	Cec	13	C6
Brigantine Golf Links	At	20	B1
Buck Hill Falls GC	Mnr	1	C4
Buena Vista GC	At	15	B6
Bunker Hill GC	Sms	10	F1
Caesars Pocono Palace Resort	Mnr	1	F6
Cantiague Pk GC	Nsu	8	F3
Cedar Cr GC	Oc	16	D2
Center Square GC	Mnt	9	B4
Center Valley Club	Leh	5	B6
Centerton GC	Sal	14	E6
Central Valley GC	Orn	3	E2
Chantilly Manor GC	Cec	13	A4
Charleston Springs GC	Mom	11	B4
Cherry Valley GC	Mnr	5	D1
Chesapeake Bay GC	Cec	13	F2
Christopher Morley Pk GC	Nsu	8	D3
Clayton Pk GC	Del	14	A2
Clearview Pk GC	Que	8	C3
Cliff Pk GC	Pke	2	B3
Cobbs Cr GC	Ph	14	C1
Cohanzick CC	Cmb	18	D2
Colonial Terrace GC	Mom	11	F4
Cranbury GC	Mer	10	E3
Cream Ridge GC & CC	Mom	10	F5
Cricket Hill GC	Pke	1	E1
Cruz Farm GC	Mom	11	E4
Crystal Springs GC	Ssx	2	F5
Culver Lake GC	Ssx	2	D4
Darlington Co Pk GC	Brg	3	D6
Deerwood CC	Bur	15	C1
Delaware Co GC	Del	13	F2
Delcastle GC	NC	13	D3
Douglaston GC	Que	8	D4
Dover Par 3	NC	17	E5
Dunwoodie GC	Wch	8	B1
Dyker Beach GC	Kng	7	F5
Eagle Cr GC	Ket	18	A5
Eagle Lodge CC	Mnt	9	C6
Eagle Ridge GC	Oc	11	D6
East Orange GC	Esx	7	B3
Eastlyn GC	Cmb	19	A1
Ed Porky Oliver GC	NC	13	F3
Eddy Farm Resort Hotel GC	Orn	2	D1
Eisenhower Pk CC	Nsu	8	F4
Emerson GC	Brg	7	F1
Evergreen Pk GC	Mnr	1	D6
F D Roosevelt GC	Ph	14	D2
Fairway Valley GC	War	6	A3
Fairways GC & CC	Buk	9	E4
Farmstead G & CC	Ssx	2	E5
Fernwood CC	Mnr	1	F6
Fernwood GC	Esx	7	C3
Five Ponds GC	Buk	9	E4
Flanders Valley GC	Mrr	6	D3
Forest Pk GC	Que	8	B4
Fox Hollow GC	Buk	9	B2
Fox Hollow GC	Hnt	6	D5
Francis Byrne GC	Esx	7	C3
Freeway GC	CaC	14	F3
Frog Hollow GC	NC	17	D1
Galloping Hill GC	Uni	7	C4
Gambler Ridge GC	Mom	10	F5
Garrison GC & CC	Put	4	B2
Garrisons Lake GC	Ket	17	E3
General Washington GC	Mnt	9	A5
Glen Brook CC	Mnr	1	C6
Glen Cove GC	Nsu	8	F3
Glenwild Greens GC	Pas	3	B6
Golden Pheasant CC	Bur	15	C1
Golf Pk at Rehoboth	Sux	21	E4
Great Gorge GC	Ssx	2	F4
Great Gorge Golf Resort	Ssx	2	E5
Greate Bay Resort GC	CM	19	E3
Green Knoll GC	Sms	6	E5
Green Pond CC	Nth	5	C4
Green Pond GC	Mrr	7	A1
Green Ridge GC	Orn	2	F2
Greentree GC	At	19	D2
Hamilton Trails CC	At	19	E1
Hammonton CC	At	15	C5
Hanover CC	Bur	10	F6
Harbor Pines CC	At	19	E2
Hartefeld Natl GC	Che	13	D3
Hendricks Field GC	Esx	7	E3
Hickory Hill GC	Orn	3	C3
Hidden Acres GC	Ssx	2	C3
Hideaway Hills GC	Mnr	5	A2
High Mtn GC	Brg	7	D1
High Pt CC	Ssx	2	C3
Highlands CC	Put	4	A2
Hillsborough CC	Sms	10	C1
Holly Hills GC	Sal	14	C6
Hominy Hill GC	Mom	11	D3
Horsham Valley GC	Mnt	9	D4
Howell Pk GC	Mom	11	D4
Hyatt Hills GC	Uni	7	C5
Indian Spring GC	Bur	15	B2
Jeffersonville GC	Mnt	9	B5
John F Byrne GC	Ph	9	F6

NAME	TERR	MAP	GRID
Jonathans Ldg GC	Ket	18	A5
Jones Beach St Pk GC	Nsu	8	F5
Jumping Brook GC	Mom	11	F4
Juniata Pk GC	Ph	9	E6
Karakung GC	Ph	14	D1
Kissena Pk GC	Que	8	C4
Knob Hill CC	Mom	11	B3
Knoll East GC	Mrr	7	B2
Knoll West GC	Mrr	7	B2
Kresson GC	CaC	15	B2
La Tourette GC	Rmd	7	E5
Lake Isle CC	Wch	8	C1
Lake Lackawanna GC	Ssx	6	D1
Lakewood CC	Oc	11	C5
Latona G & CC	At	15	A6
LaTourette Pk GC	Rmd	7	E6
Lido GC	Nsu	8	E5
Limekiln GC	Mnt	9	D4
Loch Nairn Golf Links	Che	13	C2
Locust Valley GC	Buk	9	B1
Macoby Run GC	Mnt	9	A2
Mainland GC	Mnt	9	B3
Maple Moor GC	Wch	4	D6
Maple Ridge GC	Gle	14	E3
Marine Pk GC	Kng	8	A5
Mattawang GC	Sms	10	E1
Mays Ldg CC	At	19	E1
Meadows at Middlesex GC	Mer	10	E3
Meadows GC	Mrr	7	C2
Mercer Oaks GC	Mer	10	D3
Mermaid Swim & Par 3 GC	Mnt	9	C5
Merrick Road GC	Nsu	8	F5
Middletown CC	Buk	10	A4
Midway Par 3 GC	Sux	21	E4
Millburn GC	Uni	7	B4
Mine Brook GC	Mrr	6	C2
Miry Run CC	Mer	10	E4
Moccasin Run GC	Che	13	A1
Monroe CC	Orn	3	D3
Morrisville Golf Farm	Buk	10	C4
Mosholu GC	Brx	8	B2
Mount Airy Lodge Resort GC	Mnr	1	C5
Mount Pocono GC	Mnr	1	B5
Mountain Manor Inn GC Resort	Mnr	1	E6
Mountain View CC	Mer	10	C3
Neshaminy Valley GC	Buk	9	F4
New Jersey Natl GC	Sms	6	E5
North Woodmere GC	Nsu	8	D5
Northampton Valley CC	Buk	10	A4
Oak Ridge GC	Uni	7	B5
Ocean Acres CC	Oc	16	C4
Ocean City GC	CM	19	E3
Ocean Co GC at Atlantis	Oc	16	B6
Ocean Co GC at Forge Pond	Oc	11	E5
Old Ldg GC	Sux	21	E4
Old Orchard CC	Mom	11	F3
Olde Masters GC	Del	14	A1
Orchard Hills GC	Brg	7	F1
Otterkill CC	Orn	3	D1
Overpeck GC	Brg	7	F2
Oxford Valley GC	Buk	10	B4
Paramus G & CC	Brg	7	E1
Pascack Brook G & CC	Brg	7	F1
Passiac Co GC	Pas	7	C2
Paxon Hollow GC	Del	14	B1
Pebble Cr GC	Mom	11	E3
Pelham/Split Rock GC	Brx	8	C2
Pennsauken CC	CaC	14	F1
Pennsburg GC	Mnt	9	A2
Phillip J Rotella CC	Rck	3	F4
Pinch Brook GC	Mrr	7	B3
Pine Barrens GC	Oc	11	C5
Pine Brook GC	Mom	11	C3
Pinecrest CC	Mnt	9	D3
Pinelands GC	CaC	15	A5
Pitman GC	Gle	14	E3
Plainfield West GC	Mid	7	B5
Pocono Manor Inn Resort	Mnr	1	B5
Pomona GC	At	15	F6
Ponderlodge GC	CM	19	A6
Pound Ridge GC	Wch	4	F4
Princeton CC	Mer	10	E3
Putnam GC	Wch	4	D4
Quail Brook GC	Sms	6	F6
Ramblewood CC	Bur	15	A1
Rancocas GC	Bur	10	B6
Raritan Ldg GC	Mid	7	A6
Rivervale CC	Brg	3	F6
Rock Manor GC	NC	13	F3
Rockland Lake North GC	Rck	4	B5
Rockland Lake South GC	Rck	4	B5
Rockleigh GC	Brg	8	A1
Rockview GC	Ssx	2	D2
Rolling Greens GC	Ssx	2	D6
Rolling Turf GC	Mnt	9	A3
Royce Brook GC	Sms	6	E6
Rutgers GC	Mid	7	A6
Sanctuary GC	Wch	4	C3
Sand Barrens GC	CM	19	C5
Sawmill GC	Nth	5	C3
Saxon Woods GC	Wch	8	C1
Scenic Farms GC	Orn	3	C2
Scotch Hills CC	Uni	7	B5
Scotland Run GC	Gle	14	F4
Scranton Mun GC	Wyn	1	A1
Seaview Marriott Golf Resort	At	20	A1
Shark River GC	Mom	11	F4
Shawnee Inn	Mnr	1	E6
Silver Lake Pk GC	Rmd	7	E5
Skippack GC	Mnt	9	B4
Sky View G & CC	Ssx	2	E6
Skytop GC	Mnr	1	C4
Somerton Springs Golf Facility	Buk	9	F5
South Shore GC	Rmd	7	D6
Southmoore GC	Nth	5	B3
Spook Rock GC	Rck	3	E5
Spooky Brook GC	Sms	6	F6
Sprain Lake GC	Wch	8	B1
Spring Meadow GC	Mom	11	E5
Springfield CC	Del	14	B1
Springfield Golf Ctr	Bur	10	C6
Sterling Farms GC	Ffd	4	F5
Stony Ford GC	Orn	3	C1
Stonybrook GC	Mer	10	C2
Summit Mun GC	Uni	7	B4
Sunset Valley GC	Mrr	7	C1
Tamarack GC	Mid	11	A1
Tamcrest GC	Brg	8	A1
Tamiment Resort	Pke	1	F5
Tara Greens GC	Mid	11	A1
Terra Greens GC	Mnr	1	D6
The Pines at Clermont GC	CM	19	C4
The Salt Pond GC	Sux	21	F6
The Spa GC	Ssx	2	F5
Three Little Bakers GC	NC	13	D4
Town & Country Golf Links	Sal	14	C5
Tumblebrook GC	Leh	5	B6
Twin Brook GC	Mom	11	E4
Twin Willows GC	Mrr	7	C1
Twin Woods GC	Mnt	9	C3
Twining Valley GC	Mnt	9	E5
Two Bridges GC	Mrr	7	C2
Upper Perkiomen GC	Mnt	9	A2
Vails Grove GC	Wch	4	E2
Valley Forge GC	Mnt	9	B6
Valleybrook GC	CaC	14	F3
Van Cortlandt Pk GC	Brx	8	A2
Vandegrift GC	NC	17	E1
Walnut La GC	Ph	9	D6
Warrenbrook GC	Sms	7	A5
Washington Twp Mun GC	Gle	14	F4
Water Gap CC	Mnr	5	E1
Wedgewood GC	Leh	5	A6
Wedgwood CC	Gle	14	F3
Weequahic Pk GC	Uni	7	D4
Westbury CC	Gle	14	D3
Westover GC	Mnt	9	B5
Westwood GC	Gle	14	D3
White Oaks CC	Gle	14	F6
Whitetail GC	Nth	5	A4
Wild Oaks GC	Sal	14	A6
Willow Brook GC	Leh	5	A5
Willowbrook CC	Bur	10	A6
Woodlake GC & CC	Oc	11	E5
Woodland Hills GC	Nth	5	C5
Woods Golf Ctr	Mnt	9	C5
Wyncote GC	Che	13	A3

Indian Reservations

NAME	TERR	MAP	GRID
Powhatan Renape Nation	Bur	10	C6

Information Centers

NAME	TERR	MAP	GRID
Atlantic City	At	20	A2
Bay Country	QA	17	A6
Connecticut	Ffd	4	F2
Delaware	NC	13	D5
Delaware	NC	13	F4
Dover Air Force Base	Ket	18	A5
Fort Mott St Pk	Sal	13	F5
Gateway Natl Rec Area	Mom	12	A1
Morristown Natl Hist Pk	Mrr	6	F3
New Jersey	At	15	C6
New Jersey	Brg	3	F6
New Jersey	CM	19	C5
New Jersey	CM	19	D4
New Jersey	Gle	14	A4
New Jersey	Hnt	6	B6
New Jersey	Hud	7	F4
New Jersey	Mer	10	C4
New Jersey	War	5	E1
New York	Nsu	8	D4
Newtown Square	Del	14	B1
Pennsylvania	Buk	10	A5
Pennsylvania	Del	14	A3
Pennsylvania	Mnr	1	B6
Pennsylvania	Pke	1	D2
Pennsylvania	Pke	2	D2
Sea Isle City Tourist	CM	19	D5
University of Delaware	NC	13	C4
Valley Forge Natl Hist Pk	Mnt	9	A5

Islands & Points

NAME	TERR	MAP	GRID
Artificial Is	Sal	17	F1
Bakeoven Pt	Ket	18	A2
Bay Pt	Cmb	18	C3
Beadons Pt	Cmb	18	C2
Ben Davis Pt	Cmb	18	C3
Biles Is	Buk	10	D5
Cape Henlopen	Sux	21	E3
Cape Horn	Oc	16	B6
Cedar Pt	Sal	13	F4
City Is	Brx	8	C2
Cohansey Pt	Cmb	18	B2
Coney Is	Kng	7	F5
Coney Is	Kng	8	A6
Davids Is	Wch	8	C2
Delaware Pt	NC	17	F2
Dinner Pt	Oc	16	C5
East Pt	Cmb	18	F4
Egg Is	Oc	16	D5
Egg Is Pt	Cmb	18	E4
Ellis Is	Hud	7	F4
False Egg Is Pt	Cmb	18	D4
Finns Pt	Sal	13	F5
Flat Is	Oc	16	D5
Fowler Is	Cmb	18	F4
Gaunt Pt	Oc	16	B6
Goose Pt	Ket	18	B3
Graveling Pt	Oc	16	B6
Great Is	At	20	A2
Great Is	Wch	4	D5
Gull Is	CM	19	C5
Gull Is	CM	19	D5
Hart Is	Brx	8	C2
Hewlett Pt	Nsu	8	C2
Hylands Pt	Cec	13	A6
Island Pt	Cmb	18	C4
Liberty Is	Hud	7	F4
Liston Pt	NC	17	F2
Manursing Is	Wch	8	E1
Matinecock Pt	Nsu	8	E2
Oyster Pt	Oc	16	D5
Parsonage Pt	Wch	8	D1
Pea Patch Is	NC	13	E5
Pelican Is	Oc	16	E1
Pigeon Pt	NC	13	F4
Reedy Is	NC	13	F6
Reedy Pt	NC	13	F6
Rikers Is	Brx	8	B3
Ring Is	CM	19	C6
Roach Pt	Cec	13	A6
Rockaway Pt	Que	8	A6
Rocky Pt	Nsu	8	F1
Rose Pt	Oc	16	C5
Sands Pt	Nsu	8	D2
Sandy Hook Is	Mom	11	F1
Sandy Hook Is	Mom	12	A1
Sandy Islands	Oc	16	E4
Seven Islands	Oc	16	B6
Sludge Pt	Mom	12	A2
Story Is	Oc	16	C6
Thorofare Is	Oc	16	D5
West Pt Is	Oc	16	E1
Whispering Is	Oc	11	E6

Lakes & Streams

NAME	TERR	MAP	GRID
Abbotts Pond	Sux	21	A2
Albertson Brook	At	15	C4
Albertson Brook	CaC	15	C4
Alder Cove	Sal	18	A1
Alexauken Cr	Hnt	10	A2
Alloway Cr	Sal	14	A6
Alloway Lake	Sal	14	B6
Amawalk Res	Wch	4	D3
Andover Br	QA	17	C4
Andrews Lake	Ket	17	F6
Appoquinimink River	NC	17	E1
Aquashicola Cr	Mnr	5	A2
Ariel Cr	Wyn	1	B1
Arthur Kill	Mid	7	D6
Arthur Kill	Rmd	7	D6
Arthur Kill	Uni	7	D6
Assawoman Canal	Sux	21	E6
Assunpink Cr	Mer	10	D4
Assunpink Cr	Mer	10	E4
Assunpink Cr	Mom	10	E4
Atlantic City Res	At	19	F1
Atlantic Ocean	CM	19	E6
Atlantic Ocean	CM	22	C3
Atlantic Ocean	Kng	8	B6
Atlantic Ocean	Mom	11	F6
Atlantic Ocean	Mom	12	C4
Atlantic Ocean	Nsu	8	B6
Atlantic Ocean	Oc	11	F6
Atlantic Ocean	Oc	16	E6
Atlantic Ocean	Que	8	B6
Atlantic Ocean	Sux	21	F3
Atsion Lake River	Bur	15	C4
Back Channel	CaC	14	E1
Back Cr	Cec	17	A2
Backbird Cr	NC	17	E2
Bamber Lake	Oc	16	B2
Barnegat Bay	Oc	11	E6
Barnegat Bay	Oc	16	E3
Barnegat Inlet	Oc	16	E3
Barrett Run	Cmb	18	C1
Barton Run	Bur	15	B2
Bass River	Bur	16	A6
Batsto River	Bur	15	D3
Beaver Dam Pond	Orn	2	D1
Beaver Lake	Ssx	2	F5
Beaverdam Lake	Orn	3	E1
Becks Pond	NC	13	D5
Bells Lake	Gle	14	F3
Big Elk Cr	Cec	13	B3
Big Elk Cr	Che	13	B3
Big Elk Cr East Br	Che	13	B2
Big Elk Cr West Br	Che	13	B3
Big Meadow Run	Mnr	5	D1
Big Mill Pond	Ken	17	C3
Big Pond	Orn	2	E1
Biles Cr	Buk	10	C4
Bisphams Mill Cr	Bur	15	E1
Black River	Mrr	6	D3
Blackwater Cr	Sux	21	E5
Blairs Pond	Sux	21	A2
Blind Br	Wch	4	D6
Blooming Grove Cr	Pke	1	E2
Bog Brook Res	Put	4	E1
Bohemia River	Cec	17	A1
Boonton Res	Mrr	7	B2
Boyd Corners Res	Put	4	E1
Brandywine Cr	Del	13	F2
Brandywine Cr	NC	13	E2
Brandywine Cr East Br	Che	13	E1
Brandywine Cr West Br	Che	13	C1
Breakwater Hbr	Sux	21	E3
Brigantine Inlet	At	20	C1
Brindle Lake	Oc	10	F6
Broadkill River	Sux	21	C3
Brodhead Cr	Mnr	1	C5
Bronx River	Wch	4	C6
Brooks Lake	Wyn	1	B1
Buckshutem Cr	Cmb	18	E1
Buckwha Cr	Mnr	5	A2
Budd Lake	Mrr	6	D2
Burrs Mill Brook	Bur	15	D2
Bushkill Cr	Mnr	1	E4
Bushkill Cr	Nth	5	C3
Bushkill Cr	Pke	1	E5
Butler Res	Mrr	7	B1
Byram Lake Res	Wch	4	D5
Byram River	Ffd	4	D5
Cabin John Cr	Cec	17	A1
Canistear Res	Ssx	3	A5
Captain Hbr	Ffd	4	E6
Cedar Cr	Cmb	18	D3
Cedar Cr	Oc	16	C2
Cedar Cr	Sux	21	B2
Cedar Cr Millpond	Sux	21	B2
Cedar Run	Oc	16	C4
Centennial Lake	Bur	15	B3
Cherry Cr	Mnr	5	C1
Chesapeake & Delaware Canal	Cec	13	B6
Chesapeake & Delaware Canal	NC	13	B6
Chester River	Ken	17	A4
Chester River	QA	17	A4
Choptank River	Crl	17	C6
Christiana River	Cec	13	C4
Christiana River	NC	13	C4
Churchmans Marsh	NC	13	E4
Clark Br	CaC	15	C4
Clendaniel Pond	Sux	21	A2
Clinton Res	Pas	3	A5
Clove Brook	Ssx	2	E3
Cohansey Cove	Cmb	18	B3
Cohansey River	Cmb	18	B2
Cohansey River	Cmb	18	C1
Converse Lake	Ffd	4	E5
Cooks Cr	Buk	5	C6
Cooper River	CaC	15	A2
Cooper River Lake	CaC	14	F1
Corson Inlet	CM	19	E4
Country Lake	Bur	15	F1
Cow Marsh Ditch	Ket	17	D6
Cross River Res	Wch	4	E3
Crosswicks Cr	Bur	10	E5
Crosswicks Cr	Mer	10	E5
Crosswicks Cr	Mom	10	E5
Croton Falls Res	Put	4	D2
Croton River	Put	4	E1
Croton River	Wch	4	D3
Culbreth Marsh Ditch	Ket	17	D6
Culvers Lake	Ssx	2	C4
Cypress Br	Ken	17	C3
Cypress Br	NC	17	C3
Cypress Swamp	Sux	21	C6
Deep Cr	NC	17	D1
Deep Cr	Sux	21	A4
Deep Run	At	15	B6
Deer Head Lake	Oc	16	D2
Deforest Lake	Rck	4	A5
Delaware and Raritan Canal	Mer	10	E3
Delaware and Raritan Canal	Mid	10	E3
Delaware and Raritan Canal	Sms	10	E3
Delaware Bay	CM	19	A5
Delaware Bay	CM	22	A1
Delaware Bay	Cmb	18	A2
Delaware Bay	Cmb	18	C5
Delaware Bay	Cmb	19	A5
Delaware Bay	Ket	18	A2
Delaware Bay	Ket	18	C5
Delaware Bay	NC	17	F2
Delaware Bay	Sal	18	A2
Delaware Bay	Sux	21	D1
Delaware River	Buk	5	E6
Delaware River	Buk	9	F1
Delaware River	Buk	10	A2
Delaware River	Buk	10	A6
Delaware River	Bur	9	F6
Delaware River	Bur	10	A6
Delaware River	CaC	14	A4
Delaware River	Cmb	17	F1
Delaware River	Del	14	A4
Delaware River	Gle	14	A4
Delaware River	Hnt	5	E6
Delaware River	Hnt	9	F1
Delaware River	Hnt	10	A2
Delaware River	Mer	10	A2
Delaware River	Mnr	1	E6
Delaware River	NC	13	E5
Delaware River	NC	14	A4
Delaware River	NC	17	F1
Delaware River	Nth	5	D3
Delaware River	Orn	2	B1
Delaware River	Ph	9	F6
Delaware River	Ph	10	A6
Delaware River	Ph	14	A4
Delaware River	Pke	2	A5
Delaware River	Pke	2	B1
Delaware River	Sal	13	E5
Delaware River	Sal	14	A4
Delaware River	Slv	2	B1
Delaware River	Ssx	2	A5
Delaware River	War	1	E6
Delaware River	War	2	A5
Delaware River	War	5	D3
Dennis Cr	CM	19	B4
Derby Pond	Ket	17	F5
Diamond Pond	Sux	21	C3
Dividing Cr	Cmb	18	E4
Double Run	Ket	18	A6
Dragon Cr	NC	13	C6
Drawyer Cr	NC	17	D1
Duck Cr	Ket	18	A3
Duhernal Lake	Mid	11	B2
Dyke Br	Ket	17	F4
East Bay	Nsu	8	F5
East Br	Put	4	E2
East Br Big Elk Cr	Che	13	B2
East Br Brandywine Cr	Che	13	E1
East Br Croton River	Put	4	E2
East Br Res	Put	4	F2
East Br White Clay Cr	Che	13	C2
East River	Brx	8	B3
Echo Lake	Pas	3	B6
Elk Cr	Cec	13	B4
Elk River	Cec	13	B6
Elk River	Cec	17	A1
Fairview Lake	Ssx	2	B6
False Hook Channel	Mom	12	A1
Farrington Lake	Mid	11	A1
Flagler Run	Mnr	5	D1
Flat Brook	Ssx	2	A5
Forest Lake	Orn	3	E3
Fork Br	Ket	17	E4
Forked River	Oc	16	E3
Fox Hollow Lake	Ssx	2	D6
Franklin Lake	Brg	7	D1
Friendship Cr	Bur	15	D1
Garrisons Lake	Ket	17	E4
German Br	QA	17	A6
Gibson Cr	At	19	C2
Glenmere Lake	Orn	3	B3
Gravelly Br	Sux	21	A4
Gravelly Run	Ket	17	D4
Grays Br	Sux	21	A6
Great Bay	At	16	B6
Great Bay	At	20	B1
Great Bay	Oc	16	B6
Great Bohemia Cr	Cec	17	B1
Great Cedar Swamp	CM	19	C4
Great Egg Hbr	Gle	15	A4
Great Egg Hbr Bay	At	19	E3
Great Egg Hbr Bay	CM	19	E3
Great Egg Hbr Inlet	At	19	F3
Great Egg Hbr Inlet	CM	19	F3
Great Egg Hbr River	At	15	A4
Great Egg Hbr River	At	19	D1
Great Egg Hbr River	CaC	15	A4
Great Sound	CM	19	C5
Great Swamp Br	At	15	C4
Great Swamp Br	CaC	15	C4
Green Pond	Mrr	6	F1
Greenwood Br	Bur	15	E1
Greenwood Lake	Orn	3	C4
Griscom Swamp	At	19	D3
Hackensack River	Brg	7	F3
Hackensack River	Hud	7	F3
Hamburg Cove	NC	13	E5
Hammonton Cr	At	15	D5
Hanover Lake	Bur	15	F1
Haven Lake	Sux	21	A2
Haynes Cr	Bur	15	B2
Hays Mill Cr	CaC	15	B3
Hempstead Hbr	Nsu	8	D2
Hereford Inlet	CM	19	C6
Herring Br	Ket	18	A4
Herring Cr	Sux	21	E5
Hobb Lake	CaC	15	A5
Hollow Cr	Put	4	B2
Hoopes Res	NC	13	E3
Horicon Lake	Oc	11	C6
Hospitality Br	At	15	A5
Hospitality Br	Gle	15	A5
Howells Pond	Ssx	2	D6
Hudson Br	Ket	17	E6
Hudson River	Brg	8	A2
Hudson River	Brx	8	A2
Hudson River	Dut	4	A1
Hudson River	Hud	7	F4
Hudson River	NYC	7	F4
Hudson River	NYC	8	A2
Hudson River	Orn	3	F1
Hudson River	Put	4	A1
Hudson River	Wch	4	A4
Hudson River	Wch	8	A2
Indian Br	Gle	14	F5
Indian Mills Br	Bur	15	C3
Indian River	Sux	21	C5
Indian River Bay	Sux	21	E5
Indian River Inlet	Sux	21	F5
Isaac Br	Ket	17	E5
Island Pond	Orn	3	E3
Jade Run	Bur	15	D1
Jamaica Bay	Kng	8	B5

NAME	TERR	MAP	GRID
Jamaica Bay	Que	8	B5
Jarvis Sound	CM	22	B1
Jenkins Sound	CM	19	C6
Jones Inlet	Nsu	8	E6
Kenisco Res	Wch	4	C6
Kettle Run	Bur	15	B3
Keyport Hbr	Mom	11	D2
Kill Van Kull	Hud	7	E5
Kill Van Kull	Rmd	7	E5
King Pond	Cmb	18	E4
Kirk Lake	Put	4	C2
Lackawaxen River	Pke	1	D1
Lackawaxen River	Wyn	1	D1
Lake Absegami	Bur	16	A5
Lake Aeroflex	Ssx	2	D6
Lake Ariel	Wyn	1	B1
Lake Barnegat	Oc	16	D2
Lake Carasaljo	Oc	11	D5
Lake Galena	Buk	9	D2
Lake Girad	Ssx	2	F5
Lake Henry	Wyn	1	B1
Lake Hopatcong	Ssx	6	D1
Lake Illif	Ssx	2	D6
Lake Kanawauke	Orn	3	E4
Lake Kemah	Ssx	2	C5
Lake Lackawanna	Ssx	6	D1
Lake Laura	Pke	1	E3
Lake Lenape	At	19	D1
Lake Mahopac	Put	4	C2
Lake Mohawk	Ssx	2	D6
Lake Nockamixon	Buk	9	D1
Lake Owassa	Ssx	2	C5
Lake Parsippany	Mrr	7	A2
Lake Sebago	Rck	3	E4
Lake Silver Mine	Orn	3	F3
Lake Skannatat	Orn	3	E4
Lake Stahahe	Orn	3	E4
Lake Takanassee	Mom	12	A3
Lake Tappan	Brg	4	A6
Lake Tiorati	Orn	3	F3
Lake Valhalla	Mrr	7	B1
Lake Waccabuc	Wch	4	E3
Lake Wallenpaupack	Pke	1	C2
Lake Wallenpaupack	Wyn	1	C2
Lake Wallenpaupack	Wyn	1	D1
Lake Welch	Rck	3	F4
Lamington River	Hnt	6	D5
Lamington River	Sms	6	D5
Landing Cr	At	15	E6
Laurel Res	Ffd	4	F4
Lawrence Brook	Mid	11	A1
Layton-Vaughn Ditch	Sux	21	A4
Lehigh River	Leh	5	B5
Lehigh River	Nth	5	B5
Leipsic River	Ket	17	E4
Lewes & Rehoboth Canal	Sux	21	E3
Little Bay	At	20	B1
Little Bohemia Cr	Cec	17	B1
Little Bushkill Cr	Pke	1	F5
Little Egg Hbr	Oc	16	C6
Little Neck Bay	Brx	8	C3
Little Neck Bay	Nsu	8	C3
Little Neshaminy Cr	Buk	9	E4
Little Northeast Cr	Cec	13	A4
Little Pocono Cr	Mnr	5	D1
Little River	Ket	18	A4
Locklin Pond	Wyn	1	C1
Long House Cr	Pas	3	B4
Long Is Sound	Ffd	4	F6
Long Is Sound	Ffd	8	D2
Long Is Sound	Nsu	8	D2
Long Is Sound	Wch	8	D2
Long Marsh Ditch	QA	17	B5
Love Cr	Sux	21	D4
Lower Lake	Pke	1	D3
Lower New York Bay	Kng	7	E6
Lower New York Bay	Mom	11	E1
Lower New York Bay	Que	7	E6
Lower New York Bay	Rmd	7	E6
Lower New York Bay	Rmd	11	E1
Ludlam Bay	CM	19	D4
Makepeace Lake	At	15	C6
Manahawkin Bay	Oc	16	D4
Manalapan Brook	Mid	11	B3
Manalapan Brook	Mom	11	B3
Manasquan River	Mom	11	C4
Manasquan River	Mom	11	E5
Manasquan River	Oc	11	E5
Manhasset Bay	Nsu	8	D3
Mannington Cr	Sal	14	A5
Mannington Meadow	Sal	14	A5
Mantua Cr	Gle	14	D3
Manumuskin River	Cmb	19	A3
Maple Br	Sux	21	A3
Marshalls Cr	Mnr	1	E5
Martins Cr	Nth	5	D2
Mason Br	Crl	17	B6
Mason Br	QA	17	B6
Masseys Millpond	Ket	17	E4
Maurice River	Cmb	18	F2
Maurice River	Cmb	18	F4
Maurice River Cove	Cmb	18	E4
Maurice Run	Sal	18	F1
McGinnis Pond	Ket	17	F6
McMichael Cr	Mnr	5	C1
Menantico Cr	Cmb	19	A2
Menantico Lake	Cmb	19	A1
Meredith Br	Ket	17	D6
Merrill Cr Res	War	5	E3
Metedeconk River	Oc	11	E6
Mianus Res	Wch	4	E5
Mianus River	Wch	4	E4
Middle Bay	Nsu	8	E5
Middle Br Res	Put	4	D2
Mill Cr	Ket	17	E3
Mill Cr	NC	13	D3
Mill Cr	Oc	16	C4
Mill Cr Cove	Sal	13	F6
Miller Cr	Sux	21	E6
Millsboro Pond	Sux	21	C5
Millstone River	Mer	10	F3
Millstone River	Mid	11	A3
Millstone River	Mom	11	A3
Millstone River	Sms	6	E6
Minsi Lake	Nth	5	E2
Mirror Lake	Bur	15	F1
Mispillion River	Ket	21	B1
Mombasha Lake	Orn	3	D3
Mongaup River	Orn	2	C1
Mongaup River	Slv	2	C1
Monksville Res	Pas	3	B5
Monocacy Cr	Nth	5	B4
Moodna Cr	Orn	3	F2
Morris Lake	Ssx	2	E6
Morris Millpond	Sux	21	C5
Mossmans Brook	Pas	3	A5
Mount Misery Brook	Bur	15	F1
Mountain Lake	War	6	A2
Muddy Br	Ket	17	F4
Muddy Br	Ket	18	A4
Muddy Run	Sal	18	E1
Mudstone Br	Ket	17	E5
Mullica River	At	15	F5
Mullica River	Bur	15	F5
Murderkill River	Ket	18	A6
Musconetcong River	Hnt	5	E5
Musconetcong River	Hnt	6	A4
Musconetcong River	Mrr	6	C2
Musconetcong River	War	5	E5
Musconetcong River	War	6	C2
Nacote Cr	At	16	A6
Nantuxent Cove	Cmb	18	C3
Navesink River	Mom	11	F2
Nescochague Cr	At	15	D4
Neshaminy Cr	Buk	9	F3
Neshaminy Cr	Buk	10	A4
Neversink River	Orn	2	E2
New Croton Res	Wch	4	B4
New Croton Res	Wch	4	D4
Newark Bay	Hud	7	E5
North Br Cooper River	CaC	15	A2
North Br Forked River	Oc	16	C2
North Br Jade Run	Bur	15	D1
North Br Manasquan River	Mom	11	C4
North Br Metedeconk River	Oc	11	C5
North Br Mt Misery Brook	Bur	16	A1
North Br Pennsauken Cr	Bur	15	A1
North Br Raritan River	Sms	6	D5
North Stamford Res	Ffd	4	F5
Northeast Cr	Cec	13	A4
Northeast River	Cec	13	A6
Noxontown Lake	NC	17	D1
Oakford Lake	Oc	10	F6
Oldmans Cr	Gle	14	B4
Oradell Res	Brg	7	F1
Oranoaken Cr	Cmb	18	E4
Oscawana Lake	Put	4	B2
Oswego Lake	Bur	16	A4
Oswego River	Bur	16	A4
Oswego River	Oc	16	A4
Oyster Cove	Cmb	18	B2
Oyster Cr	Oc	16	C3
Palatine Lake	Sal	14	D6
Papakating Cr	Ssx	2	D5
Parvin Lake	Sal	14	E6
Pascack Brook	Brg	3	F6
Pascack Brook	Rck	3	F6
Passaic River	Brg	7	E3
Passaic River	Esx	7	C2
Passaic River	Mrr	6	F4
Passaic River	Mrr	7	C2
Passaic River	Pas	7	E3
Passaic River	Sms	6	F4
Passaic River	Uni	7	B4
Passaic River	Uni	7	C2
Paulins Kill	Ssx	2	C5
Paulins Kill	Ssx	2	D6
Paulins Kill	War	2	B6
Paulins Kill	War	5	F1
Paupackan Lake	Wyn	1	C1
Peach Lake	Put	4	E2
Pearce Cr	Cec	17	A1
Pecks Pond	Pke	1	E3
Peekskill Hollow Cr	Wch	4	B3
Pennsauken Cr	Bur	15	A1
Pennypack Cr	Mnt	9	F5
Pennypack Cr	Ph	9	F5
Perkiomen Cr	Mnt	9	A4
Philipse Br	Put	4	A2
Pine Lake	Oc	11	C6
Pine Meadow Lake	Rck	3	E4
Pinecliff Lake	Pas	3	B5
Pinks Br	Ket	17	D4
Pochuck Cr	Orn	3	A3
Pocomoke River	Sux	21	B6
Pocono Cr	Mnr	5	D1
Pocono Peak Lake	Wyn	1	B3
Pohatcong Cr	War	5	E4
Pompton River	Mrr	7	C1
Pompton River	Pas	7	C1
Pratt Br	Ket	17	F6
Presidential Lakes	Bur	15	F2
Promised Land Lake	Pke	1	D3
Prospertown Lake	Oc	11	A5
Providence Cr	Ket	17	D3
Pump Br	CaC	15	B4
Putnam Lake	Ffd	4	E5
Quaker Cr	Orn	3	E3
Raccoon Cr	Gle	14	C3
Rahway River	Mid	7	C5
Rahway River	Uni	7	C5
Ramapo River	Brg	3	D6
Ramapo River	Orn	3	D4
Rancocas Cr	Bur	10	A6
Raritan Bay	Mid	11	D1
Raritan Bay	Mom	11	D1
Raritan Bay	Rmd	7	D6
Raritan River	Mid	11	B1
Raritan River	Mrr	6	D3
Raritan River	Sms	6	F6
Red Clay Cr	NC	13	D3
Red Mill Pond	Sux	21	D3
Reed Br	Gle	14	E5
Reeds Bay	At	20	A1
Rehoboth Bay	Sux	21	E4
Reservoir No 3	Orn	2	D2
Reynolds Pond	Sux	21	B3
Rockaway Inlet	Que	8	A6
Rockwood Lake	Ffd	4	E4
Round Valley Res	Hnt	6	B5
Run Lion Br	QA	17	B4
Rutgers Cr	Orn	2	F3
Rye Lake	Wch	4	D6
Saddle River	Brg	3	E6
Saint Jones River	Ket	18	A5
Salem Cove	Sal	13	F6
Salem River	Sal	14	A5
Salem River	Sal	14	B5
Sandy Hook Bay	Mom	11	E1
Sandy Hook Channel	Mom	12	A1
Sassafras River	Cec	17	A2
Sassafras River	Ken	17	A2
Saucon Cr	Leh	5	A6
Saucon Cr	Nth	5	A6
Saw Mill River	Wch	4	C5
Sawmill Br	NC	17	E2
Schuylkill River	Che	9	A5
Schuylkill River	Mnt	9	A5
Schuylkill River	Mnt	9	C6
Schuylkill River	Ph	9	C6
Schuylkill River	Ph	14	D1
Scotchman Cr	Cec	17	B1
Scotland Run	Cmb	14	F6
Scotland Run	Sal	14	F6
Scull Bay	At	19	F3
Seely Brook	Orn	3	D2
Sewell Br	Ken	17	C4
Sewell Br	Ket	17	C4
Shearness Pool	Ket	18	A3
Shingle Kill	Orn	2	D1
Shohola Cr	Pke	2	A1
Shrewsbury River	Mom	11	F3
Silver Bay	Oc	16	E1
Silver Lake	Ket	17	F4
Silver Lake	NC	17	D1
Silver Stream Res	Orn	3	E1
Sixmile Run	Mid	10	F1
Sixmile Run	Sms	10	F1
Skippack Cr	Mnt	9	B4
Skit Br	Bur	15	D3
Sleeper Br	At	15	C4
Sleeper Br	CaC	15	C4
Smyrna River	Ket	17	F3
South Br Jade Run	Bur	15	D1
South Br Raritan River	Hnt	6	B4
South Br Raritan River	Hnt	6	B5
South Br Raritan River	Sms	6	D6
South River	At	19	B1
South River	Mid	11	B1
Southwest Br	Bur	15	B2
Splitrock Res	Mrr	7	A1
Spring Cr	Ket	18	A6
Springers Brook	Bur	15	D3
Springton Res	Del	14	A1
Spruce Run	Hnt	6	A4
Spruce Run Res	Hnt	6	B5
Stamford Hbr	Ffd	4	F6
Stephen Cr	At	19	C1
Sterling Lake	Orn	3	C4
Stickle Pond	Mrr	7	B1
Stillwell Lake	Orn	3	F2
Stoney Run	Mnr	1	D5
Stow Cr	Cmb	18	A2
Stow Cr	Cmb	18	B1
Stow Cr	Sal	18	B2
Sunset Lake	Cmb	18	D1
Sunset Lake	NC	13	D5
Swan Bay	Bur	16	A6
Swartswood Lake	Ssx	2	B6
Swimming River Res	Mom	11	D3
Tacony Cr	Mnt	9	E6
Tacony Cr	Ph	9	E6
Tappahanna Ditch	Ket	17	D5
Tidbury Cr	Ket	17	F6
Timber Lakes	Gle	15	A5
Titicus Res	Wch	4	E3
Tohickon Cr	Buk	9	B1
Tohickon Cr	Buk	9	D1
Tomahawk Lake	Orn	3	D2
Toms River	Oc	11	B5
Toms River	Oc	16	D1
Townsends Inlet	CM	19	D5
Trap Pond	Sux	21	A6
Tub Mill Pond	Ket	21	A1
Tuckahoe Cr	Crl	17	B6
Tuckahoe Cr	QA	17	A6
Tuckahoe River	At	19	B2
Tuckahoe River	Cmb	19	B2
Tulpehocken Cr	Bur	15	E4
Tulpehocken Cr West Br	Bur	15	E4
Turners Cr	Ken	17	A2
Tuxedo Lake	Orn	3	D4
Twin Lakes	Pke	2	B2
Unami Cr	Buk	9	B1
Unicorn Br	QA	17	B4
Union Lake	Cmb	18	F1
Upper Bay	Hud	7	F5
Upper Bay	Kng	7	F5
Upper Greenwood Lake	Pas	3	B4
Van Sciver Lake	Buk	10	C5
Voshell Pond	Ket	17	F5
Wading River	Bur	15	F5
Wagamons Pond	Sux	21	B3
Walker Lake	Pke	2	B1
Wallenpaupack Cr	Pke	1	B2
Wallenpaupack Cr	Wyn	1	B2
Wallkill River	Orn	2	F3
Wallkill River	Orn	3	A3
Wallkill River	Orn	3	B1
Wallkill River	Ssx	2	E6
Wallkill River	Ssx	2	F3
Wampus River	Wch	4	D5
Wanaque Res	Pas	3	C5
Wanaque River	Pas	3	C5
Waples Pond	Sux	21	C3
Washington Canal	Mid	11	B1
Wawayanda Cr	Orn	3	B4
West Br Big Elk Cr	Che	13	A3
West Br Brandywine Cr	Che	13	C1
West Br Res	Put	4	D1
West Br White Clay Cr	Che	13	B3
West Lake Res	Ffd	4	F2
Westcott Cove	Ffd	4	F6
White Clay Cr	Che	13	C3
White Clay Cr	NC	13	C3
White Clay Cr East Br	Che	13	C2
White Clay Cr West Br	Che	13	B3
White Marsh Run	Cmb	18	E2
Whitney Lake	Wyn	1	D1
Wickecheoke Cr	Hnt	10	A1
Wickham Lake	Orn	3	C3
Wiggins Mill Pond	NC	17	D2
Wildwood Lake	Wyn	1	B1
Wissahickon Cr	Ph	9	D6
Woodcliff Lake	Brg	3	F6
Wyoming Lake	Ket	17	F5
Yellow Brook	Mom	11	D3

Military & Federal Features

NAME	TERR	MAP	GRID
Belle Mead General Depot	Sms	6	D6
Belle Mead General Depot	Sms	10	D1
Camp Charles Wood	Mom	11	E3
Dover Air Force Base	Ket	18	A5
East Jersey Prison	Mid	7	C5
Evans Area Fort Monmouth	Mom	11	F4
Fort Dix Mil Resv	Bur	15	E1
Fort Dix Mil Resv	Oc	10	F6
Fort Dix Mil Resv	Oc	11	A6
Fort Dix Mil Resv	Oc	16	A1
Fort Hamilton	Kng	7	F5
Fort Monmouth	Mom	11	F3
Killcohook Coordination Area	Sal	13	F5
Lakehurst Naval Air Engineering Station	Oc	11	B6
McGuire AFB	Bur	10	E6
Mid-Orange Correctional Facility	Orn	3	C3
Military Ocean Terminal Bayonne (US Army)	Hud	7	E4
National Guard Training Station	NC	13	E5
New York St Mil Resv Camp Smith	Wch	4	A3
Picatinny Arsenal (US Mil Resv)	Mrr	6	F1
Sievers-Sandberg US Army Resv Ctr	Sal	14	A3
Sing Sing St Corr Facility	Wch	4	B5
Tobyhanna Army Depot	Mnr	1	A4
US Army Corps of Engineers	Sal	13	F5
US Coast Guard Lifeboat Station	CM	22	A1
US Coast Guard Resv	CM	22	B1
US Coast Guard Training Ctr	CM	22	B1
US Govt Resv (Aeronautical Communications Sta)	Bur	16	A3
US Mil Acad at West Pt	Orn	3	F2
US Mil Acad at West Pt	Orn	4	A2
US Mil Resv	Mom	11	E5
US Mil Resv	Mrr	3	A6
US Mil Resv	Mrr	7	A1
US Naval Air Station Willow Grove	Mnt	9	E4
US Naval Resv	Ph	14	D2
US Naval Resv (Warren Grove)	Bur	16	B4
US Naval Resv Earle Ammunition Depot	Mom	11	D3

Mountain Peaks

NAME	TERR	MAP	GRID
Bald Mtn	Brg	3	D5
Baldpate Mtn	Mer	10	B3
Buckingham Mtn	Buk	9	F3
Cushetunk Mtn	Hnt	6	C5
Diamond Mtn	Rck	3	E4
Graham Mtn	Orn	2	F1
Hall Mtn	Hnt	6	C4
Haycock Mtn	Buk	9	D1
Hickory Mtn	Pas	3	C5
High Mtn	Brg	3	D5
High Mtn	Pas	7	D1
High Point	Ssx	2	D3
Jericho Mtn	Buk	10	A3
Kittatinny Mtn	Ssx	2	B5
Mount Nimham	Put	4	D1
Musconetcong Mtn	Hnt	5	F5
Pohatcong Mtn	War	5	F4
Rock Hill	Buk	9	C2
Schunnemunk Mtn	Orn	3	E2
Scotts Mtn	War	5	F3
South Beacon Mtn	Dut	4	A1
Sterling Mtn	Orn	3	C4
Taylor Mtn	Orn	3	B4
Upper Pohatcong Mtn	War	6	A3

Parks & Recreation

NAME	TERR	MAP	GRID
Allaire St Pk	Mom	11	E4
Allaire St Pk	Mom	11	E5
Allamuchy Mtn St Pk	Ssx	6	C1
Allamuchy Mtn St Pk	War	6	C2
Allentown St Farm	Nth	5	A4
Ashbrook Resv	Uni	7	B5
Barnegat Lighthouse St Pk	Oc	16	E3
Bear Mtn St Pk	Rck	3	F3
Bear Mtn St Pk	Rck	4	A3
Bellevue St Pk	NC	14	A3
Belmont Pk	Nsu	8	D4
Big Pocono St Pk	Mnr	1	B6
Blauvelt St Pk	Rck	4	A6
Branch Brook Pk	Esx	7	D3
Brandywine Batl St Pk	Del	13	E2
Brandywine Cr St Pk	NC	13	F3
Bronx Pk	Brx	8	B2
Brookdale Pk	Esx	7	D2
Campgaw Mtn Co Resv	Brg	3	D6
Cape Henlopen St Pk	Sux	21	E3
Cape May Pt St Pk	CM	22	A1
Central Pk	NYC	8	A3
Cheesequake St Pk	Mid	11	C1
Clarence Fahnestock Mem St Pk	Put	4	B1
Clausland Mtn Co Pk	Rck	4	A6
Clay Pit Ponds Preserve	Rmd	7	D6
Clementon Lake Amusement Pk & Splash-World	CaC	15	A3
Colonial Pk	Sms	6	F6
Corsons Inlet St Pk	CM	19	E4
Croton Pt Pk	Wch	4	B4
Cunningham Pk	Que	8	C4
Darlington Co Pk	Brg	3	D6
Davella Mills Co Pk	Esx	7	D2
Davidsons Mill Pond Pk	Mid	11	A2
Delaware & Raritan Canal St Pk	Hnt	9	F1
Delaware & Raritan Canal St Pk	Mer	10	D4
Delaware & Raritan Canal St Pk	Sms	10	E1
Delaware & Raritan Canal St Pk	War	5	F6
Delaware Canal St Pk	Buk	5	E6
Delaware Seashore St Pk	Sux	21	F5
Delaware Water Gap Natl Rec Area	Mnr	1	F6
Delaware Water Gap Natl Rec Area	Mnr	5	E1
Delaware Water Gap Natl Rec Area	Nth	5	E1
Delaware Water Gap Natl Rec Area	Pke	2	A4
Delaware Water Gap Natl Rec Area	Pke	2	B3
Delaware Water Gap Natl Rec Area	War	1	F6
Delaware Water Gap Natl Rec Area	War	2	A4

NAME	TERR	MAP	GRID
Delaware Water Gap Natl Rec Area	War	5	E1
Double Trouble St Pk	Oc	16	C2
Duke Is Pk	Sms	6	D6
Eagle Rock Resv	Esx	7	C3
East Freehold Co Pk	Mom	11	D3
Edgelake Pk	Uni	7	B5
Eisenhower Pk	Nsu	8	F4
Elk Neck St Pk	Cec	17	A1
Estell Manor Co Pk	At	19	D2
Evansburg St Pk	Mnt	9	B4
Fairmount Pk	Ph	9	D6
Fairmount Pk	Ph	14	D1
Fantasy Is Amusement Pk	Oc	16	D6
Farny St Pk	Mrr	3	A6
Farny St Pk	Mrr	7	A1
Flushing Meadows Corona Pk	Que	8	B3
Forest Pk	Que	8	B4
Fort Delaware St Pk	NC	13	F6
Fort Dupont St Pk	NC	13	E6
Fort Mott St Pk	Sal	13	F5
Fort Wadsworth Pk	Rmd	7	F5
Fort Washington St Pk	Mnt	9	C5
Fox Pt St Pk	NC	14	A3
Franklin D Roosevelt St Pk	Wch	4	B3
Galloping Hill Pk	Uni	7	C4
Garret Mtn Resv	Pas	7	D2
Gateway Natl Rec Area	Kng	8	B5
Gateway Natl Rec Area	Mom	11	F1
Gateway Natl Rec Area	Mom	12	A1
Gateway Natl Rec Area	Que	8	B5
Gateway Natl Rec Area	Rmd	7	E6
Georges Is Pk	Wch	4	A4
Goosepond Mtn St Pk	Orn	3	D3
Gouldsboro St Pk	Mnr	1	A4
Graeme St Pk	Mnt	9	E4
Graham Hill Co Pk	Wch	4	C5
Green Lane Res Pk	Mnt	9	A2
Greenwich Pt Pk	Ffd	4	F6
Hacklebarney St Pk	Mrr	6	C4
Harriman St Pk	Orn	3	F3
Harriman St Pk	Orn	4	A2
Harriman St Pk	Rck	3	F3
Hempstead Lake St Pk	Nsu	8	D4
High Pt St Pk	Ssx	2	D3
High Tor St Pk	Rck	3	F4
High Tor St Pk	Rck	4	A4
Highland Lakes St Pk	Orn	3	B1
Historic New Bridge Ldg Pk	Brg	7	F1
Holts Ldg St Pk	Sux	21	E5
Hook Mtn St Pk	Rck	4	B5
Hopatcong St Pk	Ssx	6	D1
Howell Co Pk	Mom	11	D4
Hudson Highlands St Pk	Put	4	A1
Hudson Highlands St Pk	Put	4	A2
Island Beach St Pk	Oc	16	F2
Jackson St Pk	Oc	11	B5
Jacobsburg Environmental Education Ctr	Nth	5	B3
Johnson Co Pk	Mid	7	A6
Jones Beach St Pk	Nsu	8	F5
Keansburg Amusement Pk	Mom	11	E1
Kissena Pk	Que	8	C4
Kittatinny Valley St Pk	Ssx	2	D6
La Tourette Pk	Rmd	7	E6
Lake Towhee Co Pk	Buk	9	C1
Lenape Pk	Uni	7	C4
Liberty St Pk	Hud	7	F4
Lincoln Pk	Hud	7	E4
Long Pond Ironworks St Pk	Pas	3	C5
Louis Morris Pk	Mrr	6	F3
Lums Pond St Pk	NC	13	D6
Marine Pk	Kng	8	A5
Mercer Co Central Pk	Mer	10	E3
Minisink Battleground Natl Hist Site	Slv	2	A1
Mohansic Co Pk	Wch	4	B3
Monmouth Batl St Pk	Mom	11	C3
Monmouth Co Pk	Mom	11	C4
Morristown Natl Hist Pk	Mrr	6	F3
Mountain Cr Summer Water Pk	Ssx	3	A4
Mountain Reserve Pk	Pas	7	D1
Neshaminy St Pk	Buk	10	A6
New Brooklyn Pk	CaC	15	A4
Nockamixon St Pk	Buk	9	D1
Nomahegan Pk	Uni	7	C4
North Br Pk	Sms	6	D6
North Hudson Pk	Hud	7	F3
North Hudson Pk	Hud	8	A3
Nyack Beach St Pk	Rck	4	B5
Ocean Co Pk	Oc	11	D5
Old Croton Trailway St Pk	Wch	4	B6
Old Troy Pk	Mrr	7	B3
Ommelanden Pk	NC	13	E5
Overpeck Co Pk	Brg	7	F2
Palisades Interstate Pk	Brg	8	B1
Parvin St Pk	Sal	14	E6
Passaic River Pk Area	Sms	6	F4
Patriots Ballpark	Sms	6	F6
Pelham Bay Pk	Brx	8	C2
Pigeon Swamp St Pk	Mid	11	A2
Planting Fields Arboretum St Hist Pk	Nsu	8	F2
Preakness Valley Pk	Pas	7	D1
Princeton Batl St Pk	Mer	10	D3
Promised Land St Pk	Pke	1	D3
Prospect Pk	Kng	8	A5
Rahway River Pkwy	Uni	7	B4
Rahway River Pkwy	Uni	7	C5
Ralph Stover St Pk	Buk	9	E1
Rancocas St Pk	Bur	15	B1
Raritan Bay Waterfront Pk	Mid	11	C1
Red Bank Batl Pk	Gle	14	D2
Ridley Cr St Pk	Del	14	A1
Ringwood St Pk	Pas	3	D5
Riverbank St Pk	NYC	8	A3
Roberto Clemente St Pk	Brx	8	A2
Rockefeller St Pk	Wch	4	C5
Rockland Lake St Pk	Rck	4	A5
Roosevelt Co Pk	Mid	7	B6
Rosedale Pk	Mer	10	C2
Round Valley Rec Area	Hnt	6	B5
Saddle River Pk	Brg	7	E1
Sagamore Hill Natl Hist Site	Nsu	8	F2
Seth Pierrepont St Pk	Ffd	4	F2
Shark River Co Pk	Mom	11	E4
Shore Sports Arena	Oc	16	D1
Six Flags Great Adventure Theme Pk & Wild Safari	Oc	11	A5
Six Mile Run Pk Res	Sms	10	F1
Six Mile Run St Pk	Sms	10	E1
Skylands Pk	Ssx	2	D5
South Mtn Resv	Esx	7	C4
Spring Lake Co Pk	Uni	7	B5
Spruce Run Rec Area	Hnt	6	A5
Stephens St Pk	Mrr	6	C2
Sterling Forest St Pk	Orn	3	C4
Stony Pt St Pk	Rck	4	A4
Storm King St Pk	Orn	3	F1
Storm King St Pk	Orn	4	A1
Swan Pt Nat Area	Oc	11	E6
Swartswood St Pk	Ssx	2	C6
Tallman Mtn St Pk	Rck	4	B6
Tamaques Resv	Uni	7	B5
Tenafly Nature Ctr	Brg	8	A1
Thomas Bull Mem Co Pk	Orn	3	C1
Thompson Pk	Mid	11	A2
Thompson Pk	Mom	11	F3
Tobyhanna St Pk	Mnr	1	A4
Trap Pond St Pk	Sux	21	A6
Tyler Arboretum	Del	14	A1
Tyler St Pk	Buk	10	A4
US Mil Acad at West Pt Michie Stadium	Orn	4	A2
Valley Forge Natl Hist Pk	Che	9	A5
Valley Forge Natl Hist Pk	Mnt	9	A5
Valley Stream St Pk	Nsu	8	D4
Van Cortlandt Pk	Brx	8	A2
Voorhees St Pk	Hnt	6	A4
Wall Stadium	Mom	11	E4
Ward Pound Ridge Resv	Wch	4	E3
Warinaco Pk	Uni	7	C5
Washington Crossing St Pk	Buk	10	A2
Washington Crossing St Pk	Mer	10	B3
Washington Rock St Pk	Sms	7	A5
Watchung Mtn Pk	Sms	6	E5
Watchung Resv	Uni	7	B4
Wawayanda St Pk	Pas	3	A5
Wawayanda St Pk	Ssx	3	A4
Weequahic Pk	Esx	7	D4
West Essex Pk	Esx	7	B3
West Essex Pk	Esx	7	C2
White Clay Cr Preserve	Che	13	D4
White Clay Cr Preserve	NC	13	D4
White Clay Cr St Pk	NC	13	C4
Winterthur Gardens	NC	13	E3
Yogi Berra Stadium & Mus	Pas	7	D2

Points of Interest

NAME	TERR	MAP	GRID
Abbotts Mill	Sux	21	A2
Absecon Lighthouse	At	20	B2
African American Mus	Nsu	8	E4
Air Victory Mus	Bur	15	B1
Allaire Village	Mom	11	D4
Allee House	Ket	17	F3
American Helicopter Mus	Che	13	F1
American Labor Mus	Pas	7	D1
American Merchant Marine Mus	Nsu	8	C3
Ashland Nature Ctr	NC	13	D3
Atlantic City Boardwalk	At	20	A2
Atlantic City Convention Hall	At	20	A2
Barnegat Bay Decoy & Baymens Mus	Oc	16	C5
Barnegat Lighthouse	Oc	16	E3
Barratts Chapel	Ket	18	A6
Bartlett Arboretum	Ffd	4	F5
Batsto Hist Village	Bur	15	E5
Bayonne Bridge	Rmd	7	E5
Bedford Hist Dist	Wch	4	E4
Black River & Western RR	Hnt	10	B1
Bordentown Hist District	Bur	10	D5
Boscobel Mansion Restoration	Put	4	A1
Bowers Beach Maritime Mus	Ket	18	B6
Brandywine River Mus	Del	13	E2
Bronx Zoo	Brx	8	B2
Bronx-Whitestone Bridge	Que	8	C3
Brooklyn Battery Tunnel	NYC	7	F4
Brooklyn Bridge	NYC	8	A4
Brooklyn Mus	Kng	8	A4
Buena Vista	NC	13	E5
Butterfly Camping Resort	Oc	11	C5
Cape May Bird Observatory & Education Ctr	CM	19	C5
Cape May Lighthouse	CM	22	A1
Cape May Migratory Bird Ref	CM	22	A1
Cape May Nature Ctr	CM	22	B1
Cape May Zoo	CM	19	C5
Cape May-Lewes Ferry	CM	22	A1
Cape May-Lewes Ferry	Sux	21	F2
Caramoor Ctr For Music & The Arts	Wch	4	E4
Carey Stadium	CM	19	F3
Chestnut Neck Battle Monument	At	16	A6
Clara Barton School Thomas Paines Home	Bur	10	C5
Cohanzick Zoo	Cmb	18	D1
Cowtown Rodeo	Sal	14	B5
Cradle of Aviation Mus	Nsu	8	E4
Craftsman Farms	Mrr	7	A2
Cross Bay Bridge	Que	8	C5
Cumberland Co Fairground	Cmb	18	E1
Discovery House	Mid	11	A1
Discovery Sea Shell Mus	CM	19	E3
Display World Stone Mus	Mid	11	B2
Dover Air Force Base Air Mus	Ket	18	A5
East Jersey Olde Towne	Mid	7	A6
East Pt Lighthouse	Cmb	18	F4
East Windsor Fairgrounds	Mer	10	F3
Edison Natl Hist Site	Esx	7	D3
Edward Hopper House	Rck	4	B5
Eisenhower Mem Pk Mus	Nsu	8	F4
Ellis Is Ferry	NYC	7	F4
Fairy Tale Forest	Pas	3	A6
Falaise-Guggenheim Estate	Nsu	8	D2
Finns Pt Rear Range Lighthouse	Sal	13	F5
Fisher Martin House	Sux	21	E3
Fort Hancock	Mom	11	F1
Frelinghuysen Arboretum	Mrr	7	A3
Garden St Discovery Mus	CaC	15	A2
General Grant Natl Mem	NYC	8	A3
George Washington Bridge	NYC	8	A2
Gingerbread House	Ssx	2	E5
Goethals Bridge	Rmd	7	D5
Goshen Hist Track & Harness Racing Hall of Fame	Orn	3	C2
Gravies Pt Mus & Preserve	Nsu	8	E2
Great Falls & Natl Landmark District	Pas	7	D2
Greenwich Tea Burning Monument	Cmb	18	B2
Gregory Mus	Nsu	8	F3
Grover Cleveland Birthplace	Esx	7	C2
Hamilton Grange Natl Mem	NYC	8	A3
Hammond Mus & Oriental Stroll Gardens	Wch	4	F3
Hancocks Br St Hist Site	Sal	14	A6
Havens Homestead Hist Site	Oc	11	E5
Hereford Inlet Lighthouse & Gardens	CM	19	C6
Hermitage Mus	Brg	3	E6
Historic Boonton	Mrr	7	A2
Historic Burlington Co Prison Mus	Bur	10	C6
Historic Cold Spring Vil	CM	22	B1
Historic Houses of Odessa	NC	17	D1
Historic Speedwell	Mrr	7	A3
Historic Walnford	Mom	10	F5
Holland Tunnel	NYC	7	F4
Hudson River Mus	Wch	8	B1
Hudson Valley Childrens Mus	Rck	4	B5
Hunterdon Co Arboretum	Hnt	6	B5
Indian King Tavern Mus	CaC	14	F2
Island Field Mus	Ket	18	B6
James Fenimore Cooper House	Bur	10	B6
Jane Voorhees Zimmerli Mus	Mid	11	A1
Jenkinsons Aquarium	Oc	11	F5
John Jay Homestead	Wch	4	E3
Knox Hdq	Orn	3	F1
Lakota Wolf Preserve	War	5	E1
Land of Make Believe	War	6	A2
Leamings Run Gardens & Colonial Farm	CM	19	C5
Lewes Ferry Terminal	Sux	21	E3
Liberty Is	Hud	7	F4
Lincoln Tunnel	NYC	7	F3
Longwood Gardens	Che	13	D2
Lost River Caverns	Nth	5	C6
Lucy The Elephant	At	19	F3
Lyndhurst	Wch	4	B6
Manhattan Bridge	NYC	8	A4
Manitoga Nature Ctr	Put	4	A2
Marine Pkwy Bridge	Kng	8	B6
Matchbox Rd Mus	Sal	14	F6
Metz Bicycle Mus	Mom	11	C3
Mid Atlantic Ctr For The Arts	CM	22	A1
Millbrook Village Hist Site	War	2	A5
Miniature Kingdom	War	6	A3
Minisink Battleground Natl Hist Site	Slv	2	A1
Mispillion Lighthouse	Sux	21	C1
Museum of Nat History	NC	13	E3
Museum Village	Orn	3	D2
Nanticoke Indian Mus & Pow Wow	Sux	21	D5
Nassau Co Mus of Art	Nsu	8	E3
Nassau Vets Mem Coliseum	Nsu	8	E4
Navesink Light Station at Twin Lights Hist Site	Mom	12	A2
New Hope Steam Railway & Mus	Buk	10	A2
New Jersey Childrens Mus	Brg	7	E1
New Jersey Ctr for the Visual Arts	Uni	7	B4
New Jersey Meadowlands Sports Complex	Brg	7	E3
New Jersey St Police Mus	Mer	10	B3
New Jersey Vietnam Veterans Mem	Mom	11	D2
New Windsor Cantonment St Hist Site	Orn	3	F1
New York Botanical Garden	Brx	8	B2
Northlandz	Hnt	6	C6
Nothnagle Log Cabin	Gle	14	C3
Noyes Mus	At	20	A1
Old Etna Furnace	At	19	C3
Old Saint Annes Epis Church	NC	17	D1
Old Sussex Co Courthouse	Sux	21	B4
Old Tennent Church	Mom	11	C3
Old Westbury Gardens	Nsu	8	E3
Outerbridge Crossing	Rmd	7	D6
Oxford Furnace Hist Site	War	6	A3
Oyster Cr Nuclear Power Plant	Oc	16	D3
Paper Mill Playhouse	Esx	7	C4
Pennsbury Manor	Buk	10	C5
Pennypacker Mills Hist Site	Mnt	9	A3
Peters Valley Craft Ctr	Ssx	2	B4
Philipsburg Manor	Wch	4	B5
PNC Bank Arts Ctr	Mom	11	D2
Popcorn Pk Zoo	Oc	16	D2
Port Penn Mus	NC	13	E6
Prallsville Mills	Hnt	10	A1
Proprietary House	Mid	7	C6
Queens-Midtown Tunnel	NYC	8	A3
Queensboro Bridge	NYC	8	A3
Red Bank Batl Pk	Gle	14	D2
Reedy Pt Patrol Station	NC	13	F6
Rehoboth Art League	Sux	21	E4
Renault Glass Mus	At	15	E6
Rockefeller Ctr	NYC	8	A3
Rockingham Hist Site	Sms	10	E2
Rockwood Mus	NC	13	F3
Saddle Rock Grist Mill	Nsu	8	D3
Sagamore Hill Natl Hist Site	Nsu	8	F2
Saint Georges Chapel	Sux	21	D4
Saint Paul Natl Hist Site	Wch	8	B2
Salem Nuclear Power Plant	Sal	17	F1
Sandy Hook Lighthouse	Mom	11	F1
Sea Girt Lighthouse	Mom	11	F5
Sea Life Mus-Marine Mammal Stranding Ctr	At	20	B2
Shea Stadium	Que	8	C3
Sleepy Hollow Cem & Old Dutch Church	Wch	4	B5
Smithville Mansion	Bur	15	D1
Somers Mansion	At	19	E3
South Jersey Mus of American History	CaC	15	A3
Southeast Mus	Put	4	E2
Space Farms Zoo & Mus	Ssx	2	D4
State Capital (Trenton)	Mer	10	C4
Staten Is Ferry	NYC	7	F5
Statue of Liberty Natl Monument	Hud	7	F4
Steamboat Dock Mus	Mom	11	D1
Sterling Hill Mine & Mus	Ssx	2	E6
Stone Hbr Bird Sanctuary	CM	19	C6
Stony Pt Batl	Rck	4	A4
Storm King Art Ctr	Orn	3	E1
Storybook Land Fun Pk	At	19	E1
Sugar Loaf Village	Orn	3	C3
Sunnyside	Wch	4	B6
Tappan Zee Bridge	Wch	4	B6
The Crayola Factory	Nth	5	D4
Thomas A Edison Mem Tower And Mus	Mid	7	B6
Throgs Neck Bridge	Que	8	C3
Tinicum Rear Range Lighthouse	Gle	14	D2
Towne of Hist Smithville	At	20	A1
Triborough Bridge	NYC	8	A3
Turtle Back Zoo	Esx	7	C3
UN Hdq	NYC	8	A3
US Army Communications Mus	Mom	11	F3
US Bicycling Hall of Fame	Sms	6	E6
US Mil Acad at West Pt Michie Stadium	Orn	4	A2
USGA Natl Hdq Golf House Mus & Library	Sms	6	E5
Van Bunschooten Mus (Daughters of Amer Revolution)	Ssx	2	E3
Van Cortlandt Manor	Wch	4	B4
Vernon Valley Great Gorge Action Pk	Ssx	3	A4
Verrazano Bridge	Kng	7	F5
Vollendam Windmill Mus	Hnt	5	D5
Washington Hdq Hist Site	Orn	3	F1
Washingtons Hdq	Wch	4	C6
Waterloo Village	Ssx	6	C1
Wetlands Institute	CM	19	C6
Wheaton Village & Mus of American Glass	Cmb	18	F2
Whippany Railway Mus	Mrr	7	A3
Whitesbog Village Hist Site	Bur	15	F1
Wick House	Mrr	6	F3
Wild West City	Ssx	6	D1
Williamsburg Bridge	NYC	8	A4
Willowwood Arboretum	Mrr	6	D3
Wilmington & Western RR	NC	13	D4
Winterthur Gardens	NC	13	E3
Winterthur Gardens Mus	NC	13	E3
World Trade Ctr	NYC	7	F4
Wylands Whaling Wall	CM	22	C1
Yankee Stadium	Brx	8	B3
Yogi Berra Stadium & Mus	Pas	7	D2

NAME	TERR	MAP	GRID
Stroud	Mnr	5	D1
Tabernacle	Bur	15	D3
Teaneck	Brg	7	F2
Teaneck	Brg	8	A2
Tewksbury	Hnt	6	C4
Thornbury	Che	13	F1
Thornbury	Del	13	F1
Thornbury	Del	14	A1
Tinicum	Buk	5	E6
Tinicum	Buk	9	E1
Tinicum	Del	14	C2
Tobyhanna	Mnr	1	A5
Towamencin	Mnt	9	B4
Tredyffrin	Che	9	A6
Troy Hills	Mrr	7	B2
Tunkhannock	Mnr	1	A6
Tuxedo	Orn	3	D3
Union	Hnt	5	F5
Union	Hnt	6	A5
Union	Uni	7	C4
Upper	CM	19	D3
Upper Chichester	Del	14	A2
Upper Darby	Del	14	C1
Upper Deerfield	Cmb	14	C6
Upper Deerfield	Cmb	18	D1
Upper Dublin	Mnt	9	D5
Upper Frederick	Mnt	9	A3
Upper Freehold	Mom	10	F5
Upper Freehold	Mom	11	A4
Upper Gwynedd	Mnt	9	C4
Upper Hanover	Mnt	9	A2
Upper Makefield	Buk	10	A3
Upper Merrion	Mnt	9	B5
Upper Milford	Leh	5	A6
Upper Moreland	Mnt	9	E5
Upper Mount Bethel	Nth	5	E2
Upper Nazareth	Nth	5	B4
Upper Oxford	Che	13	A2
Upper Providence	Del	14	B1
Upper Providence	Mnt	9	A4
Upper Salford	Mnt	9	A3
Upper Saucon	Leh	5	B6
Upper Southampton	Buk	9	F4
Valley	Che	13	B1
Vernon	Ssx	2	F4
Vernon	Ssx	3	A4
Voorhees	CaC	15	A2
Wall	Mom	11	E5
Wallkill	Orn	3	A1
Walpack	Ssx	2	A5
Wantage	Ssx	2	E3
Warminster	Buk	9	E4
Warren	Sms	6	F5
Warren	Sms	7	A5
Warrington	Buk	9	D3
Warwick	Buk	9	E4
Warwick	Orn	3	B3
Washington	Brg	7	F1
Washington	Bur	15	E5
Washington	Bur	16	A3
Washington	Gle	14	E4
Washington	Mer	10	E4
Washington	Mrr	6	C3
Washington	Nth	5	D2
Washington	War	5	F3
Washington	War	6	A4
Waterford	CaC	15	C4
Wawayanda	Orn	3	A2
Wayne	Pas	7	D1
Weehawken	Brg	7	F3
West Amwell	Hnt	10	B2
West Bradford	Che	13	C1
West Deptford	Gle	14	D3
West Fallowfield	Che	13	A2
West Goshen	Che	13	E1
West Marlborough	Che	13	C2
West Milford	Pas	3	B5
West Norriton	Mnt	9	B5
West Rockhill	Buk	9	B2
West Sadsbury	Che	13	A1
West Windsor	Mer	10	E3
Westampton	Bur	10	C6
Westfall	Pke	2	C2
Westtown	Che	13	F1
Weymouth	At	19	C1
Weymouth	At	19	D1
White	War	5	F3
White	War	6	A2
Whitehall	Leh	5	A5
Whitemarsh	Mnt	9	C5
Whitpain	Mnt	9	C5
Williams	Nth	5	D5
Willingboro	Bur	10	B6
Willistown	Che	14	A1
Willistown	Mnt	9	A6
Winfield	Uni	7	C5
Winslow	CaC	15	B4
Woodbridge	Mid	7	C6
Woodbury	Orn	3	E3
Woodland	Bur	15	F2
Woodland	Bur	16	A3
Woolwich	Gle	14	B4
Worcester	Mnt	9	B4
Wrightstown	Buk	9	F3
Wrightstown	Buk	10	A3
Wyckoff	Brg	3	D6
Wyckoff	Pas	7	D1
Yorktown	Wch	4	C3

Wineries

NAME	TERR	MAP	GRID
Alba Vineyard	War	5	D5
Amalthea Cellars	CaC	15	B4
Amwell Valley Vineyard	Hnt	10	C1
Applewood Winery	Orn	3	B3
Balic Winery	At	19	C1
Banfi Vintners-Old Brookville Vineyards	Nsu	8	E2
Brotherhood Americas Oldest Winery Ltd	Orn	3	E1
Buckingham Valley Vineyards	Buk	9	F3
Cape May Winery & Vineyard	CM	22	A1
Chaddsford Winery	Che	13	E2
Cherry Valley Vineyards	Mnr	5	C2
Country Cr Winery	Mnt	9	B3
Cream Ridge Vineyards & Champagne Cellars	Mom	10	E5
Delmonicos Winery	Kng	8	A4
Four Sisters Winery & Matarazzo Farms	War	5	F2
Franklin Hill Vineyards	Nth	5	D3
In & Out Winery	Buk	10	A3
Joseph Zakon Winery	Kng	8	A4
Kings Rd Vineyard	Hnt	5	F5
La Follette Vineyard & Winery	Sms	10	E1
Loukas Wines	Brx	8	B2
Marimac Vineyards	Cmb	18	C2
Nassau Valley Vineyards	Sux	21	D3
New Hope Winery	Buk	9	F2
North Salem Vineyard	Wch	4	E2
Peace Valley Winery	Buk	9	D3
Poor Richards Winery	Hnt	5	F6
Renault Winery	At	15	E6
Rushland Ridge Vineyard & Winery	Buk	9	F4
Sand Castle Winery	Buk	9	E1
Slate Quarry Winery	Nth	5	B4
Smithbridge Winery	Del	13	F2
Sylvin Farms Winery	At	15	F6
Tamuzza Vineyards	War	5	F2
Tomasello Winery	At	15	C4
Twin Brook Winery	Che	13	A1
Unionville Vineyards	Hnt	10	C1
Valenzano Winery	Bur	15	D3
Warwick Valley Winery	Orn	3	A3

Key to Abbreviations

Acad	Academy	Dr	Drive	Mem	Memorial	Resv	Reservation
Admin	Administration	E	East	Mgmt	Management	RI	Rhode Island
Al	Alley	Envir	Environment	Mil	Military	RR	Railroad
Alt	Alternate	Est/Ests	Estates	Mt	Mount	S	South
Ave	Avenue	Expwy	Expressway	Mtn	Mountain	SC	South Carolina
Batl	Battlefield	Ext	Extension	Mun	Municipal	Sch	School
Bldg	Building	Frwy	Freeway	Mus	Museum	SHA	State Highway Administration
Bltwy	Beltway	GA	Georgia	N	North	Soc	Society
Blvd	Boulevard	GC	Golf Club/Golf Course	Nat	Natural	Sq	Square
Boro	Borough	Govt	Government	Nat Res	Natural Resource	St	State/Street
Br	Branch/Bridge	Hbr	Harbor	Natl	National	Sta	Station
Bus	Business	Hdq	Headquarters	Natl Batl Pk	National Battlefield Park	Tech	Technical
By-P	By-Pass	Hgts	Heights	NC	North Carolina	Terr	Terrace
CC	Country Club	Hist	Historic/Historical	NH	New Hampshire	Theol	Theological
Cem	Cemetery	Hlth Ctr	Health Center	NJ	New Jersey	TN/Tenn	Tennessee
Cir	Circle	Hwy	Highway	No	Number	Tpk	Turnpike
Co	Company/County	I	Interstate	NY	New York	Tr	Trail
Coll	College	Ind	Industrial	Ofc	Office	Trk	Truck
Comm	Community	Inst	Institution	OH	Ohio	Twp	Township
Conn	Connector	Intl	International	PA/Penn	Pennsylvania	Univ	University
Cr	Creek	Is	Island	Pk	Park	US	Federal Route
Cres	Crescent	Jct	Junction	Pkwy	Parkway	Utd	United
Ct/Conn	Connecticut	Jr Coll	Junior College	Pl	Place	VA	Virginia
Ct	Court	KY	Kentucky	Pt	Point	Vil	Village
Ctr	Center	La	Lane	Rt	Road	Voc	Vocational
DE/Del	Delaware	Ldg	Landing	Rec	Recreation	VT	Vermont
Dept	Department	Lp	Loop	Rec Ctr	Recreation Center	W	West
Dev	Development	MA/Mass	Massachusetts	Ref	Refuge	WMA	Wildlife Management Area
DMV	Department of Motor Vehicles	MD	Maryland	Reg	Regional	WV	West Virginia
DOT	Department of Transportation	ME	Maine	Res	Reservoir		

Notes